Violence in
America's Schools

Violence in America's Schools

Understanding, Prevention, and Responses

R. MURRAY THOMAS

Westport, Connecticut
London

Library of Congress Cataloging-in-Publication Data

Thomas, R. Murray (Robert Murray), 1921–
    Violence in America's schools : understanding, prevention, and responses /
    R. Murray Thomas.
        p.   cm.
    Includes bibliographical references and indexes.
    ISBN 0–275–99329–9 (alk. paper)
    1. School violence—United States.   2. School violence—United
States—Prevention.   I. Title
LB3013.32.T46   2006
371.7'82–dc22   2006024498

British Library Cataloguing in Publication Data is available.

Library of Congress Catalog Card Number: 2006024498
ISBN: 0–275–99329–9

First published in 2006

Praeger Publishers, 88 Post Road West, Westport, CT 06881
An imprint of Greenwood Publishing Group, Inc.
www.praeger.com

Printed in the United States of America

The paper used in this book complies with the
Permanent Paper Standard issued by the National
Information Standards Organization (Z39.48–1984).

10 9 8 7 6 5 4 3 2 1

Contents

Preface

The purpose of this book is to introduce school personnel, parents, and members of the general public to the realm of violence in schools. Throughout the book, the expression *school personnel* refers to preservice and inservice teachers, administrators, counselors, psychologists, social workers, clerical workers, bus drivers, and the like.

In pursuit of the book's purpose, the chapters focus on a wide variety of acts that cause people physical or psychological harm or disrupt the conduct of schooling. The book's intent is not to delve deeply into any particular type of violence. Instead, the aim is to orient readers to the types of violence and to the ways that the perpetrators of violence and their victims can be treated.

CHAPTER 1

Varieties of School Violence

Throughout this book, the word *violence* refers to any intentional actions that (a) disrupt the operation of a school's learning program, (b) cause physical harm or psychological distress for students, teachers, and other members of the school staff, and/or (c) destroy property. Violent behavior can occur within the school, on the school grounds, or near the school. Persons committing violent acts can be students, members of the school staff, or outsiders.

Not all damaging events in schools qualify as violence. Many are accidents. The distinction between accidents and violence lies in the intention of the person who commits the act. If damage is caused *on purpose* rather than being *inadvertent*, it's an instance of violence and, therefore, a matter of concern in this book. But if the damage is unintentional—an error or a mistake—it's deemed an accident and not a subject of interest here.

The contents focus on types of violence and on treatment. The types are those described in Chapters 2 through 10—deadly weapons, threats, fighting, child abuse, sexual abuse, bullying, vandalism, theft, and disruptive behavior.

While planning the book I considered three options for labeling constructive ways of responding to acts of violence. The first option was to call such ways *solving violence*. But I feared that label promised too much. Readers might think the aim of the book was to offer sure-fire cures for all sorts of violence as committed by all sorts of people under all sorts of circumstances. Making such a claim would clearly be a mistake, since research and common sense both confirm the fact that there are no universally effective cures for violent acts. Some methods of dealing with violence work well with some people in some settings but fail with other people in other settings, so I rejected *solving violence*.

The second option was *coping with violence*. But I felt that label promised too little. I suspected that readers might think I was recommending a passive approach to violence—a mere *adjusting-to* or *putting-up-with* violent acts. Hence, *coping with violence* was also cast off.

The third option—*treating violence*—came closest to what the book offers. In medical practice, a *treatment* is a physician's attempt to cure—or at least to ameliorate—a patient's ailment. Yet physicians rarely guarantee success, for they recognize that the effectiveness of any treatment depends on multiple influences, and many of those influences are neither well understood nor under a physician's control. The same is true in dealing with violence. Each treatment is a kind of experiment, an attempt whose success seems likely but cannot be certain. Thus, teachers and administrators—and parents also—need to know a variety of treatments, so if one approach doesn't work with the case at hand, others are readily available. For those reasons, throughout the book I use *treating violence* to identify the suggested ways of responding to violent acts in schools.

Chapters 2 through 10 illustrate ways in which different types of school violence have been treated. But behind all such treatment attempts—no matter which type of violence is involved—is a mode of thought that leads people to choose the methods they adopt. In other words, the way a teacher, administrator, parent, psychologist, social worker, police officer, judge, or jury *thinks about* how to respond to violence is the key determinant of the treatment that will be tried. The purpose of Chapter 11 is to suggest a mode of thought—a way of planning—that I believe leads to effective treatment. In that chapter, I propose that, when confronted with an act of violence, a person who is planning treatment can profitably be guided by a question consisting of the following six underlined variables:

In light of the type of violence in the case I now face, what treatment will best accomplish the purpose I hope to achieve with the kind of person who is to be treated under a particular set of environmental conditions, and without generating undesirable side effects (collateral damage)?

In summary, this opening chapter sets the stage for the next nine chapters, which describe types of violence and ways of treating both the perpetrators and the victims of violent acts. Finally, the last chapter describes in detail a method of planning treatments that may aid school personnel, members of the justice system, and parents in their task of choosing a profitable way to respond to violence in schools.

Now to the remaining two purposes of this opening chapter, those of (a) identifying trends in violent acts and (b) illustrating the types of violence on which the book focuses.

TRENDS IN SCHOOL VIOLENCE

Recent years' reports of the frequency of school violence offer both bad news and good news.

The bad news is that violent acts and pupils' fear of danger have continued to be common in the United States. A report by the U.S. Education and Justice Departments noted that in 2003 there were about 738,700 violent crimes involving students at schools, and 846,400 crimes away from schools. Such violence included 28 crimes of rape, sexual assault, robbery, and physical assault for every 1,000 students. The good news is that the incidence of crime in schools during 2003 was only half that of 1993, and crime in general reached a 30-year low. The rate of school violence dropped dramatically between 1993 and 2000, thereafter remaining at a constant level (Sherman, 2005). High school students who reported being in a physical fight on school grounds decreased from 16 percent in 1993 to 13 percent in 2001. The percentage of students who reported being a victim of a crime of violence or theft at school decreased from 10 percent to 6 percent (St. Gerard, 2003).

In 85,000 public schools during the 2000–2001 academic year there were 717,400 incidents of reported violence in elementary schools, 441,300 in middle schools, and 261,400 in high schools (CSI, 2004). The most common types of violence were fist fights, bullying, and shoving matches. Studies of bullying suggest that three out of every 10 students were involved in bullying—13 percent as bullies, 11 percent as victims, and 6 percent as both bullies and victims. "For children in grades 6 through 10, this translates into 3.7 million children who bully other children each year and 3.2 million who are victims" (Selekman & Vessey, 2004). During the 2000 school year, 15 percent of students in grades nine through twelve reported being in a physical fight on school property (School violence statistics, 2000). Physical attacks without a weapon and vandalism were far more frequent than such violent crimes as rape, sexual assault, robbery, or aggravated assault that were reported by about 20 percent of schools (St. Gerard, 2003). The rate of violent crime has typically risen in grades six through eight, peaked at grade nine, and declined through grade twelve (Cardman, 2003). Fights with a weapon have been most frequent in middle schools, with 21 percent of middle schools reporting 7,575 incidents during 2000 (School violence statistics, 2000).

According to analysts, three important factors contributing to the decline in school violence were (a) the installation of metal detectors for screening students in the most troubled schools, (b) the hiring of more security personnel to patrol schools, and (c) the introduction of programs designed to curb bullying that might lead to serious crimes (Sherman, 2005).

In summary, although violence in schools continues to be a significant threat to students' and teachers' welfare and to the efficient conduct of the learning program, there have been positive signs of improvement over the past decade and a half.

TYPES OF VIOLENCE

Each chapter in Part II concerns a different kind of violence. The kinds are identified by the chapter titles: deadly weapons, threats of violence, fighting, child abuse, sexual abuse, bullying and hazing, vandalism, theft, and disruptive behavior. The contents of all these chapters are cast in a similar pattern. Each begins with (a) a description of a particular type of violence, and then continues with (b) cases illustrating varieties of that type and (c) ways people have sought to treat such acts. In the following paragraphs, the general feature of each chapter is suggested by a definition of the chapter's form of violence and by two or three representative cases.

Deadly Weapons

A Definition

Deadly-weapons violence involves the use of instruments that could cause severe physical harm to victims—such instruments as a gun, a knife, a hammer, a metal water pipe, a wooden cane, a rock, a ceramic bookend, an automobile, and more.

Case 1

In recent years, the event known as *the Columbine killings* has become the prototype of deadly-weapons violence.

Shortly before lunchtime on April 20, 1999, two teenage boys—armed with sawed-off shotguns, a semiautomatic rifle, a semiautomatic pistol, and pipe bombs—walked into Columbine High School in Littleton (Colorado) where they killed 13 people (12 students, 1 teacher) and wounded 23 more before shooting themselves to death. In the days following the incident, authorities found journals and videos that the two shooters had prepared, with plans for the school attack and a neighborhood massacre, and, "if they were unable to escape from the United States, [they would hijack] an airplane which they would then crash into New York City" (Columbine, 2005).

The Columbine tragedy stimulated wide-scale speculation about reasons for the teenagers' rampage and about how such events might be prevented in the future. Many schools subsequently adopted "zero-tolerance" policies toward students who bore weapons or threatened violence. Other schools established antibullying policies on the assumption that the pair of killers in the Columbine case had been goaded into their brutal act by months of taunting by schoolmates.

Over the years following the Columbine killings, aftereffects of the event appeared in the form of motion pictures (*Bowling for Columbine* in 2002, *Elephant* in 2003), books (*Hey, Nostradamus!* in 2003, *Years of Rage* in 2005), and music videos (*Alert Status Red* in 2004) (Columbine, 2005). There was also evidence that the Columbine episode continued to influence teenagers who would engage in deadly-weapon violence. For example, youths fascinated with the Columbine massacre included the 16-year-old on Minnesota's Red Lake Indian Reservation, who, in March 2005, shot to death five students, a school security guard, and a teacher before killing himself. Two days later, in a suburb of Buffalo (New York), a 15-year-old boy was arrested, accused of plotting to blow up his high school. Authorities reported that he had purchased bomb-making materials, including gunpowder, primers, ball bearings, and pipes that were already bored out. In a search of the boy's home computer, officials found downloaded autopsy reports about the Columbine killers. Earlier in the school year, the youth had written an essay for his English class suggesting that the Columbine killers' actions had been their form of rebelling against an oppressive environment (Thompson, 2005).

Case 2

Just after students at Rockdale County's Heritage High School in Georgia had finished their Spanish class's final examination, their teacher's estranged husband burst into the classroom brandishing a long knife. As he lunged at the teacher, several boys from the class dashed forward, tackled him, and wrested the knife from his hand. When the teacher was later recovering from knife wounds in her hand and leg, she told newspaper reporters, "Those kids are my heroes. I believe God used them to save my life. I'm sorry that they were called upon to do such a huge job so early in their lives, but without them I wouldn't be alive" (Lewis, 2003).

Threats of Violence

A Definition

Threats of violence consist of any indications—physical, pictorial, spoken, or written—of a person or group intending to harm other individuals, groups, or property.

Case 1

At Hopkinton (Massachusetts) High School, a female student admitted to officials that she had scrawled a "hit list" on a wall in the girls' bathroom near the main lobby. The list threatened harm to 10 students (eight freshmen girls, an older boy, and an older girl) and a teacher.

Hopkinton Police Chief Thomas R. Irvin said, "Years ago, we would have assumed this was a prank. We can't do that anymore." He said the author of the threat could be charged with a felony for violating antiterrorism laws (Gedan, 2003).

Case 2

A surveillance videotape revealed that it was a first-grade teacher who had placed a note inside the front door of Washington-Reid Elementary School in Dumfries (Virginia). The note read: "There's a bomb in the school today." When confronted with the videotape, the distraught teacher said the note had been intended as a prank she was playing on a friend and coworker. However, her plan had gone awry as another school employee found the note first and reported it to the principal, who phoned the police.

The teacher explained in a later interview that "I played a very horrible, horrible joke on another employee at the school, and it backfired. My intention was never to harm anyone. I will be paying for that for the rest of my life."

The school principal described the teacher as one of the best on the faculty. Authorities placed her on administrative leave without pay, and the police charged her with threats to bomb, a felony carrying a minimum penalty of a year in jail (Weiss, 2003).

Fighting

A Definition

Fighting consists of individuals or groups engaging in physical and/or verbal combat with the aim of harming—or at least subduing—their opponent.

Case 1

After students had completed their final exams at Smithfield-Selma (North Carolina) High School, a fight broke out in the school's crowded lobby among students waiting to go home for the Christmas holidays. The fight started between two students but quickly engaged others who punched, kicked, wrestled, and shouted threats and obscenities. A security guard stationed in the lobby radioed for help just before the radio was knocked from his hand. In response to his call, three dozen officers (sheriff deputies, police, state troopers) arrived within minutes to stop the brawl and arrest 10 of the combatants. In response to questions about the incident, the Johnston County sheriff said, "My message to school leaders is, 'You need to make up your mind who's running the schools, you or the kids'" (Sung, 2004).

Case 2

Players from rival high school football teams appeared in a Doylestown (Pennsylvania) court to testify about their part in a scrap between North Penn High School students and Central Bucks West High School students—a fight in which four Central-Bucks players were seriously injured, two with broken jaws. Authorities reported "bad blood" between the two groups ever since they had fought during a summer football camp. On the night of the recent brawl, a caravan of 40 to 60 North Penn students and some adult companions had descended on a small group of students gathered in the Central-Bucks West parking lot in Doylestown and challenged the group to fight. Twelve juveniles and four adults were arrested; all were associated with North Penn High School. They were cited for felony rioting, simple assault, disorderly assault, and conspiracy to commit those offenses.

The Bucks County district attorney called the incident an unprovoked "vicious assault." In response, an attorney representing an accused Penn High student said, "It is rather obvious that a lot of this was instigated and set up by students from Central Bucks West, and it's rather strange that no one from Central Bucks West has been charged" (King, 2004).

Child Abuse

A Definition

The U.S. Government's Federal Child Abuse Prevention and Treatment Act defines *child abuse* as

Any recent act or failure to act on the part of a parent or caretaker which results in death, serious physical or emotional harm, sexual abuse or exploitation; or an act or failure to act which presents an imminent risk of serious harm.

Most States recognize four major types of maltreatment: neglect, physical abuse, sexual abuse, and emotional abuse. Although any of the forms of child maltreatment may be found separately, they often occur in combination. (National Clearinghouse, 2004)

Case 1

A special-education prekindergarten teacher in Naples (Florida) was charged in court with aggravated child abuse for allegedly tying two learning-disabled 3-year-old boys to chairs. According to the indictment, the teacher had tied up one child to his chair with a jump rope and the other with an apron. When one of the boys fell backward, he was left on the floor. The next day the teacher tied both children with string and put tape over one boy's mouth. When the boy cried and pulled the tape off, the teacher stuck the tape back on. This account of the two incidents was confirmed by other adults.

In the teacher's defense, her attorney contended that she had loosely placed a jump rope over one child's lap and an apron across the other child in order to teach them how to sit still in class. The attorney described the ties as a symbolic way of getting the children to sit still and concentrate on their schoolwork. He said, "There was never any malicious intent here." A report from school officials stated that the teacher had difficulty coping with her class and was "experiencing debilitating emotional distress" at the time of the episode (Abuse charges, 2003).

Case 2

Law enforcement officials in Henry County (Georgia) sought to determine whether faculty members at Eagle's Landing Middle School were guilty of failing to report suspected child abuse. According to Georgia state law, school personnel are required to report apparent home-abuse of students; failure to do so can lead to a year in jail or a $1,000 fine or both.

In the case under investigation, an 11-year-old middle-school girl had been found dead in her family's garage. She had been starved, hogtied, and beaten to death. Her father and stepmother were indicted for murder.

Authorities now sought to learn if school personnel were at fault for not reporting signs that the girl had been mistreated. During the investigation, a 12-year-old pupil said the murder victim had been a "friendly classmate who sometimes came to school with scratches, bruises, and black around her eyes" and who told "different stories to different people about how those injuries occurred." It was thus the investigators' task to learn whether members of the school staff had also noticed the signs and had suspected they were the result of continuing harsh treatment at home (Reid, 2003).

Sexual Abuse

A Definition

The expression *sexual abuse* refers to unwanted sexual acts that involve exploitation, intimidation, deception, threats, or physical force. Sexual abuse can include such diverse behaviors as obscene phone calls, exhibitionism, window peeking, exposure to pornography, offensive fondling, attempted rape, and rape. The term *child sexual abuse* means interactions between a child and an adult or adolescent where the child is being used for sexual purposes.

Case 1

A popular third-grade teacher at Zebulon Elementary School in Wake County (North Carolina) was arrested on charges of fondling a 12-year-old boy and forcing him into oral and anal intercourse. The indictment included eight counts of first-degree statutory sexual offense for a series of such acts that began in May and continued into July. If found guilty, the teacher could be sentenced up to 20 years in prison for each count.

A resident of the neighborhood in which the teacher lived reported, "You would always see a lot of children going over there. He'd take them to Burger

King. He took them shopping around, and he took them to school" (McDonald, 2003).

Case 2

Three basketball players from an Easton (Massachusetts) vocational high school were arrested for allegedly plying a 17-year-old female classmate with liquor, then gang-raping her after she passed out. The three youths faced a 10-year minimum prison sentence if convicted of drugging a person for sexual intercourse. Defense lawyers for the three youths appealed for low bail on the claim that the young woman had willingly gone with one of the alleged assailants to get money for the alcohol. The lawyers also said the woman had been unable to tell police for sure that she had been raped. Evidence collected later at a medical center supported the rape accusation (Rothstein, 2004).

Bullying and Hazing

A Definition

Bullying involves an exploiter seeking to undermine, humiliate, denigrate, or injure someone through such ways as teasing, taunting, insulting, depriving, physically assaulting, robbing, spreading rumors, and the like. The terms *harassment* and *psychological intimidation* are sometimes used as synonyms for bullying.

Hazing is a form of bullying that requires applicants to an organization to submit to activities that are humiliating, degrading, or involve the risk of emotional or physical harm. Typical hazing practices include subjecting applicants to insult, sleep deprivation, vile substances to consume, humiliating attire to wear in public, branding, beating, binge drinking, sexual stimulation, sexual assault, and more.

Case 1—Bullying

Parents of a 13-year-old girl who attended a Tampa (Florida) middle school moved their daughter to a more distant school so she might escape the bullying that the girl said she had suffered.

Her problem had begun in sixth grade the previous year when she had had a disagreement with a classmate. When asked how the trouble started, she claimed that the classmate had "told me I'd been saying things [about her]. Some of them I did say, but some of them I didn't say. Then all these people that I didn't even know hated me."

According to the girl's account, she had been bullied in a variety of ways by at least 13 schoolmates. She reported that one morning in the courtyard a group had gathered around her and called her names. Before the year's first dance, some girls warned her that they were all going to attend it. During the dance they chased her into a bathroom where she first hid, then finally slipped out to stay close to the assistant principal, afraid to venture onto the dance floor. She claimed that on other occasions books were dropped on her head and spitwads shot into her hair. She reported that assailants shoved her into lockers, tripped her on the bus, and threatened to cut off her eyebrows. She said she rarely went to the bathroom during school hours for fear of being molested.

Her mother reported that during one week at the middle school, an administrator had given the daughter a note that permitted her to leave school 5 minutes early to evade girls who waited daily near her locker. One day the family's phone number and the word "slut" appeared on a wall near the school's entrance. A janitor washed the graffiti off, but within a week it was back again. Then a message was left on the family's answering machine, with a girl's voice saying "People are going to end beating her up if she doesn't stop calling them slut and other profane names" (Ave, 2003). The parents responded by transferring their daughter to a different school.

Case 2—Bullying

The Eugene (Oregon) School District was ordered to pay $10,000 in damages to a middle-school boy who had been attacked on a school bus by a group of students. The incident drew national attention when a segment of a videotape from the bus's surveillance camera was broadcast on a television news program. According to the lawsuit, the victim's parents had reported the names of his assailants to school officials who had failed to prevent the attacks until the family took the matter to court (Bullying case, 2004).

Case 3—Hazing

A supposedly friendly "powderpuff" football game between junior and senior girls of Glenbrook (Illinois) North High School turned into a wild melee in which junior girls were slapped, punched, hit with objects, doused with paint, and smeared with mud and feces. A state attorney told reporters, "During the outburst, six junior girls were injured in a high school rite-of-passage gone bad. One victim had 10 stitches in her head. There are possible concussions. It is the kind of behavior that any community cannot tolerate and will not tolerate" (Flock, 2003).

A spectator's videotape of the incident, showing senior girls pummeling juniors, drew nationwide attention when broadcast over network television.

School authorities suspended 31 students who had participated in the event. State prosecutors cited 15 of the students—12 girls, 3 boys—for misdemeanor battery, punishable by up to 364 days in jail and a $2,000 fine. Two mothers of students were also indicted for their part in the episode. One was charged with providing alcohol to a minor after she bought three kegs of beer for her son; the son was charged with unlawful possession of alcohol by a minor. A second mother was indicted for allowing her home to be used for the consumption of alcohol by minors, because one of the kegs had been sent to her home while the remaining two were delivered to the park where the hazing took place.

School officials offered several of the 31 suspended students an opportunity to graduate with their class, although they could not participate in graduation ceremonies. They would be required to perform community service and obtain counseling. They also would need to agree not to exploit the event through book or movie contracts, and they would have to promise not to sue the school district (Flock, 2003).

Vandalism

A Definition

Vandalism is the malicious destruction, injury, or disfigurement of any public or private property without the consent of the persons who own or legally control the property.

Case 1

Vandals caused $10,000 in damage to the elementary school in the town of Viking (Minnesota) (population 90) by wrecking every room in the school during a Sunday-night break-in that left broken glass, spilled paint, overturned furniture, and smashed security cameras. A 13-year-old girl and 14-year-old boy were arrested as the apparent vandals (Minnesota, 2003).

Case 2

Two males, ages 17 and 18, confessed to setting fire to the theater at Pioneer High School in San Jose (California). The pair admitted kindling debris and stuffing it under a vending machine, then lighting a nearby bulletin board afire. According to a deputy district attorney, the 18-year-old could face up to 9 years in prison—and even more time if lawyers could prove that the damage exceeded $1 million. Under California law, the 17-year-old could also be prosecuted as an adult (Nguyen & Portner, 2003).

Theft

A Definition

The word *theft* means taking property that belongs to others without the permission of the owners of the property. *Theft* also includes individuals illegally taking property that belongs to a school district.

Case 1

In a commentary on *Youth Radio*, a student said, "In my small charter school, stealing is more common than most people would think. Recently our school's Yearbook Committee had 55 dollars stolen from a safe that was locked away in a teacher's office. This is only one of the many thefts reported by students this year. But now we're wondering if we have to put giant padlocks on our backpacks or have safes to lock away our possessions. I myself had a cell phone stolen from my purse. It was so hidden that only a person who was watching me and planning their attack could have stolen it. I bet some students feel so unsafe that they will consider switching to home schooling. . . . So if the person who stole my phone is listening, please return it to Locker 122, no questions asked" (Chu, 2005).

Case 2

The 53-year-old superintendent who had headed the Sauk Village (Illinois) School District for 15 years was jailed on multiple charges that included stealing more than $100,000 from one of Cook County's poorest school districts. He was accused not only of theft, but also of bribery, intimidation, harassment of a witness, obstruction of justice, and official misconduct. All six counts were felonies that could bring up to 30 years in prison. A retired teacher who attended the initial court hearing said that the superintendent had often told her, "'I can do anything for the good of the children.' But we didn't know it was for the good of his own children" (Ex-schools chief, 2005).

Disruptive Behavior

A Definition

The expression *disruptive behavior* refers to students' actions that seriously interfere with the efficient conduct of the school's learning program. The kinds of disruptive behavior of interest here are ones that do not involve deadly weapons, threats of violence, fighting, child abuse, sexual abuse, bullying and hazing, or vandalism. In other words, the sort of disruptive behavior of interest lies outside the above-mentioned types of violence and focuses, instead, on acts within the province of *school discipline* or *classroom management*.

Case 1

Nearly all sixth-graders at an Oklahoma City public school were suspended for disrupting class and then creating a commotion in the cafeteria. Among the F. D. Moon Academy's 147 sixth graders, 16 were temporarily dismissed for disturbing their class. In a separate incident, 120 were suspended for lifting cafeteria tables, slamming the tables to the floor, and talking back to teachers.

The suspended students were required to work at the school the following Saturday.

Moon Academy had been cited by state education officials as needing improvement because of low test scores, but the school's principal said test scores would not rise until discipline problems had been resolved. She estimated that teachers were currently spending 85 percent of their time reprimanding students (School suspends, 2004).

Case 2

A 7-year-old second-grader in a Pittsburgh elementary school served a 1-day suspension from class for violating the school district's no-profanity rule. She had told a classmate that he would "go to hell" for saying "I swear to God." Another child who overheard the word *hell* reported the matter to the teacher, who then imposed the suspension. When the accused girl's father learned of the incident, he explained that his daughter had been referring to the biblical fire-and-brimstone location and had not used *hell* as a swear word that might disturb the class. He suggested that the school review its profanity policy (Pittsburgh schools, 2004).

CONCLUSION

For convenience of discussion, incidents of violence in schools are classified throughout this book by nine types: deadly weapons, threats of violence, fighting, child abuse, sexual abuse, bullying and hazing, vandalism, theft, and disruptive behavior. However, it is clear that those types are not mutually exclusive. They are often combined. Fighting can involve deadly weapons, bullying can include threats of violence, and sexual abuse can be a part of hazing. The purpose of this opening chapter has been to describe the book's structure, identify recent trends in school violence, and introduce the nine types that are analyzed in Chapters 2 through 10.

CHAPTER 2

Deadly Weapons

Deadly weapons violence is analyzed in this chapter from five vantage points: (a) devices used as deadly weapons, (b) frequent circumstances in which weapon-violence occurs, (c) treating individuals who have committed weapon violence, (d) treating victims of weapon violence, and (e) dangerous schools and safe schools.

DEVICES USED AS DEADLY WEAPONS

As noted in Chapter 1, deadly weapons are objects that can cause severe physical harm to victims. However, neither the police nor school personnel always agree about which objects are properly classed as deadly weapons.

Guns/Firearms

For most people, when deadly weapons are mentioned, guns are likely the devices that first come to mind. The definition of *guns* or *firearms* of greatest practical importance for schools is the one included in the U.S. government's *Gun-Safe Schools Act* that was passed in 1994 and revised in 2000. The gun-safe law requires each state to adopt the provisions of that act or else to forego the millions of dollars they would receive under the Elementary and Secondary Education Act (ESEA)—including the ESEA 2001 version known as the No-Child-Left-Behind program. A firearm is:

Any weapon (including a starter gun [used in track meets]) that will be, or is designed to, or may readily be, converted to expel a projectile by the action of an explosive.

Any destructive device, which includes:

(a) Any explosive, incendiary, or poison gas, including a
    1. bomb,
    2. grenade,
    3. rocket having a propellant charge of more than four ounces,
    4. missile having an explosive or incendiary charge of more than one-quarter ounce,
    5. mine, or
    6. similar device.
(b) Any weapon that will, or that may be readily converted to, expel a projectile by the action of an explosive or other propellant, and that has any barrel with a bore of more than one-half inch in diameter.
(c) Any combination or parts either designed or intended for use in converting any device into any destructive device described in the two immediately preceding examples, and from which a destructive device may be readily assembled.

Antique firearms are not included in the definition. In addition, . . . Class-C common fireworks are not included in the definition of firearm. (Guidance concerning, 2004)

Here are three representative instances of gun violence in school settings:

A judge sentenced a 15-year-old student to prison for 50-years-to-life for having shot two students to death and wounding 13 others at Santana High School in Santee (California). The student had used a .22-caliber revolver taken from his father's gun cabinet. According to the youth's testimony in court, he launched the shooting rampage because he had been bullied in school (Lyda, 2003).

At around 7:30 a.m. in the cafeteria of the junior high school in Red Lion (Pennsylvania) a 14-year-old boy suddenly stood up and shot the school principal in the chest with a .44-caliber handgun, then shot himself in the head with a .22-caliber pistol. Both the principal and the student died from their wounds. The two guns had come from the teenager's stepfather's safe, which the boy had opened with a key. The Red Lion police chief, attempting to offer reasons behind the shootings, said, "We don't know why [but] I think that something was building inside him that he couldn't control" (Barnett, 2003).

In a classroom full of pupils at Youens Elementary School in Alief (Texas), a fifth-grader was stuffing a .380-caliber semiautomatic pistol into the backpack that he held on his lap when the gun accidentally fired, sending a bullet through his groin, through the chair on which he sat, and into the floor. Before he was helped from the classroom, he picked up the bullet to show to authorities. The police did not immediately know where the boy had gotten the gun. They estimated that he had not intended to use it to do damage but merely to show to classmates. In keeping with state law, the 12-year-old would be expelled from school for a year and placed in an alternative education program for bringing a loaded gun to school (O'Hare, 2004).

Destructive Devices

The Gun-Safe Act's "destructive devices" can include not only bombs but also such fireworks as M-80s, quarter sticks, silver salutes, cherry bombs, chasers, skyrockets, pop-bottle rockets, missile-type rockets, and mortar rockets.

A 13-year-old middle-school student in Lake Alfred (Florida) threw two homemade bombs into the livestock area of the school campus. Each bomb consisted of a plastic soda bottle filled with water and chemicals. The boy was arrested on a charge of throwing a destructive device intended to cause harm (Violence in our schools, 2005).

Fire investigators in Green Township (Ohio) estimated that youngsters playing with fireworks near Oakdale Elementary School over the weekend had tossed firecrackers through an open classroom window, setting off a blaze that caused more than a half-million dollars in damage to the building (Rutledge, 1997).

Knives, Swords, and Daggers

Like firearms, other items that obviously qualify as deadly weapons are knives, swords, and daggers.

A 51-year-old school counselor was stabbed repeatedly in the stomach and chest with a knife during an argument with a 17-year-old youth in a Springfield (Massachusetts) alternative high school. After the stabbing, the youth ran from the school and discarded the knife but was arrested a half mile away (National School Safety, 2002).

In the morning before school, a 16-year-old student at Lamar High School in Arlington (Texas) brandished a pair of two-foot-long swords as he approached a group of fellow students. When he slashed a 14-year-old freshman's face, the screams of the crowd alerted an unarmed security guard who rushed to the scene, tackled the sword-wielding youth, and held him on the ground until help arrived. The assailant was arrested and taken to jail, while the injured 14-year-old was sent to the hospital for stitches to repair the cut he had suffered (Douglas, 2005).

In the Sikh religion, males are obligated to wear a *kirpan*—a ceremonial dagger—on their garment as a symbol of the struggle between good and evil. Kirpans are typically a few inches long. When a 12-year-old Sikh student wore a kirpan to class at Sainte-Catherine-Laboure School in Quebec (Canada), school authorities suspended him. In response, the boy's family took the case to court, where the judge ruled that a kirpan was a religious symbol, the same as a cross worn by Catholic students, and should therefore be permitted. However, the school board and the parents of other students considered the dagger a dangerous weapon and took the case to a court of appeals, which reversed the earlier decision and contended that school authorities were within their rights to ban the wearing of the dagger (No kirpans, 2004).

Simulated Firearms

In some school districts, toy guns are permitted, but in others they are classified as dangerous weapons along with actual firearms. Among popular toy weapons are BB guns that shoot rubber-like plastic pellets, which, if they hit a person, do not penetrate the skin but can cause welts. The Colchester (Vermont) School District had a policy permitting students to bring BB-guns to school. But a ninth-grade Colchester boy's firing pellets at schoolmates in a restroom still resulted in his being charged with assault (Colchester Student, 2005).

Rules in most schools forbid students to bring simulated weapons onto the campus.

Shortly after noon, a student at Scripps Ranch High School in San Diego (California) phoned the County-Crime-Stoppers hotline to report that he had seen a schoolmate carry what appeared to be a black, heavy-steel gun. Police promptly arrived at the school to remove the identified 16-year-old from math class and take from his backpack an "Uzi-looking, CO2 Air soft gun" loaded with plastic pellets. The accused youth said he had bought the air gun from another 16-year-old for $150. Both the buyer and seller of the weapon were arrested, then released to face possible expulsion from school. The school district's police chief told reporters, "The message here is clear: We obviously take any type of weapon seriously." The school principal sent a letter to all students' homes to explain the air gun incident and remind parents of the ban on bringing any weapons—real or fake—to the campus (Magee & Hughes, 2005).

Laser pointers that are shaped like pistols are among the simulated guns that concern school authorities. Laser pointers—also known as laser pens—send an intense, narrow beam of red or green light at the object toward which they are aimed.

The sight of a moving red dot on a corridor wall at the high school in Hastings (Minnesota), alerted a teacher to a boy brandishing what appeared to be a small double-barreled pistol. When the teacher took the 14-year-old to the principal's office, the boy said that the simulated derringer pistol was a laser pointer that had been part of his Halloween costume. He had brought the fake gun to school to show his friends. Under the school's strict no-weapons policy, the youth could face a yearlong expulsion because, as the Hastings police chief explained, even replicas of weapons were not acceptable in schools (Schoepf, 2004).

In addition to devices that are either obvious weapons or toy replicas, a wide variety of items designed for more peaceful uses may also serve as deadly weapons, as shown by violence incidents that involve paraphernalia ranging from razor blades to snowballs.

Razor Blades

After security guards broke up a lunchtime argument between a pair of 15-year-old girls at Saginaw High School in Michigan, one of the girls phoned her 42-year-old mother and two sisters, ages 17 and 20, urging them to come to the school to talk with the principal. Following their discussion with the principal, the four stepped into the corridor where they spotted the other 15-year-old who had been involved in the earlier argument. The mother and three sisters attacked the girl, with the 17-year-old slashing the 15-year-old opponent's neck with a razor blade. Within minutes, a security guard arrived to arrest the mother and three daughters. The injured student was taken by paramedics to a hospital where she required seven stitches to close the wound. The security guard's hand had also been cut during his effort to subdue the 17-year-old and the mother. At a preliminary court hearing, the 17-year-old was ordered to stand trial for assault with intent to commit great bodily harm, while her mother faced an assault charge for attacking the security guard (Tucker, 2005).

Screwdrivers

A 15-year-old student at Independence High School in San Jose (California) was attacked in front of the school by five members of a street gang and stabbed seven times in the back with a screwdriver. One member of the gang was arrested for the attack (Violence in our schools, 2005).

Lancet Needles

Lancet needles are instruments used by diabetics to test their blood-sugar level.

Two 12-year-old boys at Memorial Middle School in Harlingen (Texas), under the guise of playing a clever joke, stuck 30 classmates with Lancet needles, then announced "Now you have AIDS." After school authorities caught the pranksters and turned them over to the police, health workers tested the 30 victims of the episode for HIV and Hepatitis B as a precautionary measure. Since all of the tests turned out negative, it was apparent that the threat had been a hoax. The two 12-year-olds were sent to a juvenile detention center, charged with aggravated assault (Violence in our schools, 2005).

Concrete

During an after-school fight between two high school youths in Bradenton (Florida), a 17-year-old killed a 16-year-old by slamming his head on the concrete driveway behind a food store. The fight was over the victim being harassed over his conduct in an earlier meeting of a school-sanctioned club whose members were mostly athletes and other popular students. At that gathering, the victim, in an effort to qualify as a club member, had removed all his clothes, which resulted in his being teased about the affair by other students, including the youth who would later kill him during the fight (National School Safety, 2002).

Pens

In the midst of a before-school fight between a sixth-grader and a seventh-grader at Mayport Middle School in Jacksonville (Florida), the sixth-grader stabbed his opponent in the neck with a pen. After teachers stopped the fight, medical personnel flew the injured boy to a hospital for treatment—with the pen still stuck in his neck—while the police arrested the sixth-grader (Violence in our schools, 2005).

Responding to an anonymous tip, police arrested a 17-year-old in Rosemead (California) for filling marker pens with an explosive that would detonate when the pen caps were removed. A search of the boy's home revealed explosive materials and books describing how to fashion homemade weapons. The youth admitted placing altered pens at different locations near Rosemead High School, where three unsuspecting passers-by picked them up, opened them, and suffered injuries when the devices exploded. The 17-year-old said he planted the pens as an act of revenge for his having been expelled from school (Thermos, 2005).

Pencils

Following a scrap between two 12-year-old boys in a Memphis, Tennessee, middle school, the 14-year-old girl-cousin of the first 12-year-old stabbed the second 12-year-old in the chest with a lead pencil. Following the attack, the wounded boy underwent surgery at a nearby hospital and remained in a serious condition in the intensive-care unit (National School Safety, 2000).

A fight between members of rival Black and Hispanic gangs at Chicago's Farragut Career Academy began in the gymnasium and spilled over into a corridor where a 16-year-old Hispanic boy was stabbed in the neck with a pencil and transported to a nearby hospital for treatment. One of the school's sixteen security guards was also injured when he attempted to separate the fighters (Student stabbed, 2005).

Keys/Pen

A confrontation between two street gangs at Pelham Prep High School in New York City sent a 15-year-old to a hospital with eight stab wounds from what authorities called "an un-conventional weapon," apparently either a set of keys or a pen. A second boy was stabbed twice in the back. The brawl began at noon on the school's second-floor stairwell and continued later in the basement. The twenty assailants involved in the fight were members of rival street gangs—Bloods and DDP (Dominicans don't play) (Mongelli & Martinez, 2005).

Box Cutters

For an unknown reason, a sixth-grade boy at Adam Stephens Middle School in Salem (Oregon) stabbed a seventh-grader in the back with an extended-blade box cutter. Although the seventh-grader knew he had been hit in the back, he did not realize he had been stabbed until another student noticed the blood. The victim was treated at a hospital for his wound, while the police charged the assailant with second-degree assault and confined him in the county juvenile detention facility along with five other students who were charged as conspirators in the attack (Violence in our schools, 2005).

Wooden Poles

As pupils at Julian Thomas Elementary School in Racine (Wisconsin) entered the campus one morning, the principal—a Ms. Apmann—saw an 8-year-old boy wielding a wooden pole that was more than 2-feet long and nearly 2 inches thick. Because the boy had a history of aggressive behavior, she ordered him to give up the pole. In response, the 8-year-old began beating the principal over the head, hitting her hard enough to break the pole into three pieces. Staff members who ran to the principal's rescue took her to the hospital for treatment. Police sent the boy to the county juvenile detention center. At a court hearing, the 8-year-old said other pupils had been bullying him, so he had brought the pole to school to defend himself. Because he had already been suspended from school five times during the school year for aggressive behavior, the judge placed him in a residential treatment center for at least 2 months and declared that the boy would not be returned home until his mother could ensure that her son attended school regularly, completed his homework, and sent an apology note to the principal (Chang, 2005; Killackey, 2005).

Baseball Bats

A Hamden (Connecticut) father—enraged over his daughter's suspension from the Sacred Heart Academy softball team for breaking team rules—pummeled the softball coach in the head and chest with a baseball bat. The father was cited for first-degree assault and reckless endangerment, charges that could result in a prison sentence of up to 20 years (Eagan & Gonzalez, 2005).

Poison

Two girls, ages 12 and 13, at Daly Middle School in Klamath Falls (Oregon) were charged with attempting to commit murder after they put rat poison in two schoolmates' milk cartons during lunch hour. No damage occurred, because the poison pellets had not yet dissolved into the liquid by the time the two victims drank the milk. The victims then noticed green crystalline pellets on the bottom of the cartons and turned the cartons over to school authorities who called the police. When a hospital medical staff examined the victims, they found that the pair had suffered no harm. The county district attorney said the serious charge of attempted murder was based on evidence that "There was some premeditation and thought before the act. It wasn't a spur-of-the-moment event" (Ore. girls charged, 2005).

A fourth-grade girl at Philadelphia's Benjamin Franklin Elementary School was arrested for attempting to poison her teacher by pouring a mixture of fingernail polish, nail-polish remover, and hand lotion into the teacher's coffee mug during class. The teacher did not use the mug and only learned about the incident from the parent of another girl who had witnessed the act. The arrest charge against the 10-year-old included aggravated assault, possession of an instrument of crime, simple assault, and reckless endangerment of another person. School officials suspended the child from school for five days while a disciplinary hearing was held. The girl faced expulsion to an alternative school for difficult pupils (Dean, 2005b).

At Grover Washington Jr. Middle School in Olney (Pennsylvania), a 13-year-old boy was convicted of attempted murder and aggravated assault for pouring toxic cleaning fluid into his teacher's juice cup. After drinking from the cup, the teacher fell ill and was treated at a hospital. A family court judge placed the boy on probation and ordered him to undergo counseling (Dean, 2005b).

Snowballs

Numerous school districts consider snowballs dangerous weapons. In Bellevue (Washington) throwing snowballs falls in the category of "exceptional misconduct, causing material disruption, damage to school property, or the infliction of injury on an employee or student." A Bellevue police officer explained, "Kids have been known to pack the snowballs with rocks or soak them in water until they freeze. Throwing such projectiles can even be considered assault." In nearby Northshore School District, snowballing is deemed "malicious mischief" (Fulbright, 2004).

Multiple Weapons

Some incidents of violence involve the use of more than one kind of weapon.

A 15-year-old who attended Pahrump Valley High School in Nevada was the first student to board the school bus one Monday morning. He stepped into the bus, held a newly sharpened samurai sword over the head of the woman driver, and ordered her off the bus. According to the boy's plan, he would use the bus the following day as his get-away vehicle after setting off shotgun shells to ignite propane tanks behind the school and blow up the school building (Paul, 2002).

At an alternative school in Caro (Michigan) a 17-year-old armed himself with a .22-caliber rifle, a 20-guage shotgun, and a package of gunpowder, then took a teacher and 15-year-old girl hostage. After holding the hostages for three hours, he shot once at the principal, released both hostages as police were preparing to enter the school building, and then shot himself in the head. He died a short time later. In trying to account for the boy's actions friends reported that he had become despondent after breaking up with his girlfriend two days earlier (National School Safety, 2002).

Summary of Attacking Devices

As the foregoing examples demonstrate, some devices are violent by their very nature and thus are generally banned from schools. Such is the case with guns, explosive devices, knives, swords, and daggers. Students are prohibited from even bringing such items to school. Other devices, by their nature, are intended for peaceful purposes but can on occasion be used as dangerous weapons—razors, pens, pencils, keys, sticks, and more. Thus, school personnel are obliged to be alert not only to the presence of actual weapons but also to the likelihood that angry students might use such common school items as pencils, pens, or tools to harm others.

FREQUENT CIRCUMSTANCES

The following examples illustrate six kinds of circumstances in which weapon violence frequently occurs. Each kind confronts school personnel with a somewhat different problem of dealing with the violence that takes place.

Street-Gang Warfare

Much of the deadly violence in large cities results from members of street gangs attacking their rivals. It is often unnecessary for a victim of such violence to be selected for attack because of his or her own actions. Simply being a member of an enemy gang is usually sufficient to warrant an assault.

At the end of the school day, a 15-year-old Los Angeles high-school student was walking home with friends when a car stopped nearby and a youth got out and questioned the student and his friends about which gang they belonged to. The assailant then shot the student dead, jumped into the car, and sped away (National School Safety, 2002).

There is little that teachers or administrators can do to stop gang confrontations that occur away from the school. However, efforts to prevent gang warfare on school property can include stationing police or security officers in schools, requiring students to pass through metal detectors upon entering school, and encouraging students to report impending gang fights.

Attack Plans

Students can be arrested for deadly weapon violence on the grounds that they planned an attack, even though they had not yet put the plan into action.

On the day that a 16-year-old apparently intended to launch a shooting massacre at Wickenburg High School in Arizona, police arrested him on charges of interfering with an educational institution, computer tampering, and two counts of attempted misconduct involving weapons. The police had been alerted to the plot by a local resident who had logged into an Internet chat room that the youth frequented. In a search of the boy's home, police found weapons and notebooks detailing the intended plan (Whiting, 2003).

A high-school staff member in Malcolm (Nebraska) called the police after he saw a 17-year-old student drinking from a flask in the school parking lot and donning a black overcoat. When the police arrived, they arrested the youth for attempted murder after they found in his car 20 homemade bombs, a rifle, and a note saying he wanted to harm everyone at the school except three of his friends (Nebraska teen's bomb, 2004).

Attempts of school personnel to forestall weapon violence can involve (a) taking seriously any evidence (students' notes, drawings, essays, and remarks) that suggests someone may be preparing an attack and (b) alerting other students to their responsibility to report to the authorities any information they have that an attack is being planned.

Reacting to Bullying

A mounting body of evidence suggests that victims of ridicule and bullying sometimes vent their frustration by using deadly weapons to strike back at their tormentors or at society in general. Classic examples of such violence are the Columbine and Red Lake cases described in Chapter 1. Violent responses to bullying can be found at any age level, as illustrated in these examples:

Two second-grade boys and an 11-year-old schoolmate were arrested Wednesday in Forsyth, Montana, charged with hiding a loaded .22 caliber handgun and a box of cartridges in a playground sandbox. One of the boys also carried a knife. The three intended to shoot and stab a third-grade girl during recess because, they said, she had teased them (Three grade-schoolers, 2004).

An 18-year-old at Lawrence Central High School in Indiana was arrested on a charge of felony intimidation for bringing an unloaded BB gun to school along with a hit list containing the names of four students and two teachers. A police officer said that the episode was "the usual thing. Basically [the student] thought he was being picked on. We believe his intention was just to scare people, to bring a little attention to himself, because the BB gun was not loaded" (Renze-Rhodes, 2004).

In the opinion of Ted Feinberg, assistant executive director of the National Association of School Psychologists:

One of the common areas that binds all of the school shooters together is all of them were the victim of bullying. Their lives were made miserable. What we have also found is many of them felt there is no other recourse to stop this behavior other than going home and getting a weapon and taking care of the bullies in a dramatic and final way. (Feinberg in Menard & Martindale, 2005)

To help teachers and administrators reduce bullying, a rapidly growing number of schools are conducting training sessions designed to equip personnel with methods of detecting bullying and of reducing its incidence through techniques described later in this book (Chapter 8: Bullying and Hazing).

Retaliating against Authority

School personnel can become targets of attacks by students who resent teachers and administrators having authority over the students during the school day.

Three boys who attended Palm Middle School in Lemon Grove (California) were confined to juvenile hall on a charge of attempted murder when their plot to kill a teacher was discovered. The intended attack was to be retaliation for the teacher's awarding one of the 14-year-olds a failing grade for his poor academic performance in her class. That boy and two companions—ages 13 and 14—brought a loaded pistol to school. One planned to distract the teacher so that another could shoot her (Soto, 2004).

As a Cumberland (Tennessee) school-bus driver was driving her morning route, a 14-year-old passenger shot her to death with a .45-caliber handgun. Although the bus smashed into a utility pole after the shooting, none of the 24 pupil passengers were injured. Observers speculated that the attack was a response to the driver's having reported the boy the previous day for using smokeless tobacco on the bus. According to the public defender who spoke at length with the boy after the arrest, "We feel he has severe mental issues. He's an A and B student and had never been in trouble before" (School bus, 2005).

Efforts to reduce violence motivated by resistance to authority can include (a) counseling or class lessons that equip students with nonviolent techniques for venting their resentment at decisions made by school authorities and (b) alerting students to the wisdom of informing school personnel of any classmates' plans to adopt violent means of striking back at authorities.

Affairs of the Heart

Love triangles and the rejection of lovers are sometimes blamed for deadly weapons violence.

A Pennsylvania high-school girl, jealous over a 16-year-old schoolmate's apparent interest in the girl's boyfriend, stalked the 16-year-old and stabbed her to death. The stalker was sentenced to life in prison (High court, 2005).

Late at night in the parking lot of Alice Maxwell Elementary School in Sparks (Nevada), two boys from rival gangs met to decide—by fighting—which one had the right to date a particular girl. Each of the intended combatants was accompanied by friends, so that what had been planned as a match between the two youths turned into a gang fight involving 20 participants. During the brawl, a 16-year-old stabbed a rival gang member in the neck and chest. The wounded teenager was treated in a hospital, where he remained in stable condition, while police arrested the stabber on suspicion of attempted murder (Violence in our schools, 2005).

In the cafeteria on the last day of class at Heritage High School in Conyers (Georgia), a 15-year-old, distressed over a broken romance, opened fire on schoolmates with two handguns. He wounded six students before falling to his knees, sticking a pistol barrel in his mouth, surrendering, and sobbing, "Oh, I'm so scared." Prosecutors charged him as a juvenile with aggravated assault, weapons violations, and cruelty to children (Pilcher, 1999).

There is apparently little that teachers or administrators can do to quell violence that results from affairs of the heart, other than to conduct lessons illustrating the outcomes of different means of competing for an admired peer's affection. Classes in English literature that include discussions of stories the students read or movies they see offer such opportunities.

Showing Off

The reason students bring weapons to school is often only to boast—to show how clever or daring they are, but without any intention of doing harm. Such was the apparent motive behind an incident at Leon Godchaux Junior High School in Reserve (Louisiana).

During math class, a 15-year-old boy reached into his pocket and accidentally discharged the .25-caliber semiautomatic handgun that was hidden there. The bullet exploded into the floor, prompting the teacher and class members to flee the room. When questioned by the police, the boy said he had been given the weapon that morning by a 14-year-old companion, who later claimed that the device was a cigarette lighter he had come across accidentally. A police officer agreed that the weapon was "small, one of those that looks like a cigarette lighter." A representative of the school board believed that the violence was not planned: "There was no intent to use or show or harm anyone with the gun. No students or employees were threatened with the gun" (Daigle, 2005).

Sometimes pupils are not clearly aware of a school's rules governing weapons and of the punishments that can result from ignoring the rules. Thus, teachers can profit from discussing such matters in class, particularly by enlivening the presentation with cases in which the rules were disregarded. In addition, school regulations can appropriately be published in student-conduct handbooks given to both the students and their parents.

TREATING INDIVIDUALS WHO HAVE COMMITTED WEAPON VIOLENCE

Episodes of deadly weapon violence can result in treatments for the perpetrators of violence and for their victims. The following discussion focuses on treating perpetrators. A later section focuses on victims.

School personnel can profit from both (a) recognizing steps in the process of treating offenders and (b) identifying the advantages and disadvantages of typical kinds of treatments.

The Process of Treating Offenders

Dealing with offenders typically involves three steps: (a) detaining the apparent assailant, (b) judging his or her guilt, and (c) applying sanctions. Whether an alleged offender is detained by school personnel or by the police depends on whether only a school regulation has been breached (such as bringing a knife to school) or a crime has been committed (such as stabbing a classmate). If the offender's misdeed has been limited to breaking a school rule, then the question of guilt is usually settled in a meeting—a *hearing*—at the school. The hearing is typically attended by school personnel, witnesses to the episode, the offender, members of the offender's family, and sometimes an attorney representing the offender. However, if the misdeed has involved breaking a criminal law, the matter of guilt is determined either:

• in a criminal court for adults (if the offender is beyond age 17, or is younger but is thought to have been fully aware of the seriousness of his or her act) where the offender can be represented by a lawyer, and the matter of guilt is decided by either a judge or a jury; or

- in a juvenile court in which there is neither a jury nor a lawyer representing the defendant, and the judge usually has more discretionary power than do judges in criminal courts for deciding on a proper disposition of the case.

Whether a deadly weapon offense is handled by school personnel or in a criminal court, two considerations that can influence the choice of a treatment are (a) zero tolerance and (b) influential conditions.

ZERO TOLERANCE

Zero tolerance, in its fundamental form, means that the punishment for an act of violence is specified in a policy statement, and the punishment is imposed without exception. Thus, a strict form of zero tolerance recognizes no extenuating circumstances and permits no negotiation of sanctions.

The 1994 federal gun-safe-schools law—when followed by the 2001 Columbine killings and September 11 terrorist planes crashing into the New York Trade Center—stimulated a growing host of school districts throughout the nation to adopt zero-tolerance responses toward deadly weapon violence. By 1999, more than 91 percent of the nation's public schools had such policies in place. The zero-tolerance movement was first applied to firearms, and then in many school systems was extended to include other forms of violence— threats, sexual abuse, child abuse, and fighting. For teachers, administrators, school boards, and much of the general public, zero tolerance offers a variety of appealing features.

As originally enacted on March 31, 1994, . . . the *Gun-Safe Schools Act* [GFSA] required each state receiving *Elementary and Secondary Education Act* funds to have in effect a state law requiring local educational agencies (LEAs) to expel from school for a period of not less than one year a student who was determined to have brought a weapon to school. The gun-safe law also required that a state's law allow the chief administering officer of the LEA in question to modify the expulsion requirement on a case-by-case basis.

The term "expulsion" is not defined by the GFSA; however, at a minimum, expulsion means removal from the student's regular educational program. Expulsion does not mean merely moving a student from a regular program in one school to a regular program in another school. (Guidance concerning, 2004)

As this description illustrates, the federal gun-safe-schools act was almost— but not quite—a firm zero-tolerance law. Although it mandated a year's expulsion from school, it did provide an opportunity for the chief administrator of a school district or state education department to alter the expulsion rule in light of facts about the case at hand.

In strict-zero-tolerance practice:

- Students and their parents know precisely the punishment that will be meted out for a specified offense.
- The people responsible for enforcing the law know exactly what sanctions to impose.
- No long-drawn-out hearings or trials are needed. Justice is automatic.

However, critics have charged that the conditions affecting one case of deadly weapon violence are not identical to conditions affecting other cases. Thus, they insist that each episode should be settled on its particular merits. They argue that the task of adjudicating a case should include consideration of such extenuating circumstances as the offender's intent, age, knowledge-of-right-and-wrong, health status, past record, and likelihood of committing future violent acts. Opponents of zero tolerance have been so disturbed about the consequences of zero-tolerance practices that they have created an Internet Web site called *ZT Nightmares* at http://www.ztnightmares.com/ that publishes descriptions of incidents submitted—usually by parents—to illustrate the injustice of zero-tolerance practices.

However, news stories in the daily press, rather than Internet Web pages, have been the chief means through which the general public learns of ostensibly unfair applications of zero tolerance, as illustrated by the following news items.

A third-grade boy was suspended from a Green Bay (Wisconsin) school for wearing a key chain that included an inch-long flat plastic replica of a gun—a key chain purchased from a restaurant vending machine. The school superintendent defended the suspension as "the importance of safety. . . . The possession of facsimile firearms is also prohibited, [including] any replica, toy, starter pistol, or other object that bears a reasonable resemblance to, or can be perceived to be, an actual firearm" (Decker, 2005).

In Palm Beach (Florida) a student was arrested and charged with "throwing a deadly missile" when he tossed an egg on Halloween (Study finds, 2003).

A 16-year-old honor student in Greenville, South Carolina, was expelled from Eastside High School for using a knife with a four-inch blade to cut out plastic name tags for a Youth-in-Government club meeting. The girl had retrieved the knife from her car to use as she and fellow club members were in the school library preparing for the meeting. When the student's parents filed a lawsuit against the school district, the judge reversed the expulsion on the grounds that district officials had failed to produce any evidence of how long the blade was or that the girl "possessed or used [the knife] with the intention of inflicting bodily harm or death." At the original expulsion hearing, the school principal had said she would have handled the episode differently if she had not been forced to apply the district's no-tolerance policy (Walton, 2003).

A second-grader in Alexandria (Louisiana) was expelled for bringing her grandfather's gold-plated pocket watch to school—a watch that had a tiny knife attached (Cauchon, 1999).

Two elementary-school boys in New Jersey were arrested and charged with terrorism for playing cops and robbers with paper guns (Study finds, 2003).

A sixth-grader in Tempe (Arizona) discovered that she had left a two-inch pocketknife in a compartment of her backpack. She showed it to friends and asked what she should do. "We were thinking about whether I should or shouldn't throw it away, but then again, I worried somebody would've found it," she said. Later she gave the knife to a teacher but, according to the school-district rules, she should have surrendered the knife at the moment she discovered it. After the girl was questioned for half a day, she was suspended from school for the remaining two weeks of the semester. School authorities explained that district rules permitted administrators to impose suspensions or expulsion for students found in "possession of a dangerous instrument capable of intimidating or inflicting bodily harm to another person" (Lucas, 2003).

A typical complaint critics have made about zero tolerance is that drastic sanctions applied to students who have committed minor or inadvertent offenses cause those students to suffer dire consequences and a damaged reputation from which they may never recover.

However, in response to criticisms of zero-tolerance policies, supporters of typical school discipline practices assert that reports of unreasonable punishments lead the public to a distorted impression of safety procedures in most schools. For instance, consider the following opinion from the National School Safety and Security Services Web site.

Based on our experience as school safety professionals, which includes working with educators and safety officials in over 30 states, we have found zero tolerance to have little true meaning in the day-to-day actions of most educators. Instead, this vaguely and inconsistently defined concept appears to rest more in the minds and rhetoric of politicians and academicians than it does school administrators. While a number of anecdotal incidents illustrating questionable school discipline have been used to suggest that school administrators are out of control with their administration of discipline in the name of zero tolerance, we strongly believe that the incidents cited do not reflect discipline administration in most of our nation's schools. (National School Safety, 2005b)

Influential Conditions

Unless a strict zero-tolerance policy is followed, the choice of a treatment for deadly weapon violence will be influenced by significant conditions in the case at hand.

Consider, for example, the instance of a 6-year-old first-grader in Flint (Michigan) who shot a classmate to death with a .32-caliber semiautomatic handgun. The gun was a stolen weapon that the boy's uncle— who operated a drug crack house—had received in a gun-for-drugs trade. At the time, the boy was living temporarily with his uncle after the boy's drug-addicted mother had been evicted from her home. The 6-year-old found the loaded gun under a blanket in his uncle's house and brought it to school to frighten a first-grade girl with whom he had argued the previous day. He killed the girl with a single shot (Pelley, 2000).

Authorities now faced the problem of what to do with a 6-year-old murderer. Two influential conditions weighed by the county prosecuting attorney were the child's age and home environment. The prosecutor could not charge the boy with a crime as a juvenile delinquent because, according to the law, a 6-year-old is too young to understand death and to have intentionally committed murder. The prosecutor estimated that the boy might have considered the gun just a toy. As for the child's family background, the attorney noted that the father was presently in jail for violating parole after serving time for drug trafficking and burglary. Thus, the prosecutor reasoned that,

This little guy was living in a very chaotic environment, one in which there were drugs, guns; there were people coming in and out of his house all the time. I can't imagine a worse environment for a little boy to grow up in or be around. It appears to me that he's assimilated much of what he saw, the emulation of "I'm the man; I've got the gun." You're talking about young children in an environment where the only thing [seen was] dope and guns and a few bottles of pop. We're dealing with a 6-year-old, not a 19-year-old. We're dealing with somebody who still believes in Santa Claus and Easter Bunny. (Pelley, 2000)

But the county sheriff warned that the boy was still dangerous and should be held responsible for the crime: "Whether or not he had intent, or whether or not he can form [the idea of] intent, the fact is we've got a little girl that's dead, just as if a 40-year-old man had pulled the trigger" (Pelley, 2000).

A professor of human development, who specialized in the study of violent children, said of the Flint case, "A boy that young is still very malleable no matter what he's done. . . . But he won't automatically change. If you simply turn him loose and say, 'Have a nice day' and, 'Don't do this again,' you can almost guarantee that he'll go back to this pattern of aggression. And maybe there'll be another murder down the line" (Pelley, 2000).

During a juvenile court hearing the day after the murder, the 6-year-old was sent to live with his maternal aunt. The father appealed to have the boy returned to the family after the father was out of jail. The final decision would be the responsibility of a judge who would determine whether the 6-year-old would stay with the family, be placed in a foster home, or be sent to a state facility where he would be under professional care (Pelley, 2000).

The particular conditions that a person chooses to consider when selecting a treatment usually depend on several factors, including:

- the kinds of available treatment options;
- the intended purpose of the treatment, such as (a) to prevent the offender from further deadly weapon violence, (b) to deter other potential offenders, (c) to reform the offender's general character, or (d) to avenge a weapons attack;

- the likely cost of the treatment in terms of funds, personnel, time, and bother; and

- social acceptability, in the sense of whether a kind of treatment would be judged permissible by the public or by influential groups, particularly such treatments as the death penalty, whipping, solitary confinement, or life imprisonment without the possibility of parole.

Typical Ways of Treating Offenders

Most violent-violent cases in schools result in arrest and in court trials. Laws governing such violent behavior can include a wide variety of charges and sanctions that may vary from one jurisdiction to another. Crimes typically fall under three general categories representing different degrees of seriousness. Least critical are *infractions* that usually warrant a stern warning, a light monetary fine, a period of community service, and/or probation. *Misdemeanors* are crimes resulting in a moderate level of damage; punishment can include up to a year of imprisonment (jail or juvenile detention facility), a modest fine, a substantial period of community service, and/or probation. *Felonies* are the most serious violent crimes—murder, attempted murder, crippling physical or mental harm, costly damage to property, and the like. Each of the three categories includes subclasses of crime representing differing levels of seriousness within that category. For instance, felonies can include first-degree murder, second-degree murder, first-degree manslaughter, second-degree manslaughter, and more.

The following four cases illustrate varied kinds of charges filed against perpetrators of different kinds of weapons violence.

As a 7-year-old second-grader in a schoolroom at Leawood Elementary School in Columbus (Ohio) was stuffing a .45-caliber semiautomatic pistol into his backpack, the gun fired a bullet through the boy's hand. He was taken to a hospital for treatment while the police searched for the source of the weapon. They discovered that the boy's 24-year-old brother owned the pistol and had hidden it under a sofa where the 7-year-old had found it. No criminal charges were drawn against the 7-year-old, but his adult brother was cited for negligent assault, a third-degree misdemeanor (Violence in our schools, 2005).

During a lunchtime altercation between two girls at Kensington High School in Philadelphia, an 18-year-old stabbed a 15-year-old in the back with a paring knife, which the assailant tossed into a trash container as she ran from the scene. The 18-year-old was arrested and charged with aggravated assault, simple assault, recklessly endangering another person, and possession of an instrument of a crime (Woodall, 2005).

A 16-year-old girl was cited for attempted murder after stabbing a 17-year-old girl multiple times with a steak knife as the pair fought during geometry class at Chicago's Marshall High School. Authorities were mystified over how the stabber had been able to bring the knife into the school without its being spotted by the school's metal detectors and scanners. Another student said she thought the 16-year-old had hidden the weapon in her shoe (Jacobson, 2005).

A 19-year-old sophomore at Wyandotte High School in Kansas City (Kansas) was arraigned on four felony counts after he shot off a handgun in a school restroom. The charges against him included possession of a firearm at a school, possession of a firearm by a felon, criminal discharge of a firearm, and obstruction of justice (Newbury, 2004).

After an offense has been proven in court, a specific treatment for the offender is set. Each type of treatment is accompanied by its particular advantages and disadvantages, as illustrated in the following examples of six types—execution, incarceration, expulsion, suspension, probation, and pardon.

Execution

If the goal of treatment is to eliminate any possibility that offenders will commit another crime, then killing them is the surest way to achieve that aim. And—at least theoretically—executing criminals should save the cost incurred if they received long prison terms rather than being executed. But in actual practice, keeping felons for years on death row while their appeals drag laboriously through the court system can prove to be very expensive.

For both moral and practical reasons, execution has become increasingly less popular than it was in the past. Some critics question the morality of a justice system that intentionally deprives people of their lives. "If killing is evil and warrants punishment, then why should the state indulge in that evil?" Critics also object to execution on the grounds that increasingly sophisticated forensic techniques (such as using DNA evidence from crime scenes) have shown that innocent people too frequently have been judged guilty of violent crimes and condemned to death.

Sometimes offenders avoid a death penalty if they make the job of prosecuting attorneys easier by confessing to a crime rather than fighting criminal charges in a costly court trial.

In order to escape execution, a 19-year-old student at a rural Missouri boarding school for troubled youths confessed to slaying a 16-year-old schoolmate by bludgeoning the younger teen, then slashing his throat. Prosecutors withdrew a demand for the death penalty after the accused waived his right to a jury trial, thereby permitting the judge to assign (a) one lifetime sentence in prison for the murder, and (b) a second concurrent 50-year sentence for armed criminal action. The 19-year-old had told police that he killed his schoolmate to prevent him from revealing the 19-year-old's plan "to take over the school and start a cult like the Branch Dravidians" (Youth gets life, 1997).

Incarceration

The most frequent punishment meted out to those who commit weapons crimes is imprisonment. From the viewpoint of public safety, imprisonment has the advantage of limiting offenders' future misdeeds by removing them from general society. The only offenses they can commit while locked up are ones limited to the facility in which they are kept. But a disadvantage of incarceration as a treatment for students is that it too often defeats the purpose of schooling—of enabling the young to acquire knowledge and skills that enable them to prosper throughout a law-abiding lifetime. Unless a juvenile detention center, jail, or prison has an efficient education program (which most do not), incarcerated youths lose the opportunity to better themselves educationally. Instead, what they usually learn is how be more active, dedicated criminals by dint of instruction from their fellow inmates.

The length of time and the place in which an offender will be locked up depends both on the seriousness of the crime and the offender's age. Age in such cases is used as a likely indicator of the offender's intent and understanding of the gravity of his or her misdeed. Children below ages 10 or 12 are usually assumed by the law to be under "the age of reason," thus lacking informed judgment about moral matters. Youths between about age 12 to 17 or 18 are thought to be more aware of moral issues than are younger children, but they are still considered immature, thoughtless, and irresponsible. Consequently, the rules governing how such offenders are treated are usually different from the ones governing the handling of adult criminals. Although such rules can vary somewhat from state to state, it is common practice for child and young-adolescent lawbreakers to be tried in juvenile courts and, if sentenced to confinement, to spend their time in juvenile detention facilities rather than adult jails or prisons. Furthermore, the records of their crimes are typically sealed and not available to the police or attorneys when the offenders reach adulthood. However, if youths appear to have a mature capacity to understand the seriousness of their act and had intended to do the harm that resulted from their violent behavior, they can be tried as adults. In that event, they face the prospect of being incarcerated in an adult prison or even executed.

The following examples illustrate three kinds of violence that led to imprisonment.

When a cafeteria worker at Bull Run Middle School in Virginia discovered that her 12-year-old son had brought two rifles, a shotgun, and ammunition to school, she locked the weapons in her van. Later in the day, the boy retrieved the guns and took them into the school, where he held hostages for a brief time. The boy was sentenced to four months in a juvenile detention facility on felony-weapons and abduction charges. His mother served a three-month jail term for having weapons on school property (Glod, 2005).

A 14-year-old middle-school student in Lake Worth (Florida)—tried in court as an adult for the shooting death of a seventh-grade teacher—was convicted of second-degree murder and sentenced to 28 years in prison without the possibility of parole (Randall, 2001).

In the Pahrump (Nevada) bus-hijacking incident described earlier, when the samurai-sword-wielding 15-year-old drove off with the school bus, police were alerted and gave chase as the boy sped toward the California border. After California patrolmen stretched nail-strips across the highway ahead of the bus, the boy swerved into the desert and the bus overturned. The youth was returned to a Nevada court, where the judge ruled that, even though the boy was still a juvenile, he would be tried as an adult on the grounds that threatening a bus driver with a sword was "as serious as someone robbing a store with a gun." The court's decision meant that the youth, if convicted and sentenced to imprisonment, would serve his time in a state prison rather than in a juvenile detention center (Waite, 2003).

Suspension

Being suspended from school means that the accused is prohibited from coming to school for a specified period of time. Suspensions are of two main kinds that represent either the complete punishment or an investigative interim.

A complete-punishment suspension consists of the person—a student or a staff member—being banned from attending school for a particular number of days or weeks as the entire penalty for a weapons violation. As soon as the specified period of time has passed, the offender is permitted to return to school without further sanctions. For example, a girl was assigned to serve a 2-week suspension for bringing a pair of pointed scissors to school in her purse. A middle-school boy was suspended for 3 weeks for aiming a gun-like water pistol at a classmate. An 8-year-old was suspended for striking a teacher in the face with his jacket (Chang, 2005).

An investigative-interim suspension is a period of time during which a weapons incident can be studied to determine exactly what happened, the extent of harm, who was involved, who deserves blame for the episode, and what treatment is warranted on the basis of fact-finding.

At Carson Junior High School in Mesa (Arizona) a 12-year-old student was given a 10-day suspension for taking a loaded .38-caliber pistol to school. The suspension was intended to give police time to search out the details of the episode. The boy told police he brought the weapon to scare off rival gang members who, he said, planned to rape female members of his gang. He faced a likely sentence of a year in a juvenile detention center (Melendez, 2003).

Two advantages of suspensions are that they remove alleged offenders from the school setting, and the punishment may convince the wrongdoers to mend their ways in the future. However, if the suspension involves keeping a student out of school, it defeats the purpose of schooling by taking away the offender's opportunity to pursue the learning program. Some schools, in order to avoid this disadvantage, require students to spend their suspension at the school, continuing to study while in a detention room away from their classmates (Howard & Shinkle, 2005).

Expulsion

Expulsion (dismissal) differs from suspension in that expulsion removes a student or staff member permanently from a school.

A 15-year-old boy at Dunbar High School in Lexington (Kentucky) faced expulsion after being charged with bringing a handgun onto school grounds—a class-D felony. The weapon was discovered when a teacher suspected the student was carrying a firearm and alerted an in-school law-enforcement officer who questioned the boy and found a pistol "on his person" (Jones, 2003).

In some people's opinion, expelling a student is such a drastic sanction that they go to great lengths to have the penalty lifted.

Officials at Forest Park High School in Woodbridge (Virginia) expelled a 17-year-old for allegedly building crude bombs from plastic bottles, aluminum foil, and household cleaners, then assigning friends to plant the explosives at elementary schools throughout Prince William County. The accused youth responded to his expulsion by taking the matter to federal court where he denied playing any role in placing bombs in schools. However, Forest Park officials claimed that he was the person who had taught companions how to build the bombs that they had placed in the schools. According to school officials, even if the 17-year-old was not directly responsible for the bombings, the expulsion was warranted because he had admitted exploding several bombs throughout the community the same weekend that the explosions occurred at the elementary schools. That act in itself was a violation of school policies governing out-of-school behavior (Barakat, 2004).

Probation

Probation is the practice of permitting a law-breaker to be spared detention or imprisonment and be free to move about the community under supervision. Probation assumes two main forms. In one form, the offender spends no time in confinement. In the other form, a period of probation follows a time of incarceration. For example, a student convicted of stabbing a schoolmate may be committed to a juvenile detention facility for 1 year, then placed on probation for an additional 2 years. During those 2 years, the student may continue to attend school. To earn probation status, an offender must agree to conditions set by the court or by the school district, with a probation officer assigned to supervise the student's behavior to ensure compliance with the conditions.

In recent years, more school districts have established school-based-probation programs in which a probation officer located in a school is responsible for (a) making sure offenders adhere to the rules of their probation and (b) fostering offenders' social adjustment and reform. For instance, under the state of Pennsylvania's plan, school-based probation officers—in addition to monitoring students' conduct—are expected to:

• provide assistance to school personnel who are making decisions about court-supervised youth;

• provide immediate intervention services for offenders who come into conflict with schoolmates or school personnel;

- in collaboration with school officials, work to reduce in-school and out-of-school suspensions, tardiness, absenteeism, and dropouts;
- provide in-service training for school officials about probation services and the juvenile-justice system; and
- encourage parental involvement in school activities (Fifth Judicial District, 2005).

The benefit of school-based probation is that it increases the contact between the officers and the youths. Being located in the school also permits officers to check attendance, discipline records, and other information about probationers on a daily basis, as well as to check with teachers about academic progress. Consequently, officers develop more substantial personal relationships with youths, resulting in improved communication and understanding. (Office of Juvenile Justice, 2004)

A further benefit of probation is that it costs far less than keeping offenders in jail, prison, or a juvenile hall.

A disadvantage of probation, compared to incarceration, is that it does not ensure the safety of other students and school staff members since it allows offenders to roam about the school and community. In addition, probation officers who have a large number of students to supervise lack sufficient time to attend to offenders who are in need of guidance.

Pardon

The term *pardon* refers to the act of forgiving an individual for a crime and relieving him or her of penalties typically assessed for that crime. Pardons are granted whenever authorities—such as a school board or a juvenile-court judge—believe that extenuating circumstances associated with the accused's misdeed warrant the person being absolved of blame.

In keeping with Indiana state law, an 18-year-old student at Goshen High School was expelled for a year for bringing a rifle and ammunition onto school property. However, the youth was pardoned by school authorities after he explained that he was a member of the Indiana National Guard and that a friend had borrowed his car and rifle to go target shooting. When the student later drove his car to school, he was unaware that his friend had left the gun and ammunition in the trunk. After hearing this explanation and listening to witnesses who attested to the guardsman's good character, the administrators decided not to file charges and to allow the youth to return to school (Student expelled, 2004).

For individuals who have been accused of a violent act, a pardon has the advantages of absolving them of blame and enabling them to maintain the reputation of being law-abiding. However, whether his or her good name is thus regained depends on whether everyone who heard the original report of the alleged misdeed will also hear the later report that the accused has been judged faultless.

TREATING VICTIMS OF WEAPON VIOLENCE

Victims of violence are of two kinds, direct and indirect. Direct victims are persons who have been the object of a weapon attack—ones who have been shot, stabbed, or beaten by an assailant. Indirect victims are people who have suffered from either witnessing the attack or learning about it. Three treatments that can be offered to victims are personal counseling, compensation, and the opportunity to transfer to another school.

Crisis Counseling

Each year, more school systems develop counseling procedures designed to help students and staff members cope with the distress they have suffered as a result of weapons violence.

After a 14-year-old at Southwood Middle School in Palmetto Bay (Florida) fatally cut the throat of a fellow student in a school bathroom, authorities arranged grief-counseling sessions for the schools' students and teachers. The victim of the stabbing was described as a quiet, well-behaved honors student (Pinzur, Santana, & Rabin, 2004).

Two psychologists spent more than six weeks at Rocori High School in Cold Springs (Minnesota), offering crisis counseling to students and faculty members in the wake of a shooting episode in which a 15-year-old boy killed two schoolmates. The shooter was charged with murder and tried in court as an adult (Post, 2004).

Typical of the advice provided for counselors, teachers, and administrators who engage in crisis and grief counseling are the suggestions offered by the psychologists in the Rocori case. The day after the shooting, therapists began with the American Red Cross Critical Incident Debriefing model that involved having a group of students who had witnessed the episode share with each other their experiences at the time of the killing. However, because their recall of horrific impressions appeared to traumatize members of the group, the psychologists quickly changed to an approach that focused on the question, "How are you getting through today?" As a result, students began sharing their coping techniques with each other rather than their fears and distress. The counseling emphasis was thereafter on the more successful approach of the therapists serving as facilitators, encouraging students to problem-solve rather than the therapists forcing their own agenda by directly proposing solutions (Rollins, 2005).

The psychologists told the students they didn't have to say anything in the group or even be in the group for that matter. [Students] were allowed to sit by themselves in another room adjacent to the group instead of listening to the others. Those who needed to tell their stories in more detail were provided with "safe rooms," where they could receive individual counseling. An important part of the counselors' role ... was to let the students know that the trauma-related symptoms and feelings they were experiencing—anger, sadness, anxiousness, and trouble concentrating, sleeping or eating—were normal and would heal over time. (Rollins, 2005)

Compensation

There are various kinds of compensation that victims may receive as reparations for the harm they have suffered. Perhaps the most common kind is victims' satisfaction at knowing that their assailants have been punished by imprisonment, social disgrace, required servitude (cleaning up the campus, community service), and the like. Such satisfaction derives from the principle of *lex talionis*—ensuring that the punishment fits the crime and that wrongdoers get their "just deserts." It serves to fulfill victims' desire for revenge.

Compensation may also assume the form of offenders being obliged to admit their guilt, to apologize, and to express remorse for their misdeed. Some offenders are required to repay victims in money, goods, or services.

Transfer

Students who have been either the direct or indirect victims of weapons violence may be permitted to change to a different school if the school in which a violent act occurred is considered by parents to be unsafe or if that environment continues to remind students of tragic events.

DANGEROUS SCHOOLS AND SAFE SCHOOLS

Whereas the foregoing discussion has focused on treatments to apply after weapons violence has occurred, the following section concerns ways to prevent violence from occurring. Such ways consist of proactive steps taken to avert violent acts, or at least to reduce their frequency. The first portion of the section addresses the problem of dangerous schools. The second portion suggests ways to make schools safe.

Dangerous Schools

Included in the U.S. government's No-Child-Left-Behind Act (NCLB) that was passed by Congress in 2001 was a provision (Section 9532) that allowed students in a persistently dangerous school to transfer to a safe school. The government's way of getting states to adopt this policy was to withhold federal No-Child funds from states that failed to comply. Under the law, states have been obligated to compile a list of persistently dangerous schools each year, with states being free to set their own standards about which sorts of violence to include. School districts are required to inform parents if their child's school is persistently dangerous, and those parents have the right to transfer their child to a safe one.

The U. S. Department of Education urged states to seek advice from parents and other community members when they spelled out what the phrase *persistently dangerous schools* was intended to mean and to "review and revise" those definitions every year to make them more reflective of the actual threats of violence students may face. Different states, with this opportunity to define *persistently dangerous* as they chose, came up with somewhat different definitions. Thus, standards were not uniform across the nation, so the number of ostensibly dangerous schools has varied significantly from one state to another. A 2003 survey revealed that forty-four states and the District of Columbia reported not even a single unsafe school. Among the remaining six states, Pennsylvania reported twenty-eight schools as dangerous, Nevada eight, New Jersey seven, Texas six, New York two, and Oregon one. This meant that only fifty-two of the nation's 91,000 public schools were deemed unsafe, as judged by the states' varied definitions of "persistently dangerous" (Nealis, 2003).

Not only did the lack of consistency among definitions contribute to extensive underreporting of school violence, but also the bad image in the public's mind of a school being labeled "dangerous" caused many principals and superintendents to avoid reporting violent acts. As a result, critics of the NCLB dangerous-school plan have claimed that the way the federal provision is worded and interpreted has concealed the need for greater efforts and funds to increase school safety. For instance, as school officials keep

their statistics of school crime down to avoid the "persistently dangerous" label, they may simultaneously reduce their opportunities for obtaining funds for school violence prevention programs, since the absence of [supportive] data will prohibit them from demonstrating a need for such programs. (National School Safety, 2005a)

In addition, because so few schools have been listed as unsafe, parents have been deprived of the NCLB law's opportunity to transfer their children out of schools, which are, in fact, hazardous but not officially designated as such.

In summary, while the intent behind the NCLB dangerous-schools provision has been lauded, the plan's implementation has been so badly flawed that the plan may have caused more harm than good.

Developing Safe Schools

Rather than depending on the federal government's dangerous-schools program, school systems on their own initiative have introduced a variety of measures to make schools safer from weapons violence. Which measures a given school will adopt depends on such variables as (a) the frequency of weapons problems in the past, (b) the level of crime and disorder in the surrounding community, (c) the expense—in terms of money and personnel—of the various safety procedures, and (d) how much officials want the school to resemble a prison rather than a pleasant, welcoming site of learning opportunities. The following are among the more popular safety practices recently adopted by American schools.

Security Guards

More schools each year are employing professionally trained security guards whose tasks include (a) patrolling the school and surrounding campus before, during, and after classes are in session, (b) supervising the operation of video-surveillance cameras, alarm systems, and metal detectors, (c) detaining students and visitors who are suspected of carrying weapons, (d) stopping fights, and (e) alerting the police to security problems.

There continues to be controversy over the question of whether it is better for security guards to be unarmed rather than to carry a pistol, a stun gun, or a baton.

A stun gun or Taser is a device that fires

a pair of pronged darts that latch onto clothing or skin and send a 50,000-volt shock into the body in five-second bursts, which overrides the subject's central nervous system, causing uncontrollable contraction of the muscle tissue and instant collapse. The darts are attached to wires, which can reach up to 21 feet. People who have been "tased" report extreme, debilitating pain. (Stelzer, 2005)

Stun guns are in widespread use by police and, in some school districts, are carried by officers assigned as security personnel in schools. Because some people have died after being stun-gunned, parents and school personnel often object to equipping security guards with Tasers. In early 2005, a 14-year-old Chicago boy went into cardiac arrest after being "tased"; and the Miami, Florida, police revised their stun-gun policy after officers stunned both a 6-year-old boy in a school office and a 12-year-old girl truant who was trying to escape (Jacksonville police, 2005; Stelzer, 2005).

A typical baton is a steel stick used for hitting an assailant. Some batons, like telescopes, can be extended to a length of 16 or 24 inches. Others, like a stun gun, emit an electrical charge that momentarily shocks an assailant into a helpless state.

Two advantages claimed for arming security guards are that (a) the sight of a gun in a guard's holster deters potentially dangerous students or visitors from misdeeds and (b) if an armed offender actually fires his or her weapon, a guard can immediately stop further assault by shooting the offender. Proponents of the practice of arming guards contend that, in such cases as the Red Lake massacre cited in Chapter 1, fewer lives would be lost if guards carried weapons.

The first victim in the Red Lake incident was an unarmed guard who tried to stop the youth who did the killing. However, critics have claimed that having gun-toting police patrolling school corridors casts a depressing jail-like aura over what is supposed to be a friendly, appealing, setting in which students spend much of their time.

Security guards can be trained and supervised by the school system itself, or else the system can contract-out such services. The author of a study of security-guard practices in six large school systems (Atlanta, Baltimore, Montgomery County [Maryland], Philadelphia, St. Louis, and Washington, DC) concluded that:

We noted a greater level of professionalism, diligence, and a strengthened security posture at the schools using in-house security services. . . . An in-house security-guard force provides for a more professional working environment and . . . tends to be much more manageable. Further, the [school system] benefits more from its own in-house comprehensive security training and does not have to rely on training from an outside source that might not understand the rules and regulations unique to their school jurisdiction. (Andersen, 2005)

School districts have been cautioned to obtain bids from several companies if they plan to contract-out their security services. The Washington, DC public schools, in failing to obtain competitive bids, overpaid a security contractor by $11.4 million (McElhatton, 2004).

Entry-Control Techniques

The likelihood of deadly violence is obviously reduced if procedures are in place to prevent weapons from being brought onto school grounds. Such entry-control procedures include:

Placing a guard at the campus entry gate to check the identification of auto drivers and passengers; requiring students and staff to have a vehicle parking sticker in order to park on the campus.

Limiting the number of doors through which people can enter the school, with greeters at those doorways watching for signs of weapons; locking other exterior doors to prevent access from outside; labeling those doors inside: "For emergency exits only—Alarm will sound if opened."

Informing students and visitors that anyone walking around the campus during class hours will be (a) challenged for a pass or student identification card and (b) subject to search or scanning by a metal detector.

Ensuring that when a student is suspended or expelled, his or her identification card is confiscated, and—in large schools—making that student's picture available to the school's security staff (Green, 1999).

Metal Detectors

Particularly in high-crime neighborhoods, schools have increasingly employed portal, scanner, and X-ray metal detectors as entry-control devices.

A *portal* metal detector is a doorway-like framework through which students, staff members, and visitors must pass as they enter the school. Any object a person wears or carries that will conduct electricity—and particularly such metal items as handguns or knives—sets off an alarm (noise or flashing light) as the person walks through the frame. Then the operator of the detector must discover whether the sensed object is a weapon or, rather, is a benign piece metal, such as a belt buckle or coin.

A *scanner* is a handheld, battery-operated device that looks rather like a cell phone with an antenna or wand attached. The scanner operator, by moving the wand around and close to a student's body, can rather accurately locate sources of electrical-conductive material that are in or on the student's clothing or body. When the scanner senses such an item, it makes a squealing noise, alerting the operator to discover whether the item is something that could serve as a weapon.

If a school is attempting to do a complete screening of students each morning, the handheld metal detector will more likely be used as a supplement to portal metal detectors. . . . Handheld detectors allow the security staff to more accurately locate the source of an alarm on a student's body, after a student has already walked through a portal system and caused an alarm. (Green, 1999)

An X-ray detector reveals the shape of objects in such containers as book bags, backpacks, briefcases, handbags, and boxes without the need to open the containers. When the shape of an object suggests that it might be an illegal item (gun, knife, or an explosive), the package can be opened to determine whether it is, indeed, a potential weapon.

Although metal detectors generally do their job well, their use is accompanied by three bothersome problems. First, they slow the process of students and staff members entering school, particularly if scanners are used. Second, it is expensive to train and pay personnel to operate detector systems efficiently. Third, the use of detectors adds to the penitentiary-like atmosphere of a school—an atmosphere that students and teachers can find unpleasant.

Despite their usefulness, metal detectors are not foolproof. As a report for the school board in Dade County, Florida, observed: "Students become creative. They pass weapons in through windows to friends, hide knives and other sharp instruments in shoes and in a girlfriend's hair. They manage to find creative ways to bring weapons to school" (Constitutional Rights Foundation, 2005).

The installation of metal detectors has not always been greeted with universal student approval.

At the outset of the Fall 2005 semester at New York's DeWitt High School, security guards explained to groups of returning students that metal detectors had been installed. Therefore, when students arrived at school each day, they would need to line up, remove metal from their pockets, take off belts, and walk through a metal detector. Their bags would also be scanned by an X-ray machine, and no one would be allowed to leave the building at lunchtime. In response to the new regulations, the students circulated a protest petition and skipped classes to join a 1,500-strong peaceful march two miles to the Department of Education where they could meet the administrators who had agreed to hear their objections to the new security procedures. During the hearing, student representatives voiced their grievances. Then school officials pointed out why tighter security seemed needed—DeWitt Clinton's crime rate was 60% higher than that of any other New York school of similar size, and the school had suffered 13 major crimes during the previous school year. Although officials were unwilling to undo any of the new security measures, guidance counselors agreed to meet with students to determine if any changes could reasonably be made (Santos, 2005).

Video Surveillance Cameras

Like metal detectors, video cameras in classrooms, corridors, entry ways, and school buses have become increasingly popular as school officials have sought better methods of monitoring students' and visitors' behavior. But the adoption of video surveillance has been relatively slow as a result of concerns about (a) the costs of video arrangements (from $75,000 to $100,000 for a 16-camera system) and (b) video cameras' potential for violating individuals' right to privacy. By early 2005, only 191 of New York City's 1,356 public schools had camera systems. However, all twenty-five schools currently under construction and all future New York schools would be equipped with cameras (Lombardi, 2004).

Video cameras can serve several useful purposes. They enable school personnel at a remote location—such as the main office—to see events that occur at the fifteen, twenty, or thirty sites of cameras around the school. Students' and visitors' awareness that cameras are recording their movements helps deter them from weapons violence. And the resulting magnetic tape records of events are useful for identifying offenders and for judging their actions. Even when taped images are a bit blurred, offenders often confess their misdeeds when shown pictures of the incident. In court cases or school hearings, such tapes contribute evidence toward a just judgment of what happened.

However, video surveillance is accompanied by fears of unreasonable privacy invasion. In response to such fears, school boards sometimes establish rules governing the use of video cameras. Consider the guidelines suggested by the Information and Privacy Commission in Ontario (Canada):

Video cameras should only be installed in identified areas of schools where video surveillance is a necessary and viable detection or deterrence activity.

Equipment should never monitor the inside of areas where students and staff have a reasonable expectation of privacy (such as clothing-change rooms and washrooms).

Students and staff should be fully notified about the video surveillance program through clearly worded signs. Schools should not use hidden cameras.

Strict controls are needed to ensure the security and the integrity of the recorded images.

Retention periods need to be set [for the recording tapes]. We recommend that tapes that have not been used as part of an investigation should be erased after not more than 30 days. (Alfonso, 2003)

Crime-Prevention Roles for Students

Probably the best protection against weapons violence comes from students' willingness to discover and report the presence of weapons in school or to report schoolmates' attack plans.

The National Crime Prevention Council has suggested the following ways students can contribute to a safe school environment.

Refuse to bring weapons to school and refuse to keep silent about those who carry weapons.

Report any threats or crimes immediately to school authorities or police.

Report suspicious behavior or talk by other students to a teacher or counselor at your school. You may save someone's life.

Learn how to manage your own anger effectively. Find out ways to settle arguments by talking it out, working it out, or walking away rather than fighting.

Help others settle disputes peaceably. Start or join a peer-mediation program in which trained students help classmates find ways to settle arguments without fists or weapons.

Set up a teen court in which youths serve as judge, prosecutor, jury, and defense counsel. Courts can hear cases, make findings, and impose sentences, or they may establish sentences in cases where teens plead guilty. Teens feel more involved in the process than in an adult-run juvenile justice system.

Start a school crime watch. Consider including a student patrol that helps keep an eye on corridors, parking lots, and groups, and a way for students to report concerns anonymously.

Become a peer counselor, working with classmates who need support and help with problems.

Create a welcoming environment for students. Get to know new students and those who are unfamiliar to you. (Menard & Martindale, 2005)

More school systems are introducing programs in which students are taught alternatives to violence for coping with their conflicts with classmates or school staff, and teachers are being trained to spot violence-prone children and to intervene when violence escalates (Carter, 2003).

At a growing rate, school officials have urged students, staff members, and parents to use crime-watch hotlines for reporting evidence of weapons violence. For example, police in Fort Worth (Texas) praised students at Southwest High School who had used a hotline to report a classmate's bringing a gun to school (Kovach, 2004).

Revised School Designs

Security concerns have become high-priority considerations in architects' school designs. For example, when Supai Middle School in Scottsdale (Arizona) was razed and rebuilt in 2002, it was constructed in a courtyard style that required visitors to enter through the office. Previously, visitors could wander around the campus without reporting to the office. Under a similar plan, the aging elementary school in Tualatin (Oregon) was replaced in 2004. The new school consisted of a single building, with the office by the main door so the staff could control who came and went. In contrast, the old campus had several buildings, allowing people to go directly to classrooms and avoid the office. To cope with the problem of having multiple buildings to monitor, officials at Sandy High School in the Oregon Trail School District installed a thirty-two-camera surveillance system. And the new high school in Clackamas (Oregon) was built to optimize clear lines of sight through corridors, avoiding small alcoves and places with blocked views; a door-locking system enabled the staff to put the entire 2,000-student school on lockdown within seconds (Lopez, 2005).

Officials also make schools safer when they:

Enclose the campus with a robust fence that forces people to consciously trespass, rather than allowing uninhibited, casual entry.

Install classroom doors that teachers can lock from either the inside or outside.

Ensure that the school building and classroom areas can be locked off from the gym and other facilities that are used during off hours.

Provide a drop off/pickup lane for buses only.

Build single-stall bathrooms to reduce bathroom confrontations and problems.

Add secure skylights that allow light in but are less vulnerable to entry than typical windows.

Minimize the number of flat roofs from which an assailant could fire a gun.

Locate buildings and other student gathering areas back from streets, driveways, or parking areas by at least 50 feet.

Install security alarms in administrative offices and rooms containing high-value property, such as computers, VCRs, shop equipment, laboratory supplies, and musical instruments (Green, 1999).

CONCLUSION

The three aims of this chapter have been to (a) illustrate the nature of deadly weapons violence with vignettes from school systems around the nation, (b) suggest ways of treating both the perpetrators and victims of weapons attacks, and (c) identify methods of improving the security of schools so as to minimize weapons violence. Closely linked to weapons violence are the threats of violence described in Chapter 3, and fights in Chapter 4.

CHAPTER 3

Threats of Violence

Threats consist of menacing indications—physical, pictorial, spoken, or written—that a person or group intends to harm individuals, groups, or property. Threats can assume many forms, can be directed at various intended victims, and can cause diverse types of damage. This chapter's analysis views threats from five perspectives: (a) forms of threats, (b) circumstances often associated with threats, (c) threat consequences, (d) treating individuals who make threats, (e) treating those who are the targets of threats, and (f) reducing the incidence of threats.

FORMS OF THREATS

Two vantage points from which the form of threats can be inspected are those of the media employed and the kind of harm intended.

Media Used for Issuing Threats

The channels through which threats are issued range from face-to-face confrontations to students' personal journals and works of fiction.

Face-to-Face Confrontations

From the viewpoint of the person who issues a threat, the advantages of direct, face-to-face encounters can include (a) the possibility that the recipient will be frightened into doing what the threatener hopes and (b) the threatened person's reaction can be seen and promptly countered. From the vantage point of the threatened individual, face-to-face episodes (a) reveal who the threatener is (no anonymity) and (b) permit an immediate response. Such encounters frequently accelerate into extended arguments or physical fights that may or may not further the welfare of the combatants.

When a 16-year-old sophomore at the high school in Tiverton (Rhode Island) told a classmate that he was going to shoot him, the classmate reported the incident to a teacher who alerted the police. The subsequent investigation revealed that the same threat had been made on separate occasions to two other sophomores—one after a football game, the other during lunchtime in the school cafeteria. When police confronted the threatener at his home, they confiscated seven guns that belonged to his father (Teen said to threaten, 2003).

A history teacher from Lawrence Central High School in Indiana was arrested by police on a charge of intimidation for verbally threatening harm to a 17-year-old student. The incident occurred at a theater where the student worked collecting patrons' tickets as they entered. Not only was the teacher seen cursing the youth, but he was also observed giving money to a pair of men whom the teacher had summoned to the theater by cell phone after his encounter with the student. The two men then asked theater employees where they could find the student (Ryckaert, 2005).

Drive-by Threats

Some direct threats are not issued face to face but are shouted from a distance.

Six Santee (California) boys, ages 15 to 17, were arrested at West Hills High School and Chaparral High School on suspicion of stalking as a hate crime against Blacks and Asians and for participating in a street gang. The six, all members of a white-supremacy gang, repeatedly drove by a non-white student's house screaming racial insults and raising their arms in a Nazi salute (Sanchez & Arner, 2005).

Publicly Issued General Threats

The term *general threat* means menacing people in general rather than threatening particular individuals or groups. Such threats are typically motivated by the threateners' ill-defined anger or frustration over their plight, so they randomly strike out at the world. Or the motive may be simply to do mischief or gain attention.

At the end of the school day at Rhoades Elementary School in Wayne Township (Indiana), two boys—ages 10 and 11—shouted that there was a bomb in the building. After the school was evacuated, a search of the building failed to produce any explosives. The shouters were taken into custody and charged in juvenile court with false reporting and disorderly conduct. False reporting would qualify as a felony if filed against an adult. In a letter sent to all parents of children at Rhoades Elementary, school officials explained, "You never know if it's a threat or it's a rumor. Our policy is to investigate all threats and take appropriate action."

An executive from the Indiana Association of Public School Superintendents warned, "You can't make jokes or comments like that. It's like boarding an airplane nowadays—the things you once said aren't funny anymore" (O'Neal, 2003).

Anonymous Notes

Unsigned notes are written threats whose authors do not identify themselves. For threateners, such notes have the advantage of frightening the people who are the targets of the threats without exposing the writers to blame and retribution. For recipients of threats, the anonymity aspect can prove very stressful, leaving the victims wondering who among their acquaintances are seeking to harm them.

Students at Mounds View High School in Arden Hills (Minnesota) were sent home on the day officials found an anonymous note whose author threatened to bomb the school. The note contained racial references that worried African-American parents whose children were members of a student population that was 84 percent white and 5 percent black (Boyd, 2003). A written hit-list of "People to Kill" was discovered in the hands of an Indiana high school student whom authorities suspended from school while the episode was being investigated. The school-district superintendent said, "We don't know if it was a prank or if it was just mindless doodling by a student. But it's being taken very seriously" (Gillaspy, 2003).

Sometimes students who write anonymous threats seek to hide their identity by listing their own names among the intended victims. An example of such a ploy appeared at Montgomery Village Middle School in Gaithersburg (Maryland).

A crumpled note found on a hallway floor threatened death to 23 people, including students, teachers, and administrators. The note was discovered by two 13-year-old girls, who handed it to school officials. Three weeks later, a second note, found in another hallway, threatened death to the two girls who had given the first note to school authorities. Since the handwriting on the two notes was similar, police obtained a warrant to search the two girls' homes. In one home they found evidence that one of the girls was the author of both notes. The police charged the 13-year-old with disturbing the activities at a school, making a false statement to a police officer, and making a false statement to a school official. An attorney hired to defend the accused girl said the revelation that the 13-year-old had written the notes came as a complete surprise, "because until yesterday nobody ever indicated at any time during the investigation that she was anything but a victim" (Snyder, 2005).

Graffiti

Graffiti threats take the form of menacing phrases or drawings painted or penned (a) on walls, windows, or sidewalks of such public places as schools or (b) on property belonging to the people who are being threatened—cars, schoolbooks, backpacks, and clothing.

A message scribbled on the wall of a girls' bathroom at Martha's Vineyard Regional High School in Massachusetts read "On Dec. 12th 'I' will pull a Columbine." A search of students' lockers by the police failed to provide clues about who had written the threat. However, officials reported that they did have a list of suspects as a result of handwriting analyses and of videotapes from security cameras that photographed students entering and leaving the bathroom on the day that the scrawled threat appeared (Stearns, 2003).

Phone Calls

People who phone threats usually do so in order to keep their identity secret or to avoid directly facing those at whom the threat is aimed. However, the attempt to mask one's identity is defeated if school authorities or the police are able to trace the cell phone or home from which the call was made.

Phone calls are a great boon in combating violence when the caller's intent is either to warn school authorities of an impending attack or to identify the perpetrator of a violent act that has already occurred.

After being tipped off by an anonymous phone call, police in Dutchtown (Louisiana) arrested two high-school youths—ages 17 and 19—on one count of terrorizing, which constituted a felony punishable by up to 15 years in prison. The apparent plot was discovered when a caller phoned Dutchtown High School, accusing the two youths of planning some type of disturbance. The police who searched the students' homes found papers about the 1999 Columbine killings, along with poems written by the youths about their being bullied. In additional writings, the pair referred to themselves as "The Trenchcoat Mafia," an allusion to a group in the Columbine episode. Among the youths' drawings, police found one in which a student was "blowing the brains out of a particular teacher." Another pictured the two plotters on a school roof, "celebrating around dead bodies hanging out of windows." A police investigator reported, "This is not just a case of kids just talking to be cool. These students had plans all worked out." When questioned about their plot, the boys said it was only fantasy, a joke they never intended to carry out. Although no weapons were found in the youths' homes, there was evidence that the pair had obtained information about how to purchase shotguns and rifles (Two students, 2004).

Mailed Letters

A long-established route for sending threats is the postal service. Anonymous notes sent through the mail permit threateners to phrase their warnings carefully and illustrate them with intimidating drawings, photos, or copies of letters or newspaper articles. However, authors of such missives run the risk of the police and school authorities being able to recognize the source of the threats by analyzing handwriting, finger prints, postal marks, spelling and grammar in the letter, computer files, and the like.

Letters filled with death threats and racial slurs were mailed to two Black students and one Hispanic student at the 3,300-student Trinity International University, a Christian institution in Deerfield (Illinois). The letters prompted Trinity authorities to transfer more than 40 ethnic-minority students out of dormitories and into a hotel until police discovered that the author of the letters was a 19-year-old Black student who was unhappy at the university and wanted to convince her parents that the school was dangerous. She had hoped that publicity about the threats would accomplish her aim. Instead, she was charged with a hate crime, a felony carrying a penalty of up to five years in prison (Colias, 2005).

Computer Messages

As all of the nation's schools now provide personal computers for students and staff members, threats of violence have increasingly been issued through a school's computer network.

The message "I am going to kill you" was received on the computer printers in two teachers' classrooms at Smith Middle School in Chapel Hill (North Carolina). Because the school's computer system provided a record of who sent which messages from which computers, authorities were able to identify the boy who had made the anonymous threats. School officials doubted that the messages were aimed at specific teachers, because the school's printers were not identified by user, so the student might not have known to whom he was sending the notes (Ataiyero, 2005).

Cyber Threats

In keeping with the meaning of cybernetics as "the study of communication systems and their control," messages sent over the computer Internet have become known as *cyber threats*. Several of the Internet's services (e-mail, chat rooms, and instant-messaging) have been used both for issuing threats and for discovering threats so that potential damage can be averted.

Hints of a plot to randomly kill occupants of Wickenburg High School in Arizona were picked up by a citizen who logged into an Internet chat room that was frequented by the 16-year-old boy who was planning the attack. The police, alerted by the citizen, arrested the boy after a search of his home yielded weapons and notebooks detailing the attack plan. Authorities estimated that the youth hoped to become famous by carrying out an escapade similar to the Columbine massacre (Whiting, 2003).

Confessions to a Confidant

Criminal law recognizes that certain of society's professionals bear the obligation not to reveal confidential information that they receive from their patients, clients, and parishioners. Those professionals include physicians, psychiatrists, psychologists, lawyers, and such religious functionaries as ministers, priests, rabbis, and imams.

The matter of client confidentiality becomes a knotty problem for professionals if their clients reveal plans to carry out violent acts. On one hand, professionals are breaching client confidentiality if they warn the police or school officials of clients' plans that have been shared with their confidants during private sessions. On the other hand, the professionals may be placing innocent people at risk by not revealing such plots. If professionals remain silent and then the planned violence occurs, they might be held liable by the victims. However, if such plans are revealed and then no violent acts occur, then the confidants might be sued by the client or the client's family.

In Snellville (Georgia) a 14-year-old student was arrested after telling his psychologist he planned to set off bombs at his school, and the psychologist told the police of the plot. According to Georgia law, a psychologist or psychiatrist is permitted the discretion of deciding whether to warn either the police or intended victims of a possible attack by a potentially violent patient. In this case, the psychologist believed his teenage client was such a grave danger to the welfare of the school's inhabitants that he was willing to violate the patient-confidentiality rule and reveal the boy's intention to the police (Osinski, 2004).

Only a few states have laws (a) requiring warnings of likely violence to be issued and (b) providing immunity from litigation for professionals who give such warnings. State licensing codes often require professionals to consider certain factors before revealing a client's likely violent acts. Those factors include: Is there a clearly defined victim? Is the potential victim in clear and imminent danger? Is there a likelihood the threatened violence could actually occur?

Gestures

Cultures can differ in the sorts of gestures that imply violent intent. In one society, snapping one's thumb from one's teeth toward an intended victim or planting a kiss on the victim can signal imminent attack. In another culture, raising one's middle finger toward an opponent can portend an attack. Such traditions pose problems of interpreting gestures in societies that are becoming increasingly multicultural. In recent years, school personnel have apparently become more sensitive to the likely seriousness of threat gestures.

A fifth-grade boy at Parsons Elementary School in Gwinnett County (Georgia) was suspended from school for "disrupting class" by making a hand gesture as if he were shooting a pistol at a classmate. A school spokeswoman said the suspension was appropriate in view of "this incident and the child's past disciplinary history. The fifth-grader has committed four discipline infractions this school year, including a threat to kill other children" (Dodd, 2004).

Students' Journals and Works of Fiction

School authorities face the problem of determining if a threat has actually been issued whenever they are confronted with a student's personal diary, journal, or work of fiction that includes incidents of violence. The question becomes, "Is it fair to accuse a student of truly threatening harm to others if the student has written a story or poem that includes characters who plan attacks on others?" This issue was at the core of a case in a Georgia high school.

When a 14-year-old honor student passed her private diary to a friend during art class, the teacher seized the journal, later read it, and reported to authorities the content of one of the numerous stories the girl had written. The tale told of an unnamed student falling asleep in class and dreaming that she shot a teacher, ran from the classroom, and was killed by a security guard. In the story, the school bell then rang, wakening the student from her dream. She collected her books and went to her next class.

The day after the diary was seized, school police removed the 14-year-old from class. After a closed-door hearing, Fulton County school officials expelled her from Roswell High School for "inappropriate writings that describe the threat of bodily harm toward a school employee" (Taylor, 2003).

At the hearing, the student's act of writing such story had been defended by her parents, Georgia's poet laureate, and the editor of Georgia State University's literary magazine. The poet laureate testified that "In my opinion, based on my experience as a writer and with more than 20 years of teaching creative writing, this piece of work is clearly an imaginative piece, a piece of fiction—totally non-threatening" (Taylor, 2003).

The girl's father said, "The school system is asking her to cede her First Amendment right and her right to due process. The school system is saying they decide what is an appropriate topic to write about and what is an inappropriate topic. Creative writers, or people who create art, write about what's happening in their society. Her writing reflects a full gamut of emotions. . . . We're not saying this shouldn't have been brought to our attention. But the decision was made to expel her without any understanding of the fact that this was just a story" (Taylor, 2003).

Another case in San Jose (California) confronted officials with the same question: Can a serious threat reasonably be inferred from a student's literary efforts?

A poem written by a 15-year-old boy at Santa Teresa High School included the line "For I can be the next kid to bring guns to kill students at school." Classmates who read the poem reported it to school authorities, who responded by expelling the poem's author from school. Furthermore, a district court sentenced him to 90 days in juvenile hall for writing verse deemed too violent. When an appeals court sustained that sentence, supporters of the youth took the case to the California Supreme Court, where a dozen published authors—including a Nobel laureate and a Pulitzer-Prize winner—defended the teenager, arguing that "violent imagery is a literary device that has been employed by poets as far back as Geoffrey Chaucer and William Shakespeare. . . . [Poetry] is an artistic medium particularly well-suited for the examination of one's own potential for depravity. The developing genre of 'dark poetry' is merely a continuation of this literary tradition" (Literary luminaries, 2003).

The matter of violent content in students' artistic productions became the subject of heated debate in Jefferson (Ohio) when a 19-year-old former student distributed copies of a self-composed song at the local high school. The question debated in court after the youth's arrest was whether the lyrics were constitutionally protected free speech or a panic-provoking threat. According to a newspaper account of the event:

The aspiring rural rapper went to the high school to hawk his homemade CD. He placed copies in paper sleeves, with only an e-mail address, on the windshields of cars in the student parking lot. Concern grew when some students and parents heard [on the CD] a raucous blend of gunshot sounds and apparent references to the Columbine school shootings, suicide, and other violence-laced language about local police and the school principal.

The lyrics included such passages as "Might kill you . . . better I gotta die, which is now—click, check, splat, I pulled the [expletive] gun and the [expletive] went splat." At another point, the song implied that the intended massacre would be worse than that in the Columbine episode, and the lyrics ended with "This is a death threat."

After the 19-year-old was arrested on charges of inducing panic and of aggravated menacing, his defense lawyer argued that the youth was "merely promoting his fledgling rap music career, even if his choice of marketing location may not have been the best. The fact remains that he did not induce panic or intend to induce panic. He's not guilty of a criminal act—unless the First Amendment has been repealed and I'm unaware of it. Who puts their e-mail address on a death threat? He was looking for people to listen to his music, but I'm sure if he had it to do over, he might have done it in a different venue than the school parking lot."

In response, a prosecuting attorney noted that a variety of Jefferson High students had feared for their lives until the rapper was arrested. Jefferson's chief of police said, "I'm all in favor of free speech, but when people are in a panic because of it, that changes things. He [the rapper] made a death threat. When he gets out of jail, we'll be watching him." (Scott, 2004)

School personnel, the police, and the courts have been puzzled about what sanctions, if any, should be applied to students who create songs or poems that appear to target particular individuals—creations whose composers claim are simply fantasies and not intended to lead to action. Such an incident appeared at Central High School in Brookfield (Wisconsin).

When a 15-year-old honor student sold schoolmates a compact disc (CD) of rap songs he had produced on his home computer, school authorities who heard the music were appalled by lyrics that denigrated classmates, the school, and the boy's own mother. One song ranted at the school principal with a host of sexually explicit slurs and a suggestion that if the principal did not leave the school, the teenage composer would "beat your ass down." The principal's immediate response was to suspend the youth from school for five days, a punishment that the superintendent of schools said was fair.

A defense lawyer representing the 15-year-old argued that no disciplinary action should be taken against the boy because he was simply "expressing himself [with] kind of like love songs and fantasies. It's a long list of outrageous things that he throws out there. I think it's an attempt to make him look like a deviant or a threat. [But] nothing about this is inherently more threatening than an Eminem CD [of songs by the much publicized rapper who had been criticized for defaming women and gays in his lyrics]. He was expressing a viewpoint about how he thought the school was operating as a police state."

Some school administrators judged the CD to be "gross disobedience or misconduct," an offense similar to making a bomb threat, bringing guns to school, and arson. They considered a five-day suspension too light a punishment and thought the boy should be expelled (Epstein, 2003).

Unintentional Threats

What appear to be deliberate threats to people's safety are sometimes no more than accidents, so it is important that officials attempt to discover the intent behind an ostensibly threatening event before they apply sanctions to the perpetrator.

While standing in line with classmates, a first-grade boy in Pembroke Pines (Florida) opened his school bag and took out a pair of police handcuffs. His surprised teacher called a school security guard who searched the bag and found a pistol. The guard then discovered that when the boy's father, a police officer, had dropped his son off at school that morning, the boy had mistakenly grabbed his father's tote bag rather than his own school bag (Frantz, 2003).

Intended Targets of Harm

The targets of threatened damage can be particular individuals, particular groups, or a school in general.

Damage to Selected Individuals

The intended victim of an attack is often a person whom the threatener regards as an enemy, such as a competitor for a girl's affection, a bully who had taunted the threatener, or a teacher who had disciplined the threatener.

For supposedly planning to kill a classmate at Barrett Middle School in Sacramento (California), a 12-year-old boy was arrested and sent to the county juvenile hall. The threat, overheard by other students, included the phase "You are on my hit list." An official explained, "We take threats very seriously. School resumed as normal [the next day]. However, a district safe-schools officer, who is also a sheriff's deputy, was present the entire day" (Lindelof, 2004).

A teacher who awarded a boy a grade of F for his inadequate academic performance was the object of a death plot at Palm Middle School in Lemon Grove (California). The intended killing was prevented when a girl told her father of the plan, and he informed school authorities who called the police. The seriousness of the threat became apparent when police found a fully loaded .25-caliber handgun that the 14-year-old and a companion had hidden under a bush on the campus. The boy who had received the failing grade intended to don a ski mask and shoot the teacher after school that day (Lyda, 2004).

Damage to Particular Groups

The object of intended violence can be any member of a despised or envied group that is defined by such characteristics as the group's ethnicity (Caucasian, Afro-American, Hispanic, or Asian), religion (Catholics, Jews, Baptists, or

Muslims), social class (poor whites, rich kids, or ones from a deteriorated part of town), school social clique (athletes, nerds, gothics, or the mentally disabled), or some other trait.

At the Jesuits' Bellarmine College Preparatory School in San Jose (California), a 15-year-old boy was arrested for posting Internet threats to kill African-Americans in general and, specifically, to lynch Blacks who attended Bellarmine. His arrest came after another student revealed the Internet messages to the school's dean of students, who then informed the police. The incident was a shock to school authorities, especially because the school's own website advertised that Bellarmine Prep strove "to educate young men of competence, conscience, and compassion." In pursuit of the goal of compassion, one Bellarmine teacher used the 15-year-old's list of Internet threats as the foundation for a lesson on Christian ethics. A student from the ethics class later reported that the messages started in a light-hearted vein but then degenerated into bitter threats—"The fact that somebody could joke about lynching African-Americans . . . was shocking." A Latino class member, in reference to his own ethnic origin, said he was upset to learn that the menacing messages came from a Bellarmine schoolmate—"Maybe he would want to target other groups, too. It scares me" (Carreon, 2004).

General Damage to a School and Its Inhabitants

Teenagers who are acutely frustrated, angry, and disappointed with their lives may strike out at some imprecisely defined source of their distress, which may be the school they attend.

Caught stealing bomb-making chemicals from a science laboratory at Saratoga High School in California, a 16-year-old was arrested on a charge of planning to blow up the school. Additional incendiary materials were later found in a closet at his home. He was one of several students who had been expelled from school for having stolen a teacher's password to a computer that contained test materials. The boy had copied test items that he later shared with schoolmates before the annual testing period. A 16-year-old girl involved in the test-item theft was arrested for sending Internet messages threatening the lives of the school principal and members of his family (Banducci, Carreon, & Suryaraman, 2004).

MOTIVES OF THOSE WHO ISSUE THREATS

Although people's intentions in issuing threats are often unclear, their motives can sometimes be inferred from the conditions surrounding their particular case.

Avenging Low Academic Marks

Students whose academic performance or general behavior has been judged as unsatisfactory by school personnel may vent their disappointment and anger by threatening violence.

After an 18-year-old at Strongsville High School in Berea (Ohio) was informed that he would not graduate because of low grades and disciplinary problems, he dropped out of school and placed a message on the Internet announcing his plan to "shoot up the school." Students who had seen the message, along with photographs of guns the youth intended to use in the attack, informed school authorities, who had the police arrest the 18-year-old. When the police searched the home of the youth's father, they seized a computer, journal, knife, and semiautomatic pistol.

The threats and other rumors of violence all but shut down the school on April 20, the sixth anniversary of the Columbine killings in Colorado. More than 2,000 of Strongsville High School's 2,500 students skipped school that day.

The youth faced a misdemeanor charge of inducing panic, which could lead to six months in jail and a $1,000 fine (O'Donnell, 2005).

Attention-Getting

People sometimes seek to draw attention to themselves as vigilant, faithful citizens of the school community by their supposedly discovering and reporting threats of violence.

A 30-year-old woman teacher and a 16-year-old schoolgirl in Clearbrook (Minnesota) were arrested by police on a charge of making terrorist threats. The arrest came after several reports that the pair were threatening to bomb the high school. According to the county prosecutor, the teacher had written the threat on a school computer, had given the printout to the student, and the student had taken it to a restroom. The student later returned to the restroom, retrieved the note as if she just happened to find it, and took it to the teacher, who then reported it to the principal as a legitimate bomb threat. While police and fire officials searched the school for a bomb, all of the students were taken to a nearby church. No bomb was found (National School Security, 2002).

Copycatting

The fact that notorious instances of violence are often followed by a rush of threats of similar acts suggests that students with grievances and perhaps a desire for attention become copycats, imitating the model provided by a notorious event. A dramatic example of copycatting was provided by the state of Pennsylvania at the time of the Columbine killings in 1999. Prior to 1999, schools received no more than one or two threats per year. But within the 50-day period following the Columbine episode, Pennsylvania school districts reported 354 threats of school violence, with the incidence of threats reaching a peak approximately a week after the shootings—on days 8, 9, and 10. Out of the state's 501 school districts, 172 reported at least one threat (Kostinsky, Bixler, & Kettl, 2001). At the same time, police in the state of New York responded to 363 reports of bombs or violence in schools, with thirty such threats during one 24-hour period (New York State Government, 1999).

Personality Disorders

Some threats apparently are not attempts to avenge ostensible wrongs or to gain attention but, rather, are the result of deviations in the personalities of the authors of threats.

Police in Waconia (Minnesota) arrested a 34-year-old cook at Clearwater Middle School on eight felony counts of making terror threats after she had mailed to the school a series of menacing letters and had left ominous messages in bathrooms. Each count could lead to a maximum five-year prison term and a $10,000 fine. When the cook was questioned about why she had sent such messages, she said she was not sure, but added that she liked to "put stuff in them that she had read about Columbine and Red Lake." The court ordered a psychiatric examination to determine whether the woman should be held responsible for her behavior (Middle school cook, 2005).

THREAT CONSEQUENCES

From the viewpoint of school personnel who are attempting to conduct an efficient learning program, three unwelcome consequences of violence threats are financial loss, study time loss, and the disruption of the school routine.

Financial Loss

Threats can result in considerable cost for investigating their source and for protecting the people and property that are at risk.

During a one-week period in Rockland (Massachusetts), graffiti scrawled in bathrooms at three schools threatened deaths on a specified date. Although the threats were never carried out, the amount of time police spent investigating the case and patrolling nearby streets cost an estimated $1,152. A police official explained, "Not only does it cost us extra in overtime pay, but it also costs us extra on townwide, routine patrol coverage. Now we have to put officers in schools where the threat is" (Vaishnav, 2003).

If the authors of threats can be identified and found guilty in court, prose-cutors can ask the judge to order those responsible or their families to pay for the police overtime costs. However, in cases of anonymous graffiti, it is usually difficult to find the culprits and bring them to trial.

Providing security services for exposing and discouraging threateners can be a very expensive business. The Washington, DC school system paid $45.6 million in 2004 to staff schools with security guards (McElhatton, 2004). That same year, New York City allocated $119.9 million for upgrading existing security systems and equipping an additional 200 schools with videocameras (Lombardi, 2004).

Loss of Study Time

Students are often afraid to attend school on days that a threatened attack is supposed to take place, so they miss class study time.

In a Rockland (Massachusetts) case, a note on a urinal in a boys' bathroom at John W. Rogers Middle School announced that "everyone will die" on November 5. The same threat was written on a toilet-paper dispenser in a girls' bathroom at the R. Stewart Esten Elementary School. As a result, on November 5 only 30 percent of Rockland High's 1,000 students went to school, while just 34 percent of the Rogers Middle School's 670 students attended along with 25 percent of Esten Elementary's 406 children (Vaishnav, 2003).

The effect on school attendance of threatened attacks was illustrated in Marysville (California) when an anonymous caller phoned police the names of three high-school students who, the caller warned, planned noon-hour shootings in three schools. The police subsequently questioned the named students and searched their homes but found nothing to confirm the caller's warning. Nevertheless, the incident resulted in heightened security measures on all 21 of the school-district's campuses, with 20 additional guards on duty at the three targeted schools. Student attendance dropped the next few days, ranging from 90 percent attendance in some schools to 20 percent in others (Nadeau, 2003).

School Routine Disrupted

The systematic conduct of a school's education program is interrupted for the entire student population when the school must be emptied in the wake of an attack threat.

A series of telephoned bomb threats caused the evacuation of the high school in Mojave (California) for several hours while police searched the building for explosives, but no bombs were found. The 16-year-old responsible for the anonymous threats was caught by police through tracing the phone number from which he had called the 911-emergency-system. A further bomb threat had also been made from a teacher's stolen cell phone that was found on the student when he was apprehended. The youth was arrested on charges of possessing stolen property and of falsely reporting an emergency (High school student, 2003).

In Eagan (Minnesota) 3,500 students were sent home early from a middle school and nearby high school after a scribbled note was found claiming that a bomb had been planted in one of the schools. Police officers and five explosive-detection dogs from neighboring agencies were pulled away from other work assignments to search the schools for bombs. The threat was identified as a hoax when police apprehended the 14-year-old boy who had written the note (Yuen, 2004).

TREATING INDIVIDUALS WHO MAKE THREATS

Four issues that warrant attention in the treatment of threateners are those of (a) identifying who made the threat, (b) adopting a way of selecting a treatment, and recognizing both (c) the school system's treatment options and (d) the criminal-justice-system's options.

Identifying the Authors of Threats

Because threats are so often anonymous, a challenge authorities frequently face is that of discovering who made the threat. The sources of information to which officials turn include student informants, teachers' observations, hand-writing analyses, files in computers that students use, weapons and journals in a threatener's possession, tapes from security cameras, and phone messages from anonymous callers.

Video-camera records of girls entering and leaving a school bathroom enabled police to identify three students suspected of scribbling a series of threats on the bathroom stalls at the high school in Waconia (Minnesota). The graffiti included a drawing of a smiling face with a bullet-hole in the forehead and such phrases as "FBI can't stop me," "Tick, Tick Tick," "Anytime now," and "He, He, He." As two federal investigators and one local officer questioned each girl for an hour in the principal's office, they discovered that one of them—a 17-year-old—had a black felt-tip marker of the type used in writing the bathroom graffiti. Confronted with the marker and video evidence, the girl confessed, claiming that she wrote the threats because she was angry at the FBI, her boyfriend, and students who had made fun of her (Adams & Wascoe, 2005).

At her court trial, the judge sentenced the girl to 35 days in jail and an indefinite period of probation during which she would be required to fulfill a long list of conditions, including the requirement that she clean the bathroom stalls that she had defaced (Adams, 2005).

The Process of Selecting Treatments

As school authorities or the police decide on a suitable treatment for some-one who has issued a threat, they are obliged to consider such questions as:

- What were the threatener's motives? If a threat was intended as no more than a prank, the sanctions applied to the threatener will be less aversive than if the threat represented a serious intent to do significant harm.

  A prosecuting attorney in Seattle (Washington) explained that what a student threatener would be charged with depended on whether the teen had taken substantial steps toward carrying out the threat and whether potential victims felt intimidated or frightened. "You have to sort through things and figure out the kid's intent. Sometimes it's just typical child behavior, or kids being morons. Sometimes these are kids making true threats, and there are also times when the threat is a window into a more serious concern" (Clarridge, 2005).

- How serious were the consequences of the threat? And how aware was the threatener of the potential consequences?

  The Seattle prosecutor added that "It's not unlawful to make a list of people you don't like, but it is unlawful to make a list and use it to intimidate or frighten people" (Clarridge, 2005).

- How likely would the threat be carried out? Three cases in the state of Washington illustrate the contrast between a threat that seems unlikely to be executed and one that seems credible.

A teenage student in Seattle was arrested for preparing a hit list, but he was never charged with a crime because his list included the radio talk-show host Rush Limbaugh, the celebrity Hilton sisters, and Christmas snow globes, along with some students and teachers. In contrast, a 16-year-old in Port Orchard who had a long history of violent behavior was charged with felony harassment for threatening to "kill everyone." In Spanaway, three teenagers were arrested and charged with conspiracy when police caught them with a map of their school, a key to the school elevator, baling wire, a suicide note, and plans for violently taking over the building (Clarridge, 2005).

- What are the threatener's legal rights? A representative of the American Civil Liberties Union has pointed out that the balance between a school's responsibilities and a student's rights is delicate.

There have been kids who've accidentally brought in tiny toys that nobody thought were weapons, and the schools have said, "You're out of here." Sometimes the spread of so-called zero-tolerance policies turns into zero common sense. (Clarridge, 2005)

This question of students' rights involves issues of due process. The legal term *due process* refers to an orderly proceeding in which a person has the opportunity to be heard and to protect his or her rights before an official body that has the power to judge alleged law violations. In school settings, a question of whether due process has been followed often arises over the ways authorities deal with threats of violence.

A 13-year-old straight-A student at Garland McMeans Junior High School in Katy (Texas) was suspended from classes for 7 days for having brought an "illicit item" to school. The girl was also stripped of her positions as president of the student council and president of the academic honor society. The "item" was a pencil sharpener in the form of a 2-inch blade, a type used by pupils in South Korea where the girl's mother had bought the instrument during a trip to East Asia. The girl's parents did not object to the school district's ban on the blade, but they objected to the severity of the punishment and to their daughter's not being accorded due process—that is, offered a proper hearing. The parents filed a lawsuit against the district in federal court, charging a violation of due process.

A school-district spokesperson defended the punishment (a) as ensuring fair treatment by disciplining all violators and (b) on the possibility that—even though the pencil sharpener was not intended to be used as a weapon—it could have posed a danger. Another official said the district strictly applied its zero-tolerance policy and that the girl's punishment could have been worse.

A professor of criminal justice at Sam Houston University criticized strict applications of a zero-tolerance policy that could lead to extremes: "The schools should be sensitive to cultural differences. If [the girl] wasn't trying to hurt anyone with [the pencil sharpener}, just take it away and discuss it with the parents" (Zuiga, 2003).

Kinds of Treatment—School-System Options

For treating people who threaten violence, alternatives typically available to school officials include suspension, dismissal, transfer, probation, and defined alternatives.

Suspension

There are two main circumstances under which a student accused of threatening violence can be required to stay away from school for a specified period of time. In the first instance, a few days' or weeks' suspension is considered sufficient punishment for the student's misdeed. In the second, the student is barred from attending school while officials investigate the episode in preparation for a hearing during which a decision will be reached about what consequences the student should face.

At a middle school in Lebanon (Indiana), officials discovered a petition urging students to "go after" the "popular kids." The teenage author of the petition was expelled and 22 of his schoolmates who had signed the petition were suspended (Hit list, 2004).

A teenager who had prepared a document titled "People to Kill" was suspended from Washington High School in Westfield (Indiana) while authorities investigated the case prior to a meeting in which a decision would be reached about expelling. The school principal said, "We don't know if it was a prank or if it was just mindless doodling by a student. But it's being taken very seriously. High school students are old enough, responsible enough, and intelligent enough to realize this is not the sort of thing that's done in this day and age. We all have memories back to Columbine" (Gillaspy, 2003).

A 9-year-old third-grader at a Franklin Township elementary school in Indiana faced criminal charges and possible expulsion for bringing an unloaded handgun to school. The school principal, after discovering the gun, sent the boy to the county juvenile-detention center on charges of possessing a firearm and intimidating schoolmates. Because the boy was a minor, his name was not released to the press. His immediate punishment was a 10-day suspension from school. A hearing was scheduled to determine if he would be permanently expelled (Murray, 2005).

Dismissal

When officials consider a threat of violence sufficiently serious, they may permanently expel the student from school. Sometimes expulsion assumes the form of a long-term suspension, after which a dismissed student can petition to return. Such was the case in Maryland's Anne Arundel County until late 2005 when the school board introduced a stricter discipline policy.

Prior to the change, expelled students typically returned quite soon, often sent to a special campus for those with a background of discipline problems. However, a survey revealed that an increasing number of regular students in schools feared harm from potentially violent classmates who had been expelled but returned to school. In addition, school principals

━ ━ ━ ━ ━ ᴣ mandatory 18-week dismissal period (which often was not actually imposed)

ᴣrect the behavior of many of the expelled students when they returned. Thus,

new policy, the required expulsion period would extend to 36 weeks.

expelled students could be assigned to two alternative schools, called *academies*

ᴣh and a senior high) that enrolled youths who were discipline problems. But

ᴣw rules which required that dismissed youths actually complete their assigned

ᴣod before being allowed back in a regular school, the two academies could

ate the 600 or more students expelled each year. The leftovers would have

ᴣheir formal education would be at an end. As a stopgap measure, school

ᴣ have dismissed youths who were under age 16 study at home under the

of a visiting teacher. However, some school board members doubted

ᴣnt would succeed, because the county's home-schooling program

ᴣents with discipline problems, it failed to cover the entire range of

ᴣbjects, and it was more costly than normal schooling. One board

ᴣome-schooling] teacher shows up for just six hours a week. Who

ᴣ are] doing when they're not home-educating?" (de Vise, 2005).

ᴣn expelled student regard the dismissal unduly dam-

ᴣare, and they may take the matter to court to have

Authorities at the private Detroit (Michigan) Country Day School dismissed a ninth-grade boy for writing two notes in which he threatened to kill a schoolmate. The notes were given to the intended victim's sister. The note-writer's parents filed a petition in court to have their son readmitted to the school. However, the judge ruled that school officials were within their rights to expel the boy, because the contract the parents had signed with the school allowed authorities to dismiss a student when "in the opinion of the school, his or her interest, or that of the school, will be best served by such action" (Garzia, 2000).

Transfer

Students who have threatened harm to others are sometimes sent to a different school, usually an alternative school designed for teenagers who have been chronic discipline problems in a regular school. The intent is to get them out of a place in which they frighten classmates and teachers and into an educational setting in which staff members are trained to deal with difficult youths.

Two sophomore boys and one freshman boy were transferred from West High School in Pueblo (Colorado) to an alternative school for their having placed schoolmates' names on a computer-generated form that asked them "if they had it in them to do harm to another person." The form had been given to them by a friend who was compiling a notebook of violent writings about classmates he disliked. That friend was suspended from school while awaiting a hearing in which officials would decide his fate. School authorities were disturbed about the notebook's contents, but they doubted that the material represented a criminal violation. The superintendent of schools said, "There were nooses drawn next to some of the names, but no words like *gun* or *death*. It's something you can't trivialize because it had the potential to be a very serious matter." No weapons were found when investigators searched the youths' homes, and none of the students named as potential victims in the notebook reported being threatened or harassed (Garner, 2003).

Probation

People who violate a school regulation or a criminal law can be assigned a penalty, such as expulsion from school or a period of months in a juvenile detention facility. But those individuals are allowed to avoid the punishment if they behave themselves properly for a stated period of time. Such an arrangement is called *probation*. However, if, during the defined probation interval, they violate the terms of the agreement, they must endure the punishment. Probation is a treatment applied whenever the threat the individual made is not considered very serious and the threatener's prospect of having to endure the punishment is expected to be sufficient to deter the miscreant from future wrongdoing.

Two 18-year-old youths pleaded guilty to spray-painting a shooting-spree message on the outside of a Weston (Massachusetts) high school. The pair was initially charged with "communicating a threat causing public alarm," a violation of the Massachusetts antiterrorism law. But in a negotiated settlement, both agreed to the lesser charge of property destruction and were assigned two years probation, during which they were obligated to perform community service (Gedan, 2003).

Defined Alternatives

School regulations sometimes specify the kinds of treatments allowable for different types of misconduct, including different types of violence threats. In such cases, authorities are restricted in the treatments from which they can choose.

A school board in Harlan County (Kentucky) had two available options for disciplining an eighth-grade boy who had been charged with second-degree terroristic threatening and unlawful possession of a weapon on school property. The board could either expel him or assign him to an alternative school that enrolled students who seemed unfit to attend any regular school. The weapon was a loaded handgun the boy had stolen from a 19-year-old who lived in his home. When the boy displayed the weapon to classmates on a school bus, they reported him to the middle-school principal (Student accused, 2003).

Kinds of Treatment—Criminal-Justice Options

Whenever threats are judged serious enough to warrant arresting those who have issued the threats, decisions must be made in the justice system about what laws have been broken and what consequences the lawbreakers should face.

Cities and states have applied a variety of laws to people who threaten school violence, with crimes ranging from misdemeanors that warrant light punishment to felonies meriting severe penalties.

While in class during final exams, two high-school girls in Chandler (Arizona) used a cell phone to call the 911 emergency number to report that someone had been shot on the Chandler High School campus. The school was immediately locked down as police searched the corridors but found no victim. After fellow students led investigators to the pair who had perpetrated the hoax, each girl was charged with a class-6 felony (disrupting an educational facility) and a misdemeanor (making a false report) (Collom, 2004).

A 15-year-old boy—who sent a menacing Internet instant-message to a girl at Yorktown High School in Arlington (Virginia)—was cited by police for making a written threat to kill, a felony that could bring a five-year prison sentence and a $2,500 fine (Student accused, 2005).

Following the destruction of the New York City trade center by terrorists piloting hijacked airliners in September 2001, states passed a spate of antiterrorist laws. As a result, in recent years individuals who plot to attack schools can be prosecuted as terrorists. However, applying terrorist legislation to threats in schools has posed knotty problems for jurists and school personnel. For instance, should an immature teenager's expressed desire to bomb the school or engage in a shooting spree be considered as serious a threat as an adult's plot to blow up an airliner or kidnap a bank president? Such a concern was faced in the following three cases, which were among the first ones within the purview of the nation's new terrorist laws.

When a 17-year-old was corresponding cross-country with a girl in Idaho via an Internet chat room, he mentioned that he planned to massacre students at the school he attended— Chippewa Valley High School in a Detroit (Michigan) suburb. The girl informed her father, who sent the information to Michigan police. They arrested the boy for violating two recently adopted state laws—threatening an act of terrorism and using a computer to make threats of terrorism, both felonies punishable by up to 20 years in prison. At the trial, the prosecuting attorney contended that the chat-room statements which the police had recovered were not idle talk but, rather, were serious threats to the lives of Chippewa students and faculty. A police search of the 17-year-old's home had yielded "weapons, ammunition, bomb-making paraphernalia, videotapes showing the teen in possession of assault weapons, a Nazi flag, and printed materials about Adolf Hitler and white supremacy."

The defense lawyer portrayed the youth as "a very angry, hurt, foolish, misguided teenager" who might belong in therapy. "But what he did when he communicated with this girl was not a criminal act" (Durbin, 2005).

The court sentenced him to a minimum of four-and-one-half years in prison (Schwisow, 2005).

Within a one-week period, felony charges of making terrorist threats were issued against three teenagers for two incidents in southeastern-Minnesota schools. At Dakota Hills Middle School, a 14-year-old boy admitted writing a note suggesting that a bomb was set to go off in the school. Six days later, two 13-year-old girls at Valley Middle School confessed that they had written a bomb threat on a school bathroom wall. In the Dakota Hills incident, security cameras enabled the police to identify the boy who had written the note. He confessed after police confronted him with handwriting samples (Yuen, 2004).

A 17-year-old student at Assabet Valley Regional Technical High School in Marlborough (Massachusetts) was arrested on multiple charges under the state's recent antiterrorism law. He was accused of writing an unsigned threatening message on a school bathroom wall— "Everyone is going to die, 11:30, 2:25, 10:04 anytime." The charges included communicating a bomb/hijacking threat with serious public alarm, threatening to commit a crime, vandalizing property, and disturbing the peace. If found guilty, he could face between 3 years and 20 years in prison and a fine of up to $50,000. Police identified the youth as the author of the threat by asking other students who they thought might have done the deed. When confronted with the accusation, the 17-year-old admitted that he had posted the first threat but denied writing a message in another bathroom that read— "Close the school or you will die tomorrow." The police, however, reported that the handwriting of the two messages was so similar that both must have been from the same person (Schworm, 2004).

TREATING THOSE WHO ARE TARGETS OF THREATS

Both direct and indirect victims of threats deserve the help of school officials and of such members of the criminal justice system as police officers, judges, and social workers. Direct victims are the individuals at whom the threats are aimed—the ones harmed if the threats are actually carried out. Indirect victims are (a) friends of the persons threatened— friends who suffer through their sympathy for the threatened ones—or (b) individuals who are frightened when they imagine that they could be victims of similar intimidation. Such individuals include schoolmates of direct victims.

Common treatments of victims include crisis counseling, removal from a threat site, and explanation.

Crisis Counseling

The same kinds of crisis counseling described in Chapter 2 can be offered to both direct and indirect victims of threats. At an increasing pace since the Columbine massacre in 1999 and the terrorist destruction of the New York World Trade Center in 2001, school systems have published information about crisis counseling for students. A typical announcement is one issued by the Wichita (Kansas) school district.

Specially trained staff provide individual and small group counseling sessions regarding personal, school, local, and national crises. The crisis counseling team coordinates services with other similar crisis counseling organizations throughout our community. A district wide Threat Assessment Team is in place to respond to, assess, and recommend action based on a threat to the safety of a school. Our threat assessors use a unique threat-assessment tool based on research by school psychologists, the Federal Bureau of Investigation, and the U.S. Secret Service. (Wichita Public Schools, 2005)

Removal from a Threatening Setting

The safety of potential victims of violence can be furthered by their leaving a site in which a threat of violence might be carried out. The removal either can be voluntary on the part of potential victims or can be ordered by authorities, such as a school principal, teachers, or the police.

In Ohio, within a one-week period, about half of the students in Maumee High School and Arcadia local schools stayed home after messages written on bathroom walls contained bomb threats (Three threats, 2005).

Nearly one-third of Windsor (Colorado) High School's 800 students stayed home after a message on a restroom wall warned them not to come to school on January 25 (USA school violence, 2005).

Explanation

Students in threatened schools need to know the nature of the threat so they can estimate the risk they face and can take steps to protect themselves. Their parents, news reporters, and members of the community also expect an explanation of threat conditions. To prepare students and their parents for emergencies that may occur, schools often include a description of crisis policies and services in a student handbook. For example, the Burwell (Nebraska) High School handbook explains that:

On occasion, it may be necessary to dismiss school early or close school for a period of time due to emergency situations. . . . Notice of any unplanned closures will be through the radio and TV news media to alert students, staff, and parents. Each school year a notice alerting the public to which stations to listen to or watch will be provided to students and their parents. (Burwell High School, 2004)

REDUCING VIOLENCE

Four ways schools attempt to reduce violence are by (a) revising school policies, (b) training staff members, (c) encouraging students to report threats, and (d) increasing security provisions.

Revise School Policies

Tragic consequences of violence in schools often lead to an improvement of school policies in an effort to prevent future tragedies.

Following the murder of a 16-year-old student by two classmates at Roosevelt High School in Seattle (Washington), the school district formulated a new threat-notification policy. The move by district officials was partially in response to a successful $250,000 lawsuit filed by the murdered youth's mother. The lawsuit was supported by evidence that several district employees had been aware of the murder plan ahead of time, but the schools' current manner of handling threats was flawed, so nothing had been done to prevent the attack. Under new regulations that the school system adopted, all lethal threats would have to be promptly reported to the district security office. Receptionists, including students who answered school telephones, would be trained in how to handle threats, and they would be required to fill out an assessment form whenever anyone called to report a potential assault (Sullivan, 2004).

Train Staff Members

Training sessions for administrators, teachers, and support staff (counselors, secretaries, bus drivers, cafeteria workers, and the like) typically focus on two sorts of knowledge—what to do when a violent act occurs and how to recognize potentially violent individuals.

When Violence Occurs

The following are typical questions addressed in training programs focusing on what to do in the event of violent acts:

- What kinds of violence should you try to stop on your own, and by what techniques? What kinds should you not try to stop on your own?
- To whom should you appeal for help, and by what means should you seek help?
- What phone numbers should you keep on hand, and where should you keep them?

One method of conducting training sessions involves the trainer organizing discussions around cases that represent the range of violent acts that conceivably could occur in the particular school. As each case is presented to the training group, participants (a) propose alternative ways they might try for coping with the violence, (b) identify skills and equipment they would need for employing each of those ways, and (c) assess the advantages and disadvantages of the various ways. One source of useful cases is this book, *Violence in America's Schools*. The cases used in these pages to illustrate types of violence can be altered to fit conditions at the school in which the training is conducted. An extensive list of additional cases is posted on the School Violence Watch Network Web page, http://www.cybersnitch.net/schoolviolencewatch.htm.

Potentially Violent Individuals

The analysis of conditions in nine episodes of school shootings over a recent 2-year period revealed seven characteristics shared in common by the shooters. All of them:

- Were white males
- Complained of being taunted by schoolmates
- Did not perform well in sports

- Hated other races and subscribed to white-supremacist, Nazi philosophies
- Enjoyed violent videos and computer games along with music with violent or satanic themes
- Were fascinated with guns and gun magazines
- Collected information from the Internet on how to build bombs (School violence, 2002).

Thus, individuals who are prone to violent acts often display a cluster of interests and habits that can serve as indicators of potential violence. Such signs have been summarized in *Early Warning, Timely Response: A Guide to Safe Schools* (OSERS, 2005). The indicators are divided into two kinds—early warning signs and imminent signs.

Early signs are traits that *may*—but not necessarily *will*—foreshadow violent acts. Because such signs may be observed in people who will never behave violently, caution is needed in interpreting what those indicators mean in any given instance. But in general, the greater the number of the following characteristics a student or staff member displays, the more likely those signs portend violent behavior.

Withdrawal from social contacts

A strong sense of isolation, rejection

Feeling picked on and persecuted

Having been a victim of violence

Creating violent writings and drawings

Uncontrolled anger

Impulsive, chronic hitting, intimidating, and bullying

Chronic discipline problems and aggressive behavior

Intolerance of people who are different from oneself

Drug and alcohol use

Gang affiliation

Inappropriate access to and use of firearms

Serious threats of violence (Blaha & Adams, 2001).

Imminent signs are characteristics suggesting that a person may soon become violent. Such signs include fighting with peers or family members, destroying property, flying into a rage on slight provocation, issuing detailed threats of lethal violence, collecting weapons, injuring oneself, and threatening suicide (Blaha & Adams, 2001).

Solicit Students' Help

Students frequently recognize signs of likely violence by schoolmates. However, either out of fear of being attacked by the potentially destructive individuals or not wanting to "snitch" on peers, such students may refrain from informing authorities of their suspicions. It is therefore important for school officials and the police to encourage students to report signals of imminent trouble. There are various ways that teachers and administrators can elicit students' cooperation, including (a) during class discussions, describe cases in which students averted tragedies by reporting schoolmates' threats of violence, (b) publicize in the press the constructive role played by student informants in preventing violence, and (c) commend students for reporting signs of impending trouble.

An eighth-grade girl at Sweetwater Middle School in Lawrenceville (Georgia) was arrested after classmates told school administrators that the girl was carrying a loaded handgun in her book bag. According to the chief of police, the girl claimed that she "brought the weapon for protection from a fellow student." Any kind of threat could not be substantiated. Nobody bullied her. Basically, her schoolmates just saw her showing the gun to people. The girl was sent to the county juvenile detention center, facing a felony charge of carrying a concealed weapon on campus. The school principal spent time reassuring the students who had reported the incident that "they did the right thing; and in the future, if they see something that is questionable, they need to report it to an adult" (Dodd, 2003).

Increase Security

The past decade has witnessed a dramatic nationwide increase in schools' security provisions. In addition to the measures described in Chapter 2 (security guards, entry-control techniques, metal detectors, videosurveillance cameras, and revised school designs), a growing number of school systems have been installing school-violence hotlines. One example is the State of Missouri's hotline that informs local schools and law enforcement agencies of actual or potential violent acts and provides for immediate intervention to prevent or minimize such acts. The hotline is staffed Monday through Friday (7:00 a.m. to 6:00 p.m.). Information gathered from callers is entered into a centralized computer database and also sent—via phone, fax, or e-mail—to appropriate law-enforcement agencies and schools. The agencies and schools then determine how a reported case should be handled (Clemens, 2005).

CONCLUSION

The purpose of this chapter has been to identify types of threats of violence, intended targets of harm, motives of those who issue threats, consequences of threats, ways of treating both the people who make threats and their victims, and efforts to reduce the incidence of threats. Cases from school systems around the nation have been included to illustrate the chapter's issues as they have appeared in various settings.

CHAPTER 4

Fighting

Fights are conflicts in which two or more combatants seek to defeat opponents in oral or physical attacks. Often a confrontation begins with verbal exchanges—accusations, curses, threats, and name-calling—and then, as tempers heat up, the encounter morphs into fisticuffs and hair pulling. Participants may be unarmed and thus obliged to depend solely on their hands and feet, or they may wield weapons—knives, rocks, clubs, guns, or the like.

Students' fear of becoming victims of fights and other forms of violence may be increasing in American schools. A 2005 survey showed that the proportion of students reporting that they felt safe at school declined between 2004 and 2005 from 88 percent to 80 percent in middle schools and from 82 percent to 74 percent in high schools. Those who participated in the survey were also more likely to report racial tensions, drug use, and fights at school. Among elementary students, for example, 75 percent reported that fighting was a problem at their school, compared with 64 percent in an earlier survey (de Vise, 2005).

Not only are students victims of fights, but also staff members. In 2003, Cleveland (Ohio) schools reported 213 assaults on teachers, 40 on security guards, and 123 on other school personnel. The 123 was a 68 percent increase over the seventy-three cases of 2002 (Reed & Okoben, 2003).

Although general trends in the incidence of fighting can be estimated, it is impossible to know exactly how many fights occur because the standards for reporting fights can vary from one school to another. Furthermore, school personnel may underreport fighting in order to protect their school's reputation as a safe place to learn. As an example of underreporting, during the 2004–2005 school year at Denver's (Colorado) Montbello High School no fights or assaults were listed, even though one student had died in a cafeteria stabbing. The Westminster school district led the Denver metropolitan area in recorded fights and assaults with 685, an increase of four over the previous year. Jefferson County, the state's largest school district with eight times more students than Westminster, reported no fights at all, a decrease from 632 a year earlier (Morson & Mitchell, 2005).

In contrast to the overall decline in violence in America over the past decade, fights at football games that required police intervention took a sharp upturn in the years 2004 and 2005. Whereas in 2003 only nine incidents were reported (two deaths, seven injuries), major incidents increased in 2004 to twenty-one (one death, twenty-two injuries) and in 2005 to thirty-one (four deaths, thirty-three injuries). School security experts noted that "football stadiums present a perfect opportunity to settle a score: a distracted crowd, an overwhelmed, and often undertrained, security staff, and access to rivals not available during school hours" (Morson & Mitchell, 2005).

In this chapter, fighting as a form of school violence is described under five headings: (a) forms of fights, (b) gangs, (c) conditions affecting fights, (d) responding to fights-in-progress, (e) the treatment of fighting, and (f) reducing the frequency of fights.

FORMS OF FIGHTS

For convenience of discussion, fights can be divided into four types in terms of the number of combatants and how well they are organized: (a) one-on-one, (b) several-on-one, (c) spontaneous groups, and (d) gang fights.

One-on-One

The simplest kind of fight involves one person clashing with another.

At Timber Creek High School in Orlando (Florida), 18-year-old Jonathan Robles was driving into the parking lot when he was cut off by another car full of students. Angry words exchanged between Robles and a passenger in the other car, 17-year-old David Roshak, led to the pair alighting from the cars and engaging in a fight. As the two rolled on the ground, Robles grasped Roshak in a headlock and bit off three-quarters of Roshak's left ear. Robles was charged by police with aggravated battery, and Roshak's ear was reattached at a hospital (Fla. student, 2005).

Several girls were milling about their lockers at Travis Academy Middle School in Dallas (Texas) when a seventh-grade science teacher told them to go to their classrooms. One eighth-grade girl was upset at being ordered to her class, so she went to a counselor's office and phoned her mother, a 45-year-old North Dallas high-school teacher. Upon the mother's arrival at the Academy, she entered the science-teacher's classroom and shouted at the teacher. When the science teacher tried to persuade the mother to move the conversation out of the classroom, the mother grabbed the teacher by the hair, jerked her out of her chair, dragged her across the floor, punched her repeatedly in the face, and kicked her several times. While some students restrained the mother, others ran to fetch the school's security officer. The science teacher sustained facial bruises, a concussion, and two broken ribs. Police cited the mother for assault with bodily injury (William B. Travis, 2005).

Several-on-One

A group of students sometimes attacks a single schoolmate.

Three incidents of groups assaulting individuals were reported during a one-week period in East St. Louis (Illinois). In the first episode, 20 boys began beating up a 15-year-old student in the high school cafeteria, then pursued him into a hallway where they knocked him to the floor and stomped on him. Two other attacks that came after an evening dance at the school involved a collection of 25 boys assaulting a 14-year-old boy and four girls attacking a 13-year-old girl (National School Safety and Security Services, 2002).

Spontaneous Groups

In a crowd gathered at an event attended by students—basketball game, soccer match, party, holiday celebration, concert, dance, or political rally—an altercation between individuals may erupt into a general melee. Such a fight is not an organized bout planned ahead of time but is a spontaneous event involving various members of a crowd.

At Jefferson High School in Los Angeles, 2,000 students were in the football stadium for a noontime earthquake drill. When a Latino boy tossed a milk carton that landed near a group of Black football players, the Blacks demanded to know who had thrown the carton. A Latino replied, "Go back to Africa." As journalists later reported, the incident that started as a food fight turned into a race riot.

The fight was over in less than 20 minutes. But for two months after that April 14, 2005, battle, Jefferson's Black and Latino students faced off in spontaneous skirmishes, orchestrated beatings, and at least two more large-scale melees. Twenty-five students were arrested, three hospitalized, and dozens suspended or transferred. Hundreds more stayed away from classes, and those who showed up did so with fear (Banks & Shields, 2005).

The Jefferson brawls were, to a significant degree, the result of demographic change. By 2005, the Black/Latino ratio had shifted so markedly that Latinos, who had represented 31 percent of the Jefferson student body in 1980, by 2005 comprised nearly 92 percent (3,547), with Blacks at 8 percent (305), and other ethnic groups less than 1 percent (17). Half of the Latinos were immigrants, mostly from Mexico. Of the 747,000 students in the entire Los Angeles Unified School District, 72 percent were Latinos, 12 percent Blacks, and 16 percent others, such as Whites, Asians, Filipinos, Pacific Islanders, and Native Americans (Banks & Shields, 2005).

Racism had become so deeply embedded in the community that "In the neighborhoods around Jefferson High School, Blacks and Mexicans live next door to each other, but— separated by language, culture, and history—they rarely interact. Immigrant children navigate a confusing cultural milieu, where Black youths can throw the N-word around, but their Mexican friends aren't allowed to use it, and popular brands of hip-hop clothing are considered off-limits to all but Blacks. Mexicans living in largely Black areas tell of being robbed, beaten, and intimidated by Blacks. Their Black neighbors complain about chickens in the yard, old cars on blocks, and harassment by belligerent street toughs allied with Latino gangs" (Banks & Shields, 2005).

Gang Fights

Physical violence often takes the form of gangs attacking each other.

At Honolulu's Farrington High School, a gang of Samoans (Hollywood's Finest Bloods) fought a Filipino gang (Bisayan Boyz) in retaliation for "mobbing one of our friends." The school principal estimated that (a) there were more than 10 gangs at Farrington, many of them representing ethnic groups, and (b) between 10 percent and 15 percent of the school's 2,500 students were gang members (Fujimori, 2005).

Competition over a girl's affection was the motivating factor behind a late-night confrontation between two teenage gangs at Alice Maxwell Elementary School in Sparks (Nevada). The original plan—one boy from each gang "fighting it out" over a girl—evolved into a gang-against-gang brawl. During the fight involving 20 participants, one youth was stabbed in the neck and transported to a hospital. The stabber, cited as an adult on suspicion of attempted murder, confessed to the charge (Alice Maxwell, 2005).

Street gangs play such an important role in school fights that the nature of gangs and their development warrants the following additional attention.

STREET GANGS

Street gangs in the United States are hardly a recent invention. They have existed since early days, especially when immigrants moved into neighborhoods dominated by people of their own ethnic heritage, and they formed gangs to protect their interests in the face of attacks by competing ethnic groups. However, the rapid increase in gangs, their violent acts, and their threat to safety in schools are mainly phenomena of the past three decades. The proportion of teenagers reporting gangs in their schools nearly doubled between 1989 and 1995, rising to 37 percent of the youths surveyed toward the end of the 1990s (Howell & Lynch, 2000).

Members of street gangs typically:

- Are from a particular ethnic group.
- Are predominantly males (90 percent).
- Adopt distinctive dress styles, colors, tattoos, insignia, jewelry, and mottos.
- Consider a particular street or neighborhood their "turf" which they guard against intruders and often mark out with graffiti.
- Are likely to use and peddle illicit drugs.
- Carry weapons—guns, knives, and clubs—at least part of the time.

The thousands of gangs in the United States vary markedly in numbers of members. Some gangs—such as the Crips and Bloods based in Los Angeles, or the Folk Nation and People Nation based in Chicago—have hundreds of members in other communities throughout the nation. At the other extreme of size, many gangs consist of a mere handful of members whose turf may be limited to a single block on a city street.

The incidence of gangs in schools is somewhat related to the size of the community, with the frequency of gangs increasing as the population approaches 50,000. The largest number of students reporting the presence of gangs in their schools appeared in cities with populations between 100,000 and 249,999 (54%), followed closely by areas with populations between 250,000 and 999,999 (53%). "Students in areas with populations of 1 million or more were slightly less likely to report gangs (51%). Even in the smallest jurisdictions (populations smaller than 1,000), 23 percent of students reported gangs in their schools" (Howell & Lynch, 2000).

In the distant past, schools were likely to be considered neutral territory by gang members who avoided confrontations with other gangs while on campus. However, in recent times gangs have viewed schools as convenient sites in which to pursue their activities, which include fighting other gangs, selling drugs, and intimidating students who have no gang affiliation. Survey results show that students in schools with gangs are twice as likely to report that they fear becoming victims of violence than are students in schools without gangs (Burnett & Walz, 1994).

Although many gang members acknowledge the importance of the educational objectives of school, school is much more important to them as a place for gathering with fellow gang members for socializing and other more violent activities . . . [and] even those gang members who had been suspended or had dropped out of school could be found on campus with their associates, effectively using the school as a gang hangout rather than as an educational institution. (Burnett & Walz, 1994)

As school personnel attempt to cope with gang-related violence, they can profit from understanding conditions that contribute to the development of juvenile gangs (William Gladden Foundation, 1992). Adolescents who feel alienated and powerless may join a gang for support because they lack such traditional sources of security as a stable and close-knit family, law-abiding companions, and a school in which teachers care about students as individuals. Alienated youths find that gang membership gives them a feeling of belonging and identity, with gang activities providing an outlet for their anger. A sense of purpose and control comes when a gang is successful in defending its turf and maintaining discipline over its membership. And gangs grow in strength when they can recruit new members and expand their territory. Hence, "both 'willing' and 'unwilling' members are drawn into gangs to feed the need for more resources and gang members" (Burnett & Walz, 1994). Students in schools heavily infiltrated by violent gangs often believe that joining a gang is their best protection against being molested, because being in a gang equips them with compatriots who will act in their defense.

Schools' ways of dealing with gang-related fighting are rather limited in scope and potential effectiveness. There is nothing school authorities can do to disband street gangs or to prevent them from recruiting new members. However, administrators do have ways to curtail gang activity on campus. Those ways include (a) employing security guards to patrol the campus and to disperse groups that appear apt to instigate a fight, (b) requiring that visitors to the campus obtain a pass from the office before they are allowed to move about the campus, (c) outlawing the wearing of gang insignia at school, and (d) suspending or expelling gang members who attempt to intimidate school-mates or try to bring alcohol, drugs, or weapons to school. Teachers may help reduce gang violence by getting to know gang members individually, treating them as worthy persons, and offering them help and encouragement with their studies.

CONDITIONS ASSOCIATED WITH FIGHTING

When school personnel understand factors that are related to fighting, they are better equipped to predict when fights are likely to occur and thus are better prepared to manage such incidents. Six of those factors are (a) the nature of the students' social/cultural backgrounds and their home/community environments, (b) the degree to which fighting is an organized activity, (c) the influence of entertainment media, (d) the increased popularity of personal-communication devices, (e) the use of alcohol and drugs, and (f) an adolescent tendency toward suicide.

Social/Cultural Backgrounds

Schools can differ dramatically in the kinds of populations from which they draw their clientele. Fights are more apt to occur in schools whose students are (a) from families in which violence is routinely used to settle disagreements and (b) from crime-infested communities—particularly big-city neighborhoods rampant with drugs, drive-by shootings, poverty, street gangs, high rates of unemployment, and low levels of education. Fights are less likely to occur in schools whose students come from (a) families in which peaceful means of negotiating disagreements are common, and (b) communities noted for their economic vitality, low rates of unemployment, lack of street gangs, and high levels of education.

On the same Friday in November 2005, officials at two chronically troubled high schools were obliged to contend with multiple fights.

At Broad Ripple High School in Indianapolis (Indiana), police arrested eight students. Three combatants (ages 14, 15, and 17) in one fight were charged with disorderly conduct. To subdue the 17-year-old, officers used pepper spray and a stun gun. A separate fight between two girls resulted in each being cited for misdemeanor, battery, and disorderly conduct. A 15-year-old girl was charged with disorderly conduct for becoming "loud and abusive" as she cursed staff members in a vice-principal's office. Two boys (ages 17 and 14), arrested for fighting after school, were cited for disorderly conduct, misdemeanor, battery with injuries, and criminal mischief (Eight broad ripple, 2005).

The principal of Mount Vernon (New York) High School closed the school at noon after four fights broke out. The disturbance began with an altercation between two students over a cell phone, then spread to include schoolmates. A 16-year-old girl, who scratched a police officer when he tried to stop a fight, was arrested for second-degree assault; and a 16-year-old boy was charged with disorderly conduct. Although in recent times the school had been relatively free from disorder, it had been the setting of numerous fights and shootings in the past, with street gangs blamed for much of the disorder (Foderaro, 2005).

Degree of Organization

Youths who engage in fights can differ markedly in the extent to which their actions represent organized efforts. The least degree of organization is observed when one student independently insults another. The greatest degree of organization is observed in skirmishes between highly structured gangs that have (a) a long history, (b) strong charismatic leadership, (c) a hierarchy of positions of power, (d) a reputation of brutal treatment of enemies and of their own members who fail to abide by the leaders' orders, (e) a large membership, (f) a source of funds (trafficking in drugs and extorting "protection money" from people who fear being attacked by the gang), and (g) symbols of membership—gang names, tattoos, mottos, passwords, or styles of dress. From the perspective of violence in schools, the more highly organized the fighters are, the more difficult it is to control fighting.

Entertainment Media

Two forms of entertainment to which children and adolescents have become addicted are television and video games. Research on the effects of violent television programs and violent video games strongly suggests that both media lead to more aggressive behavior among viewers.

During the half century that children have been watching television, educators and parents have worried that violence on television might contribute to youngsters acting more violent in their daily lives. This concern has led to the conduct of hundreds of research studies. As a result, there is now a large body of evidence supporting the contention that violence on television contributes to children and youth behaving violently. For example, Gerbner's study of the content of children's television programs revealed that, on the average, such viewing fare contained about twenty violent acts an hour; and preschool children who watched those shows were more likely to strike out at playmates, argue, and disobey authority than children who watched nonviolent programs. By the time the average American child has completed sixth grade, he or she will have watched 100,000 acts of televised violence, including 8,000 murders (Abelard, 2005).

Three prominent effects of viewing violent programs are that children may become (a) less sensitive to the pain and suffering of others, (b) more fearful of the world around them, and (c) more likely to behave in aggressive ways toward others (Abelard, 2005). The American Psychological Association, the American Academy of Pediatrics, and the American Medical Association have all concluded that scientific evidence shows a cause-and-effect relationship between television violence and aggression among the children and teenagers who watch it (Walsh, 2001).

Over the 35 years since videogames were first introduced, the videogame industry has expanded into a multibillion-dollar business, with 79 percent of American children playing computer or video games on a regular basis. Students between the ages of seven and seventeen have reported playing for an average of 8 hours a week (Walsh, 2001). Whereas many video games are suitable for young people, a growing number feature fighting, torture, intimidation, and killing. Social scientists have estimated that such games may increase children's aggressive, antisocial behavior even more than television does because:

- Children are more likely to imitate the actions of a character with whom they identify. In violent video games the player is often required to take the point of view of the shooter or perpetrator.
- Video games by their very nature require active participation rather than passive observation.
- Repetition increases learning. Video games involve a great deal of repetition. If the games are violent, then the effect is a behavioral rehearsal for violent activity.
- Rewards increase learning, and video games are based on a reward system. (Walsh, 2001)

After Anderson (2003) analyzed dozens of studies of the effect of violent video games on the young, he concluded that such games "are significantly associated with: increased aggressive behavior, thoughts, and affect; increased physiological arousal; and decreased prosocial (helping) behavior."

Expanding Technology

Studies of violence have suggested that a critical mass of participants willing to take extreme actions is needed to escalate a fight to the level of a riot. The recent dramatic rise in the use of cell phones and hand-held pagers by students has been credited for expanding the size of audiences at fights on school cam-puses and in surrounding neighborhoods. Equipped with cell phones that not only carry messages but also pictures of events, students increasingly summon others to fights as either witnesses or combatants. An example is the Manteca (California) school district where high school fights nearly turned into riots when students used mobile phones to summon spectators (Epiphany, 2003).

Use of Alcohol

A study of 208 older teenagers from thirty-seven schools in Erie County (New York) revealed that 25 percent at some time during the school year had drunk alcohol during school hours, and alcohol use was associated with increased fighting. More than one-quarter of the respondents reported physi-cally fighting at least once with other students, and 6 percent reported fighting with teachers. The survey showed that aggression at school was related to al-cohol use only during school hours, while drinking outside of school was not associated with aggression at school (Finn & Frone, 2003).

Gender

Although boys have traditionally been by far the main participants in fights, this dominance has been challenged in recent years by increasing numbers of girls engaging in shoving and punching matches, especially in large urban schools. A University of Florida study reported that by seventh grade, girls in such settings were more often involved in fights than boys.

At Boston's Martin Luther King Jr. Middle School, a 13-year-old girl was handcuffed by police after she beat up a fellow student in the hallway and bit a teacher's finger, "all because she thought the other girl's skirt was too short. Students say most fights stem from two age-old roots: rumors and cliques. Nowadays girls use their fists to settle squabbles, and they're not afraid to admit it." Girls fighting at city bus stops and on buses became so frequent that the transit police sent intervention teams to schools in an attempt to stem the growing violence. A professor of African studies at Simmons College in Boston blamed media stereotypes, particularly television programs: "I really worry about messages that are out there—especially about women of color—that we are tough brass. It's that sort of hand-on-the-hip, finger waving, 'I'm not taking any stuff from anybody' message" (Atkins, 2005b).

The analysis of 18,675, fights in Chicago schools during the 2004–2005 academic year showed that 28 percent involved girls. At a school-district hearing about violence among girls, two students reported that it was "common practice for girls to slick their faces with petroleum jelly at Chicago schools to avoid gashes from fingernails." Officials estimated that the increase in girls being cited for criminal activity over the past decade was partially a result of changing social attitudes, so that "Girls are now being arrested for behavior that 10 or 20 years ago, because of paternalism, would not have led to arrest" (Sheehan, 2005).

Suicidal Tendency

A survey of nearly 12,000 high-school students nationwide revealed that students who reported attempting suicide during the preceding 12 months were four times more likely to have been in fights than students who reported not attempting suicide. Among ones who said they had tried suicide, the percent that reported fighting was highest among ninth graders (64.5%) and decreased with each subsequent grade (Swahn, Lubell, & Simon, 2004). Thus, school counselors may be alerted to the possibility that students who are frequently involved in fights are perhaps suicide risks and thus might profit from counseling designed to cope with the depression that can lead to suicide attempts.

COPING WITH FIGHTS-IN-PROGRESS

Typical advice to school personnel on how to respond to fights-in-progress is that offered by the University of Colorado's Center for the Study and Prevention of Violence.

- Do not physically get in the middle of a fight or try to restrain fighters.
- Disperse student spectators away from the fight.
- Use your best authoritative, loud voice to let the fighters know you are there and you want the fight to end immediately. You may use commands such as: "Break it up." "Stop right there." "Everyone back off." "Move away from each other, now!"
- If you know the names of the fighters, call them by name.
- Obtain additional help from other teachers to stop the fight (School fights, 2005).
- The Missouri Center for Safe Schools recommends that each school have an intervention team composed of staff members trained in dealing with fights. If a teacher, administrator, secretary, or counselor is unable to stop a fight, the intervention team should be summoned.

It takes a minimum of four, and desirably six, adults (three per combatant), to safely separate two fighting students and physically restrain them until they regain self-control or until law enforcement arrives. The restraint team must be well trained in approved procedures for safeguarding the students and the staff members. Team members should not be wearing glasses, wrist watches, rings, or other jewelry.

Members of the team with long hair should have their hair tied back. The intervention team must know where they will take the restrained combatants while awaiting law enforcement. These separate holding areas should be private rooms free of any objects which could be used as weapons. Members of the intervention team must be capable of conducting a post-trauma debriefing with the combatants. Members of the team should have first-aid training and know how to obtain any necessary medical assistance for combatants or team members. (Missouri Center for Safe Schools, 2001)

Security guards and police officers use a variety of methods for stopping fights and subduing the combatants—batons, stun guns, wrestling holds, handcuffs, and pepper spray.

As students poured out of Cleveland's Kenney High School at the end of the day, a fight broke out in a crowd of 200 students who gathered in front of the school. The 16 police officers who arrived on the scene had the combatants under control within 10 minutes. Pepper spay was used to restrain one student who resisted arrest (Okoben, 2005).

When a pair of 18-year-old boys at Don Bosco Charter School in Kansas City (Missouri) started fighting over a 18-year-old girl during a student assembly in the gymnasium, a crowd of students descended "hooting and hollering" from the bleachers and surrounded the combatants. When two off-duty police officers arrived and ordered the crowd to disperse, the students refused to move until the officers blew pepper spray into the air from canisters. As the crowd scattered, the police arrested the pair of fighters. They also took into custody the girl who was the object of the dispute when she tried to hit an onlooker. The three were cited for disorderly conduct and fighting in public (Vendel, 2005).

THE TREATMENT OF FIGHTING

The process of dealing with fights can usefully include (a) gathering and interpreting evidence and (b) deciding how to treat a fight's participants.

Gathering and Interpreting Evidence

Three useful procedures in preparation for applying treatments are those of (a) analyzing a fight that has occurred, (b) soliciting students' help in identifying conditions that contribute to fights, and (c) assigning blame for a fight.

Analyzing Fights

Researchers who study school violence frequently offer suggestions about how to analyze episodes in order to understand what changes might be needed to reduce violence of a particular type in a particular school. An example of a scheme aimed at coping with fights is the SARA plan, portrayed by its proponents as a commonsense problem-solving model that is a "first defense against school violence" (Gavin, 2000). The acronym SARA stands for scanning, analysis, response, and assessment. The SARA model is applied whenever an act of violence, such as a fight, occurs.

The first step—scanning—involves collecting evidence relating to the act so that the conditions surrounding the event are clearly understood. This step is founded on the assumption that wise treatment can differ from one fight to another depending on the circumstances affecting each fight. Sources of evidence for the scanning phase include witnesses' accounts of the incident, school and police records of the fighters' backgrounds, videotapes of the fight, and descriptions of the participants' behavior in other settings (character witnesses' perceptions).

Step two, the analysis phase, consists of comparing the versions of the fight that have been collected from different sources in order to identify consistencies and inconsistencies among versions and the likely influence of details. The importance of evaluating the accounts from different sources has been illustrated by Gavin (2000) in the case of frequent fights in a high-school cafeteria. School staff members were puzzled about the high incidence of cafeteria fighting until students pointed out that most fights occurred on days that pizza was served. When the pizza supply was short of demand, students tried to sneak into line to get theirs before the supply ran out, and that set off fights. When the cafeteria staff ordered a larger supply of pizzas, the frequency of fights on pizza days dropped dramatically.

The response phase involves deciding what action should be taken to cope with the fight to which the SARA model is being applied. This step can profitably include the participation of several staff members who propose potential solutions, which are then evaluated by the members for the proposals' strengths and weaknesses. Then the person, or persons, responsible for selecting which actions to attempt puts those actions into practice.

The last phase, assessment, consists of evaluating how well the attempted solutions succeeded. Assessment includes answering such questions as: (a) Were the solutions applied as planned—if not, what went wrong and why? (b) Did some aspects of the solutions succeed and others fail—which and why? (c) What changes in the solutions could profitably be made—how and why?

A school resource officer at a 2,000-student high school in St. Petersburg (Florida) applied the SARA model to determine how the frequency of fights might be reduced. From police reports and student disciplinary files he learned that over one-third of the fights took place in hallways and only 6 percent in the cafeteria. It became clear that there was more adult supervision in the cafeteria than in the hallways. In addition, special-education students comprised only 14 percent of the student enrollment but were involved in 27 percent of the fights. It appeared that stationing staff members at the times and locations in hallways that fights most often occurred would be an effective deterrent to potential fighters. After this solution was applied, hallway fights decreased by 64 percent (Gavin, 2000).

Soliciting Students' Help

Students can be valuable sources of information about the where and why fights erupt, who instigates fights, and what might be done to reduce fighting. The question, then, is how can such information be efficiently collected. One useful device is a written survey in which respondents are asked such questions as the following:

• Do you feel safe at school? If not, why not?
• Are there particular places in the school or outside in which you don't feel safe? What are those places? Why do you not feel safe there?

- Where do you think kids get into fights around school?
- Why do you think they fight?
- Which kinds of kids are most likely to fight?
- What might be done to make our school a safer place?

An alternative to the written survey is a small group or class discussion. However, a typical class discussion fails to elicit each student's frank opinion because of time restraints and because some students are reluctant to have classmates hear their views.

Useful information can also be collected from teachers and other staff members, either by a written questionnaire or a discussion session.

Officials in one school discovered through such a survey that only 10 percent of the students liked the character-development program that the school had adopted, while 90 percent thought something should be done to improve the safety of routes to and from school. This information alerted the student council to develop a plan to improve the security of the routes through better street lighting, a community-watch program, and the monitoring of "corridors of safety" by teachers, parents, and older students (Belcher, 2005).

Providing Evidence of Blame

Often it is difficult to decide who was to blame for a fight. The issue of blame is important because custom dictates that lighter sanctions—or none at all—be applied persons who have been attacked and then have fought only to defend themselves. Thus, those who instigate a fight—and particularly without what school personnel would regard as "a good reason"—are the ones who deserve blame and punishment. The task of placing blame has become easier in recent years as schools have installed security cameras and employed more campus police who patrol halls and grounds.

Seven students from Landon Middle School in Jacksonville (Florida) were suspended after school administrators viewed a school-bus surveillance-camera tape showing the seven punching a 12-year-old as he cowered in his seat on the bus. Knowledge of the event and of who participated became widespread when the tape was broadcast on local and national television. The bus driver was placed on leave until authorities could determine whether he had been negligent in not preventing the fight (Seven suspended, 2004).

Treating a Fight's Participants

Two of the most popular school sanctions applied to fighters are those of suspending them from school or expelling them entirely. A third option—corporal punishment or paddling—is a popular discipline device from the past that is still used in some places but has being going out of style. Two additional alternatives are those of teaching children social adjustment techniques that do not entail fighting or of assigning student courts the responsibility for deciding how to treat fighters. In addition, at an apparently growing rate, cases of students who fight are turned over to juvenile courts and criminal courts.

Suspension

Fighters are frequently sent home for a specified period of time. The purpose of suspension is usually to give fighters time to "cool off" and to realize that fighting can invite unwelcome sanctions.

Twenty-eight high school students in Espanola (New Mexico) were suspended for their part in lunchtime fights that attracted crowds of onlookers. Twenty law-enforcement officers used pepper spray to disperse the hundreds of students who clustered around small groups of fighters (Espanola incident, 2002).

Exclusion

Students who are identified as consistently instigating conflicts with school-mates can be banned from places or activities in which the fights occur, or they can be expelled from school.

After an unusually large number of fights at the high school in Venice (Missouri)—with one altercation leaving a combatant with a broken arm—the newly appointed school board adopted a zero-tolerance policy. Participants in any future fights would be charged with disorderly conduct and turned over to the police. In defense of the policy, the superintendent said, "We need to be cautious so this doesn't get out of hand" (Aguilar, 2003).

But a question arises about whether exclusion is appropriate when fights have involved children who suffer neurological impairments that affect their social interaction skills. In other words, to what extent should the rights of an impaired pupil take precedence over the rights of nonimpaired schoolmates?

When a 9-year-old boy in Falmouth (Maine) was banned from his school's playground, his parents filed a lawsuit aimed at forcing officials to allow the second-grader access to the playground. The parents argued that their son suffered from Asperger's syndrome, an autism-like condition marked by deficiencies in social-interaction and communication skills. Children with Asperger's syndrome often misinterpret what other people say and do. Those misunderstandings easily lead to arguments and fights. Other pupils on the playground complained that the boy swore and threatened them, played roughly with younger children, and kicked one child. The teachers' aides who supervised the playground said the boy defied their commands and told other pupils that they need not obey the aides. School officials banned the boy from the playground until a psychologist could analyze the child's condition and suggest a suitable treatment plan. However, the boy's parents objected, asserting that previous assessments of the boy had been sufficient and that his suspension was an instance of prejudicial discrimination against children with neurologically based actions. The boy's mother said, "Neurologically based behaviors are not crime scenes waiting to happen."

But school authorities responded that her son's ill-treatment of other children and continual defiance of the adults who supervised the playground could not be tolerated (Leitch, 2004).

Corporal Punishment

The venerable place of the paddle, switch, and cane in American pedagogy was memorialized years ago in a familiar song.

> School days, school days,
> Dear old golden rule days.
> Reading and writing and 'rithmetic,
> Taught to the tune of the hickory stick.

Across the decades in American schools, the hickory stick has been used as a discipline device not only for dissuading fighters from future misconduct, but even more often as a response to other behaviors that school personnel regard as misconduct—insubordination, disrespect for authority, bullying, repeated tardiness, and more. Although corporal punishment has gradually diminished over the years, spanking recalcitrant pupils is still practiced in some schools, with policies governing the use of the paddle differing markedly from one district to another.

In Florida during 2003, pupils were spanked in two-thirds of the state's school systems, however not in such larger districts as Miami-Dade, Broward, or Palm Beach counties where corporal punishment was outlawed in the late 1990s. Duval County in Northeast Florida led the state in paddling during the period 1994–2004, with more than 15,000 recorded cases. A decline in the use of corporal punishment over the previous two decades was reflected in figures from 1981 and 2003. Statewide, more than 184,000 Florida students were paddled in 1981 compared to 11,000 in 2003 (Garza, 2004).

In a pattern similar to that in Florida, corporal punishment in Arkansas schools continued to decline, dropping 16 percent between 2001 (55,772 recorded cases) and 2004 (47,002 cases). Yet Arkansas still had more paddlings than nearly any other state. In 2000, only Texas and Mississippi topped Arkansas' total. The decrease in spanking was accompanied in Arkansas by a rise in suspensions, with in-school suspensions increasing by 12 percent and out-of-school suspensions by 3 percent between 2000 and 2004. Paddling varied significantly from one region of the state to another, with the highest frequency in the center and northwest. "In Chicot County, for example, administrators and teachers administered one paddling for every two students during the 2003–2004 school year. Across the state in Washington County, there was one paddling administered for every 500 students. And, some school districts, such as those in Pulaski County, don't practice corporal punishment" (Reese, 2005).

As the foregoing cases suggest, the desirability of having paddling as an option available to teachers and administrators continues to be a controversial matter. Advocates of corporal punishment contend that, for some students, a swat on the behind is the only way to get them to behave; spanking gets a unruly youth's immediate attention and the punishment is promptly over. In defense of paddling, the superintendent of one Arkansas school district said, "It's a quick, effective way to discipline students. It gets the message across and gets children back into class. It's over with. You don't miss school because of it. You're not out of the classroom but a short period of time" (Reese, 2005).

But opponents of paddling question the inconsistency of hitting children in order to cure them of fighting—"If you hit other children, then, as your teacher, I'll hit you." Opponents also argue that paddling can do physical harm and that there are more effective, humane, longer-lasting ways to foster children's peaceful responses to frustration, such ways as (a) counseling students about how to deal with problems without fighting and (b) summoning parents to discuss the matter.

In schools that still endorse corporal punishment as a discipline device, guidelines often define how the activity is to be carried out.

The Webster Parish school board in Louisiana approved a policy requiring that spanking be applied only to the buttocks with a paddle no larger than 15 inches long, 6 inches wide, and one-half inch thick; the spanking should not exceed five strokes. Each school principal was obligated to inform the school district's supervisor-of-child-welfare of the names of all faculty members designated to administer corporal punishment. At the end of the school year, a list of all students who had been spanked would be sent to the district supervisor. Parents who did not want their child paddled at school should mail the supervisor a letter to that effect. Those letters would be filed, and each principal would maintain a list of the exempt students (Richie, 2005).

In some school districts, sympathy for children's feelings and physical welfare has not been the only consideration leading to the banning of corporal punishment. The Ashland (Ohio) school board voted to outlaw corporal punishment because the district's insurance carrier would no longer offer liability coverage if paddling was permitted (Lawrence, 2004).

Sometimes the policy to allow spanking is maintained more as a threat than as a common practice.

Five out of the six school districts in North Carolina's Catawba Valley have permitted corporal punishment, but school personnel rarely turn to the paddle as a disciplinary device. The director of student services for Catawba County explained that most professional educators chose not to use corporal punishment: "It's very clear in board policy that [paddling] is the absolute last resort when every other disciplinary avenue has been exhausted." During the 2003–2004 school year, among the district's 17,000 students, only three times was paddling on clothed buttocks used. At the outset of the school year, parents had a chance to sign a form if they wished to allow their child to be spanked. The school could not paddle any child whose parents had not signed the permission form (Lacour, 2005).

In Sallisaw (Oklahoma) the school board eliminated corporal punishment in the late 1990s but left the spanking provision in the student handbook for its ostensible threat value—the belief that students would more likely behave if they thought paddling could result from misconduct. But the threat was removed from the handbook in 2005 when administrators concluded that such a threat "doesn't work any more" (Keen, 2005).

One important influence on corporal punishment practices can be the dominant culture of the community in which a school is located. If parents frequently beat their children at home, they are more likely to condone beating at school. Paddling tends to be more common in smaller rural communities in which parents are less well informed about present-day childrearing practices than are parents in urban settings who have more formal education (Lacour, 2005; Reese, 2005).

Teaching Alternatives to Fighting

Two programs, designed to reduce fighting by equipping students with peaceful ways of settling disputes, are ones introduced in Portland (Oregon) and Jefferson Parish (Louisiana).

Supported by an $8-millon federal anti-violence grant, the Portland school system instituted a district-wide program to teach children alternatives to violence for coping with their conflicts. The program included training teachers and other school employees to identify violence-prone children and to intervene promptly when violence escalated. The plan also fostered better cooperation among schools, juvenile-justice agencies, and mental health officials in dealing with students prone to violence. Observers reported that since the program was initiated, fights in Portland's schools had noticeably subsided—an apparent result of more instruction in anti-violence techniques, more school safety officers, and better risk assessment of students who seemed likely to turn violent. In launching the effort, school personnel were successful in obtaining the cooperation of students who often were aware of disturbed peers before teachers noticed them (Carter, 2003).

Administrators of two middle schools in Jefferson Parish established a one-semester character-development class for the schools' 600 sixth graders. The course of study, furnished by the Colorado-based Character Development Systems, focused on such topics as "positive identity formation," "confrontation and assessment of self," and "decreasing hedonism." The school-board member who introduced the plan said that, unlike church instruction, the program was not trying to teach students specific morals but rather to show them how morality played a role in their decision-making. "We're not trying to impose morals on anybody [but to give students] an ability to develop a morality standard in life. . . . Ideally the success of the program should be measured in an improvement in grades and reductions in suspensions, fighting, truancy and dropouts" (Nelson, 2005).

Assigning Cases to Youth Court

One alternative to arresting fighters and deciding their fate in criminal court is to have their cases judged in a student court.

Two neighbors of Willowcreek Middle School in Lehi (Utah) saw what appeared to be two boys fighting on the school grounds at lunchtime. To stop the fight, the observers phoned the police, who arrived at the school to arrest the pair of combatants and charge them with disorderly conduct. When the Willowcreek principal questioned the boys, they told him they were only playing at wrestling—just "goofing around." The principal ordered the pair to defend themselves in Lehi's Youth Court where their agemates would decide if the two should be assigned to do community service (Rolly & Jacobson-Wells, 2004).

Justice-System Options

As in cases of deadly weapons and threats of violence, the criminal justice system defines permissible sanctions for combatants who engage in different kinds of fights. The available sanctions often vary from one state or community to another.

When a bus driver for the Punta Gorda School District in Florida ordered a 13-year-old boy to fasten his seat belt, the boy refused. As the bus driver started up the aisle toward the boy who sat near the back of the bus, the boy's 15-year-old brother stepped in the way and cursed the 66-year-old driver, who then slapped the brother and grabbed his throat. The brother retaliated by pushing and punching the driver. The entire episode was recorded on videotape by the bus's security camera. Police charged the brothers with assault on a school official, a felony punishable by up to five years in a juvenile detention facility. The driver was cited for misdemeanor battery that could lead to one year in jail if he was convicted. The boy's parents objected to their sons being charged with a felony and the driver cited for only a misdemeanor. The case was complicated by the fact that Florida law demanded that all new buses include seat belts, but students were not required to use them (Boys slapped, 2005).

In a trial at a Robeson County (North Carolina) district court, three students from Purnell Swett High School were convicted on charges of disorderly conduct and failure to disperse on command for their involvement in a fight between Lumbee Indians and Blacks at the County Fair. The three were sentenced to jail time ranging from 48 to 98 hours and to community service ranging from 24 to 48 hours, plus two years' probation (Three students, 2002).

REDUCING THE FREQUENCY OF FIGHTS

Two methods that can be attempted to reduce the incidence of fighting are those of increasing security measures and of canceling events at which fights are apt to occur.

Increasing Security Provisions

As noted in Chapter 2, schools have been expanding their security measures at an increasing rate—hiring guards or police officers to maintain order on school premises, installing surveillance cameras, requiring visitors to report to the school office, and tightening rules about student behavior.

When fighting escalates in schools, a question arises about how many guards are needed to discourage disorder. This issue became the focus of debate at Olney High School in Philadelphia.

Two events on the same day brought the matter of effective security to the attention of school-safety officials. During a noontime brawl in the cafeteria, three police officers were injured. One was hospitalized with a broken nose, and the other two were treated for minor injuries. Four ninth-grade girls who had instigated the fight were expelled from school. A short time later a teacher was attacked in a hallway by two brothers who punched the teacher in the face. In response to those episodes, the president of the school-district police officers' union said the problems of violence at the 2,600-student Olney High and other Philadelphia schools were partly due to reductions in the number of police officers assigned to schools; the number had dropped from 518 to 421 over the past two years (Dean, 2004).

Canceling Potentially Dangerous Events

Such occasions as football and basketball games, holiday celebrations, parties, dances, concerts, and fairs draw audiences that can include members who are apt to turn violent, particularly if they are under the influence of drugs or alcohol. School authorities, when alerted to the probability that such individuals will be in the audience at a school event, may deem it wise to call off the activity.

After police were warned that disruptive outside groups planned to attend a scheduled blues musical fest at St. Mary's High School in Lancaster (New York), school officials announced that the concert was called off "due to unforeseen circumstances" (Police warning, 2005).

Rather than entirely canceling Friday night football games that led to fights in the stands or in nearby parking lots, school officials in the Dallas (Texas) area planned to move an increasing number of high-school football contests to Saturday afternoon (Schools may move, 2005).

CONCLUSION

This chapter has been designed to identify types of fighting, the role of gangs in school fights, conditions that affect the incidence of fighting, and ways of treating fighters and of reducing the frequency of fights. Specific cases from schools across the nation have been included to illustrate each topic as it can appear in the daily conduct of schooling.

CHAPTER 5

Child Abuse and Neglect

As suggested in Chapter 1, a useful definition of *child abuse* is the one included in the U.S. Government's Federal Child Abuse Prevention and Treatment Act where child abuse is described as:

Any recent act or failure to act on the part of a parent or caretaker which results in death, serious physical or emotional harm, sexual abuse or exploitation; or an act or failure to act which presents an imminent risk of serious harm. Most States recognize four major types of maltreatment: neglect, physical abuse, sexual abuse, and emotional abuse. Although any of the forms of child maltreatment may be found separately, they often occur in combination. (National Clearinghouse, 2004)

Because sexual abuse is so important in the lives of children and youths, it is addressed in a separate chapter—Chapter 6. Consequently, Chapter 5 is limited to matters of neglect, physical abuse, and emotional abuse.

School personnel bear three types of responsibility for combating child maltreatment. Teachers and other staff members are obligated to (a) report evidence of apparent ill treatment that students have suffered outside the school, such as in their homes, (b) avoid abusing pupils in school, and (c) report abuse at school that has been perpetrated by students or staff members. The first two of these types are the focus of Chapter 5. The third type is examined in Chapter 7 under the title "Bullying."

REPORTING ABUSE OCCURRING OUTSIDE THE SCHOOL

The federal government and every state have laws defining child neglect and abuse, with the state versions going beyond the federal statutes by stipulating

(a) who is obligated to report evidence of child mistreatment and (b) what consequences can be suffered by persons who fail to report. Teachers and other school personnel are among the individuals held responsible for reporting signs of abuse. Failing to report promptly to the proper authorities can be a criminal act—a misdemeanor or, in some cases, a felony. Over the past two decades, such laws have become more precise and strict.

Arizona's law governing the reporting of suspected abuse was altered in 2003 to specify how suspicions of school personnel had to be reported. As the director of counseling services for the Mesa Public Schools explained, "It used to be when someone told us something over the fence or made an anonymous call, our response was to encourage that person to call Child Protective Services. We can no longer wash our hands of this. We call CPS. It isn't OK for us to assume it's [the other] person's responsibility." (Juozavapicius, 2004)

States can differ in their definitions of what must be reported. For example, a distinction can be drawn between two standards for judging abuse—*harm standard* and *endangerment standard*. Under the harm standard, children are considered maltreated only if they have already suffered damage from abuse or neglect. Under the endangerment standard, children are considered abused if they are currently being treated in ways that put them at risk of harm. The frequency of child mistreatment differs according to which of these standards is used—or if both are applied. By way of illustration, a comparison of the incidence of reported maltreatment between 1986 and 1993 by the harm standard showed that a child's risk of experiencing harm-causing abuse or neglect was 50 percent greater in 1993 than in 1986. In contrast, under the endangerment standard, "the number of abused and neglected children nearly doubled from 1986 to 1993. Physical abuse nearly doubled, sexual abuse more than doubled, and emotional abuse, physical neglect, and emotional neglect were all more than two and one-half times their 1986 levels. The total number of children seriously injured and the total number endangered both quadrupled during this time" (Sedlak & Broadhurst, 1996).

Therefore, teachers and school administrators need to be aware of the particular standard used and of the rules of reporting in their state.

With the passing years, the frequency of reported child abuse has risen markedly. However, the causes of this increase are unclear. No one knows how much the increase is due to tighter child-maltreatment laws and stricter reporting requirements rather than to an actual growing frequency of abuse and neglect. But whatever the causes, it is apparent that the mistreatment of children in the United States is a major social problem. States' child-protection personnel in 2003 investigated 2.9 million referrals regarding the welfare of approximately 5.5 million children. About two-thirds (1.9 million) of the reports were accepted for investigation or assessment. More than half (57%) of the referrals were from educators, child daycare providers, foster care providers, and personnel in law enforcement, legal, social service, medical, and mental-health agencies. Around 30 percent of the complaints that were investigated included at least one child who was a victim of abuse or neglect. Fifty-eight percent of the reports "were found to be unsubstantiated (including those that were intentionally false)." The remaining 12 percent were closed for various other reasons (Child maltreatment 2003, 2005).

More than 60 percent of child victims experienced neglect. Almost 19 percent were physically abused, 10 percent were sexually abused, and 5 percent were emotionally maltreated. In addition, 17 percent were associated with "other" types of maltreatment, based on specific state laws and policies. Children ages birth to 3 years had the highest rates of victimization at 16.4 per 1,000 children of the same age group. Girls were slightly more likely to be victims than boys. Pacific Islander, American Indian or Alaska Native, and African-American children had the highest rates of victimization when compared to their national population. While the rate of White victims of child abuse or neglect was 11.0 per 1,000 children of the same race, the rate for Pacific Islanders was 21.4 per 1,000 children, the rate for American Indian or Alaska Natives was 21.3 per 1,000 children, and the rate for African-Americans was 20.4 per 1,000 children. (Child maltreatment 2003, 2005)

Forms of Maltreatment and Their Indicators

If school personnel are to fulfill their reporting obligations, they need to know which forms of maltreatment are involved and they need to recognize the symptoms of the different kinds. The following discussion focuses on three types—physical, emotional, and educational—and identifies typical signs of those types in terms of both physical and behavioral evidence. Several indicators of possible maltreatment are identified for each of the types. The more indicators of a given type that are observed, the more likely the child has indeed suffered maltreatment (Child abuse and neglect, 2005).

Physical Neglect

Physical neglect consists of parents or guardians failing to furnish children appropriate food, shelter, supervision, and/or medical care. In states' definitions of neglect, some distinguish between (a) failure to provide because of financial inability to do so and (b) failure to provide for no apparent financial reason. The latter condition constitutes neglect.

Physical Evidence

The child has been abandoned or lacks consistent supervision, is often hungry and emaciated, has unattended medical needs, displays a distended stomach, poor hygiene, unsuitable garb, or head lice. Parents or other caretakers

are deemed guilty of abandonment when the child has been left in circumstances that threaten serious harm, or the parent has failed to keep in contact
with the child or to furnish reasonable support.

Behavioral Evidence

The child says there is no caretaker at home. The child is chronically tired
and listless, falls asleep in class, steals or begs food from schoolmates, is often
absent or tardy, and is self-destructive.

A second grade teacher overhears a student say he hates going home because it is scary.
When the teacher asks why, the child says the electricity has been turned off and his mom
doesn't get home from work until dinnertime (Duncan, 2001).

Physical Abuse

The term *physical abuse* means nonaccidental injury resulting from punching, beating, kicking, biting, pinching, shaking, throwing, whipping, paddling,
stabbing, choking, hair-pulling, hitting (with a hand, stick, strap, or some other
object), burning (with cigarettes, scalding water, or a hot iron), or otherwise
harming a child. "Such injury is considered abuse regardless of whether the
caretaker intended to hurt the child" (What is child abuse, 2004).

Physical Evidence

The child has unexplained bruises, cuts, welts, bite marks, burns (as with
cigarettes), abrasions, fractures, and hair loss.

Corporal (physical) punishment is distinguished from physical abuse in that physical
punishment is the use of physical force with the intent of inflicting bodily pain, but not
injury, for the purpose of correction or control. Physical abuse is an injury that results
from physical aggression. However, physical punishment easily gets out of control and
can become physical abuse. Corporal punishment is against the law in schools in some
states, but not in others. In many families, physical punishment is the norm. (Child
abuse: Types, 2005)

Behavioral Evidence

The child is inordinately aggressive or extremely withdrawn, dislikes physical contact, complains of pain, wears clothing to cover bruises, comes to school
early and departs late as if disliking to be home, or frequently runs away.

The little girl in the front row with long dark hair and big blue eyes arrives dirty and says
she is hungry because her mother doesn't have any food. The teacher observes a fading

bruise beneath the girl's eye. Over several months, the teacher has noticed the girl's bruised legs, and arms with healing sores. The child has been referred to the school nurse because of chronic lice, dental neglect, and poor hygiene. School staff, particularly her teacher, are frustrated and suspect something is wrong at home. Calls to home generally elicit angry outbursts—Mom has made it clear she doesn't appreciate the school intruding on her family and tells the teacher as much. The teacher decides it's time to contact child protective services and file a report of suspected child abuse (Duncan, 2001).

Emotional Maltreatment

Emotional neglect is characterized by lack of attention to children's emotional needs, failing to furnish psychological care, or allowing them to use alcohol or other drugs. Emotional abuse mars a child's sense of security and worth. Abuse techniques can include constant criticism, threats, and rejection, as well as withholding love, support, or guidance. All states except Washington and Georgia include emotional or mental abuse in their definitions of child maltreatment.

Physical Evidence

The child displays delayed physical development, speech disorders, severe allergies, ulcers, and/or drug or alcohol addiction.

Behavioral Evidence

The child is inordinately aggressive or submissive, anxious, antisocial, delinquent (especially in adolescence); exhibits habit disorders (sucking, rocking, head twisting, and blinking) and/or neuroses symptoms (sleep problems, terrifying dreams, and play inhibition); has attempted suicide; reports disliking parents or guardians.

In some states, evidence of constant domestic strife and/or drug and alcohol abuse by parents or members of the family is sufficient reason for reporting likely emotional mistreatment.

Parents' Behavior and Attitudes

Hints of child maltreatment can often be inferred from parents' behavior. Such may be the case when a parent:

- Shows little concern for the child's welfare.
- Denies the existence of—or blames the child for—the child's problems in school or at home.
- Asks teachers or other caretakers to use harsh physical discipline if the child misbehaves.

- Sees the child as entirely bad, worthless, or burdensome.
- Demands a level of physical or academic performance the child cannot achieve.
- Looks primarily to the child for care, attention, and satisfaction of (the parent's) emotional needs. (Recognizing child abuse, 2003)

Educational Neglect

Rarely are there official statutes, other than compulsory education laws, which apply to parents' responsibility for the education of their children. Thus, parents are usually not formally accused of educational neglect, which is the failure to educate a child or to provide for special education needs. As a result, school personnel are seldom obligated to report evidence of parental educational neglect. However, schools can be accused of such neglect if they fail to meet standards of enabling all children to pursue an education suited to their physical and mental conditions. In effect, schools can suffer sanctions for not providing suitable services.

Behavioral Evidence

The child does not adequately acquire the skills, knowledge, and attitudes deemed suitable for his or her age and apparent physical and mental potential.

STATE DIFFERENCES

Although U.S. state and territory laws agree on the principal conditions described above, there can be important differences among states in the details. For example, fourteen states and three territories (District of Columbia, American Samoa, and Northern Mariana Islands) permit physical discipline as long as it is "reasonable" and causes no bodily harm. At least thirty states, the District of Columbia, and Guam exempt parents from neglect when they choose not to seek medical care for their children due to religious beliefs (Definitions of child abuse, 2005).

Problems in Reporting Maltreatment

As laws bearing on child neglect and abuse have become stricter, and as penalties for failing to report suspected maltreatment have increased, school personnel have found the task of deciding when to report more challenging than in the past. As noted earlier, a large proportion of referrals to child-protective agencies are dismissed as unsubstantiated. Therefore, teachers who submit reports of ostensible physical or emotional abuse are apt to be sued for libel or slander if investigators later determine that the claims were unwarranted. However, if teachers fail to report evidence of abuse and then serious injury or death results from children's mistreatment, those teachers are liable to be arrested as criminals, facing a misdemeanor or felony. At least such teachers can expect a reprimand from school administrators, with their case perhaps publicized in newspapers and news broadcasts.

Treating Abusers

The consequences imposed on abusers by law enforcement and social service agents can be affected by such conditions as (a) the kind and severity of the maltreatment, (b) the abuser's familial relationship to the child, (c) the abuser's cultural and socioeconomic status, and (d) the abuser's apparent intent. For example, consider the following cases.

On multiple occasions, an eight-year-old boy's stepfather beat the boy with a belt for coming late to supper, for changing the TV to a different channel while the step-father and mother were watching a program, for failing to clean up his bedroom, and for other similar actions. The boy's mother did not object to the beatings. The court put the father on six month's probation (he would serve a 30-day jail term if he hit the boy again) and moved the boy to a foster home.

A very shy five-year-old kindergarten girl came to school with bruises on her arms. She was from a family consisting of two parents and five children that had immigrated seven years earlier from Central America. When the teacher asked her about the bruises, the girl reluctantly admitted that they were the result of her parents tying her to a chair with ropes to keep her from leaving the house while they were away working in the lettuce fields. Sometimes the parents also put tape over her mouth to prevent her from screaming and shouting. When a social worker interviewed the parents, they told her that such practices were not uncommon in their Central American village. After the social worker filed child-abuse charges, the judge who heard the case (a) ordered the parents to stop tying the girl and taping her mouth, (b) placed the parents on one year's probation (they would be fined and jailed if they tied the girl again), and (c) ordered both parents to attend once-a-week evening classes in humane child-rearing methods for a period of four months.

Treating Victims

Attempts to aid the victims of abuse can include:

- Providing physical and/or psychological therapy to help victims recover from maltreatment.
- Removing the child from the home and placing him or her in foster care.
- Removing abused individuals from the home where they would likely suffer continued maltreatment and temporarily placing them in a juvenile detention facility until a suitable foster home or boarding school could be found.
- Assigning a teacher at school to be the particular mentor and confidant for the child.
- Assigning one or two socially skilled students as the abused one's particular companions at school.

ABUSE AT SCHOOL

Standards for what constitutes abuse at school are neither stable over time nor the same from one place to another. Paddling, slapping, or pinching that was regarded in the past as standard treatment for unruly pupils is now deemed abuse in most school districts. So also is requiring unwilling learners to stand in a corner wearing a dunce cap or to pull schoolyard weeds under the hot sun. Therefore, teachers, principals, counselors, and bus drivers have a more difficult time today than they did in the past to select effective discipline and motivation methods without placing themselves at risk for unpleasant sanctions—reprimand, reputation damage, suspension, demotion, job loss, or arrest on criminal charges.

Forms of Abuse and Their Consequences

Types of abuse in school can be physical, emotional, or some combination of the two. Furthermore, the consequences for both the victims and the perpetrators can differ from one case to another. Consider, for instance, the variety of forms of maltreatment and of outcomes in the following cases.

The music teacher in charge of the band at La Marque Middle School in Galveston (Texas) lost his job and was fined $500 when he pled guilty to a charge of disorderly conduct for putting a belt around the neck of a 13-year-old boy during band practice. According to the teacher, he had used the belt to restrain the student after the boy had held a metal microphone stand over the band-director's head and threatened to hit him with it. But the boy's mother contended that her son had done nothing to warrant restraint and that the teacher had pulled the belt tightly enough to make marks on the boy's neck before the teacher withdrew the belt and left the classroom. In addition to the $500 fine, the dismissed teacher was placed on "deferred adjudication," meaning that if he committed no criminal offenses during the next 90 days he would have no criminal record (Moran, 2003).

A fifth-grade teacher at Side Creek Elementary School in Aurora (Colorado) was charged with misdemeanor child abuse for wrapping several layers of plastic tape around an 11-year-old boy's head. The incident had begun when the teacher made a joke about pupils' need to be quiet during math class, and the boy placed a bit of tape over his own mouth. According to the lad's testimony, the teacher had said, "That's a great idea. Come to my desk," and he had wrapped several layers of tape around the boy's head. The tape covered the boy's face. The teacher paraded the 11-year-old along the school corridor for 15 minutes until two other adults told the teacher to remove the tape. The victim's mother later reported that her son had been terrified and humiliated as "The whole fifth grade witnessed it. [My son] was traumatized" (Yettick, 2005).

At Brandon Alternative School in Seffner (Florida), a 33-year-old woman, employed as a teacher aide, confronted a 13-year-old sixth-grader who had taken candy without paying for it. When the boy tried to run off, the aide grabbed him by the neck, pushed him across a desk, and held him there. The aide was later arrested for child abuse (Teacher aide, 2005).

An occupational therapist at Hope Elementary School in Durham (North Carolina) put masking tape over the mouth of a nine-year-old boy who continued to talk to a classmate after he had been cautioned to stop talking. When the boy's father, a high-school teacher, learned of the incident, he filed a complaint on the grounds that his son suffered several developmental disabilities, including cerebral palsy and severe asthma, so that the boy's life could be endangered if his breathing was restricted. School officials, in response to the complaint, removed the occupational therapist from Hope School (Hanna-Jones & Biesecker, 2005).

A Willow Grove (Pennsylvania) judge expressed strong disapproval of the spanking activities of the 61-year-old founder of Cinekyd, a school for students interested in moviemaking and broadcasting. Eight current and former male students testified that the head of the school had kissed and spanked them, and he sometimes had pulled their pants down. Other boys who spoke on behalf of the defendant said the spankings, often on the boys' birthdays, were not meant to be harmful but were, as the defense attorney suggested, "ritualistic hazing" and "kind of a fun thing to do." He argued that the boys had consented to the spankings as "part of that ritual. Clearly, there was nothing violent and nothing sexual about it." But the judge disagreed: "This is a very foolish and bizarre thing to do. A man of his age, living in the world as it is today, ought to know better" (Pritchard, 2004).

The 32-year-old principal of Johnson Elementary School in Virgie (Kentucky) was arrested after a 17-year-old youth was hospitalized for having overdosed on hallucinogenic mushrooms at the principal's home. Police founds drugs in the home and cited the principal for endangering the welfare of a minor, second-degree possession of a controlled substance, possession of marijuana, and first-degree unlawful transaction with a minor (Mueller, 2005).

In New York State, where corporal punishment has been prohibited since the early 1980s, there were 4,223 accusations of abuse reported in 2004, with schools able to verify only 35 percent of the complaints. Most of the charges that were verified involved teachers or staff members pushing students, slapping them, or grabbing their arms. The adults found guilty of mistreating students were usually counseled or had a censure note placed in their personnel files. A few lost their jobs. One teacher who stood a misbehaving boy outside the building in freezing winter weather for 10 minutes was given counseling. Another who tackled a student who had bent over to pick up a pencil from the floor was suspended for six months with pay and ordered to complete an Internet course in classroom management. Several teachers who had taped students' mouths shut received memos in their personnel files; one was suspended (Gormley, 2005).

Perplexing Decisions for School Personnel

As child-abuse laws have grown stricter, teachers and administrators have been increasingly forced to decide which discipline techniques they can adopt that will enable them to (a) maintain reasonable order in a class so that systematic learning can take place and, at the same time, (b) avoid the risk of their being charged with child abuse. To illustrate, consider the following examples of disconcerting situations.

The mother of a six-year-old kindergarten boy in Warm Springs (Georgia) gave school officials permission to spank her son if he misbehaved. She explained that the boy had been diagnosed as suffering from ADHD (attention deficit hyperactivity disorder) and, when he failed to take his medication regularly, he would become disruptive. When the mother was informed that her son had refused to write in his journal, had spat on a table, and had colored on a chair with a crayon, she gave permission to have him spanked. The spanking was administered by an assistant principal, with the head principal as a witness. That evening, when the boy was with his mother in their car, she noticed that her son would not lean back in the seat. According to her account, when they arrived home she told him, " 'Let me see your bottom' and I noticed the bruising. On one cheek the bruise was 5 by 7 inches and on the other, 5 by 6 inches. The pediatrician's office measured them." The next day she reported the incident to the sheriff's office and the department of family and children's services. The assistant principal was arrested on a charge of cruelty to children, and the school suspended further use of corporal punishment (Franklin, 2004).

The father of a five-year-old girl at Mary Lyon School in Boston complained that his daughter—diagnosed as suffering from Asperger's syndrome (a form of autism)—had been unlawfully restrained physically by teachers at the school. As a result, the parents removed their daughter from Mary Lyon School and taught her at home. The form of restraint to which the parents objected was a "basket hold" in which an adult holds a child from behind. Massachusetts state law forbids the use of restraint as a disciplinary device, permitting restraint only when children pose a serious threat to themselves or others. But what constitutes "serious threat" can be a matter of dispute. As an attorney who specialized in child disability law explained, "Students turning over desks or throwing papers or even throwing a chair isn't enough." Thus, teachers are faced with the problem of instantaneously deciding when, in the midst of a classroom crisis, the border between "mere disruption" and "serious threat" has been crossed. Mary Lyon School was designed especially for children who suffered from developmental disorders. And, according to school district officials, all teachers there had been specifically trained in proper methods of coping with children who had unusual learning needs. Consequently, a stalemate obtained between the five-year-old's parents and school officials over the question of when physical restraint was warranted (Atkins, 2005a).

Two incidents at Fairmont Park Elementary School in St. Petersburg (Florida) left school-district officials and police in a quandary about what methods to use for keeping order in school settings without violating child-abuse laws. The first episode occurred March 14, 2005, when a five-year-old kindergarten girl refused to participate in a math lesson and responded to the teacher's urgings by a series of destructive, defiant acts—tearing papers from a bulletin board, knocking objects off the teacher's desk, and jumping several times on a table. It so happened that the event was being recorded on videotape by the teacher as a self-improvement project. When the assistant principal was called to help with the recalcitrant five-year-old, she and the kindergarten teacher applied techniques advocated in a school-district inservice-training program called Crisis Prevention Intervention. They (a) let the girl know that her actions would result in consequences, (b) gave her chances to end the conflict, (c) avoided touching her, (d) defended themselves by holding up their hands to ward off the girl's punches, and (e) removed the other children from the room so they would not be hurt. For nearly an hour the standoff continued, with the assistant principal periodically telling the child that her actions were not acceptable—"You need to stop. You don't get to wreck the room." And she reinforced her orders with gestures. But each time the girl responded with a sharp "No" and continued to tear papers and break objects. Finally, the assistant principal used her cell phone to summon the police. Then she and another teacher persuaded the child to clean up part of the mess she had made and to go with them to the office; they praised her for making a good choice. In the office, the child was sitting quietly at a desk when three police officers arrived. One sternly told her, "You need to calm down. You need to do it now." Then two of the officers stood the girl up, pulled her hands behind her back, and handcuffed her as she screamed. The videotaped incident was subsequently played over national television, and the St. Petersburg Police Department set about revising its regulations on coping with unruly school children (Tobin, 2005).

The second episode at Fairmont Park Elementary appeared six months later on September 17, 2005. During an after-school recreation program, an eight-year-old girl threw a temper tantrum over a tetherball game, hit a boy, kicked off her shoes, and left the school. A supervisor, fearing for the girl's safety, phoned the police, then managed to coax the girl back into the school. When the child saw a police car arrive, she tore papers and decorations off the wall, stomped on a table, and knocked a television receiver off its stand. The officer who came did nothing to stop the girl's ranting and destruction but stood by, awaiting the arrival of the child's father. By simply observing the girl's antics, the officer was complying with the police department's new policy of not attempting to restrain a child unless the child was armed or apt to seriously injure herself or others. Whereas some people who learned of the incident praised the officer's restraint, others criticized his passive response, contending that it merely taught children that they could, with impunity, vent their displeasure through violent raving and destroying property. Once again the police department, in cooperation with school authorities, was obliged to review its policies for dealing with violent children in order to arrive at practices that promoted the welfare of (a) out-of-control pupils, (b) other children who witness violent events, and (c) school personnel who are attempting to conduct a systematic learning program (Leary & Tobin, 2005).

The Danger of False Accusations

There are at least three conditions under which school personnel can be falsely accused of child abuse:

- An accuser intentionally lied. This can happen when a student or a parent has a grievance against a teacher, administrator, bus driver, or other staff member and seeks revenge by claiming that the person committed an abusive act.

- An accuser misunderstood the law or the school policy that defines child abuse. Thus, an accuser can believe abuse has taken place, when officially it has not. The aim of most court trials and school hearings is to determine whether abuse has actually taken place according to an official definition.

- An accuser did not accurately perceive the episode of ostensible abuse. In other words, the accusation was based on "what seemed to be abuse" but actually "was not abuse." For example, a teacher, with the students' full knowledge and willing cooperation, demonstrates to a class on the playground several types of verbal and physical behavior that would constitute bullying. A passerby who witnesses a segment of the demonstration mistakenly concludes that the teacher's actions are "real" rather than "playacting" and therefore accuses the teacher of child abuse.

Damage to the reputation and career of a teacher, administrator, or other staff member can result from any of these three types of false accusation. Even when a person is exonerated of an abuse charge, the publicity that accompanied the event—as spread by news media or simply word of mouth—can linger on, leaving the accused forever under suspicion in some people's minds.

A 55-year-old man who taught English to recent immigrant pupils at Woodrow Wilson Middle School in Roanoke (Virginia) was suspended from his job while he awaited a police investigation of a child-abuse charge. School officials agreed that the teacher had a spotless record, but suspension was necessary until the issue had been resolved. The accusation had been brought by a 13-year-old boy who had come to America with his parents from India two years earlier. The teacher had been warned by a colleague who had taught the boy the previous year that the teenager was a problem—chronically rude and disruptive, taking advantage of his physical disability that kept him in a wheelchair as a result of poliomyelitis in early childhood. On the day that the supposed abuse occurred, the boy had continually interrupted the lesson, so the teacher had put his hand on the teenager's chest and told him to quiet down or he would have to leave the room. When the youth continued to disturb the lesson, the teacher ordered him out of the room. The boy went directly to the principal's office and said the teacher had hit him. In response, the principal suspended the teacher pending an investigation of the validity of the charge.

According to the boy's older sister, when the boy's parents heard of the affair "They said if [the teacher had hit their son], he deserved it. They wanted the matter dropped, and they said that they would make [the boy] go to school and apologize to [the teacher]."

During the days that the teacher was out of school, he became increasingly depressed and told his family that he would be disgraced forever if people believed he had struck a disabled student. When the police completed their two-week inquiry, they reported to the school that they had found no truth in the allegation, so the teacher was completely cleared of wrongdoing. But early the following morning, before school officials could inform the teacher of the good news, he went to a bridge 200 feet above a nearby river and jumped to his death (Dwyer, 2004).

Sometimes false accusations are not exposed until years after the putative abuse incident.

In November, 2005, a man admitted having lied when—as an eight-year-old in 1984—he had joined other children enrolled at a Manhattan Beach (California) private preschool to tell authorities that employees had forced them to play "naked games" and to witness satanic rites and animal torture that were intended to frighten the youngsters into keeping quiet about their having been molested. The 1984 court case had drawn widespread national attention and ended with the accused preschool personnel, after a two-year trial, being judged not guilty on nearly all felony charges. When the man ultimately came forward, he said that he had always felt guilty about having lied, so that now—two decades later—he wished to set an example for his own children by finally being honest about something he had done wrong in the past (Accuser, 2005).

The general counsel for the Colorado Education Association, commenting about the rapid increase in false child-abuse charges over the past two decades, said, "There is a culture now where students know how to get rid of a teacher; they know how to get a teacher removed from a classroom" (Dwyer, 2004).

Treating Abusers

As illustrated in the examples in this section, a variety of treatments have been applied to school personnel who have been accused of abusing children and youths, with the severity of sanctions usually reflecting the apparent degree of harm and the punishment provisions in the law and in school district regulations. Teachers and administrators found guilty in court of abuse are subject to fines, required community service, jail terms, restrictions on their contacts with children, or probation. Punishment applied by a school district can range from (a) a reprimand, to (b) transfer to a position that does not involve direct contact with students, (c) demotion, (d) suspension from the classroom for a specified period, (e) probation, or to (f) dismissal from the school system.

A typical instance of dismissal occurred in the case of a substitute teacher at Fuqua Elementary School in Vigo County (Indiana) when she stuck short strips of plastic tape over the mouths of six first-graders who, she said, would not stop talking. The teacher, a frequent substitute in that class, said she had taped the children's mouths only in a playful way, sticking the tape vertically over the children's lips so their entire mouths were not closed, yet they could not talk. She explained, "It was a little piece of Scotch tape. I was just joking with them. I think it's blown clear out of proportion." But the school district's director of human services announced, "That's something we don't tolerate. She's terminated" (Substitute teacher, 2005).

TREATING THE ABUSED

Efforts to help children and youths who have suffered mistreatment at school include:

- Monetary compensation, as directed by a court to pay for medical expenses and for pain and suffering that resulted from the abuse.
- Counseling and/or physical therapy to hasten a child's recovery from the ill effects of maltreatment.
- The opportunity to transfer to a different school or to be home-schooled.
- The satisfaction of knowing that the abuser was punished.

CONCLUSION

This chapter has identified two responsibilities that school personnel bear in relation to child abuse, those of (a) reporting evidence of abuse by persons outside the school—usually by persons in the child's family or neighborhood—and (b) avoiding the maltreatment of children in school.

To carry out the first of these responsibilities effectively, teachers and other members of the school staff need to (a) know how child abuse and neglect are defined by federal law and state law, (b) recognize the likely indicators of abuse as reflected in children's appearance and behavior, and (c) know how and where to report suspected neglect or maltreatment.

To fulfill the second responsibility, school personnel need to (a) know the sorts of treatment of children and youths that are proscribed in their own school district and (b) employ methods of discipline and instruction that promote children's learning progress without violating the school's rules about child abuse.

As laws and regulations bearing on child rearing and school practice have grown more comprehensive and severe over the decades, teachers' and other staff members' efforts to do their jobs without breaching those rules have become ever more difficult.

CHAPTER 6

Sexual Abuse

The forms and treatments of sexual abuse in recent decades have developed in the same pattern as the forms and treatments of physical and emotional child abuse. That is, the kinds of behavior qualifying as sexual abuse have proliferated and sanctions for abuse have become increasingly severe. Likewise, the responsibilities of school personnel in relation to sexual abuse are the same as for physical and emotional abuse. Teachers, administrators, and other staff members are obligated to (a) report evidence of sexual abuse committed by people outside the school, (b) avoid abusing students, and (c) report abuse committed by students or staff members.

In the following pages, the discussion of sexual abuse is presented as a sequence of four topics: (a) forms of sexual misbehavior, (b) abuse outside the school's jurisdiction, (c) abuse within the school's jurisdiction, and (d) the problem of false accusations.

FORMS OF SEXUAL MISBEHAVIOR

Which kinds of behavior are considered to be sexual abuse depends on how broadly abuse is defined; and definitions can differ from one time to another and from one place to another. As a result, there is an amount of confusion about what constitutes sexual misconduct and about the frequency of abuse. For example, some authors call any sort of sexual misbehavior *abuse*, whereas others limit the term *abuse* to only the more damaging and intrusive forms. Thus, under an all-inclusive definition of abuse, a male teacher's telling a female high-school student a "somewhat shady joke" involving sexual relations— and the student finds the joke offensive or at least embarrassing—will qualify as *abuse*. But under a definition that limits *abuse* to more serious invasions of the

student's sexual domain, the joke would be considered no more than a pecca-
dillo of little import.

Here are three definitions that differ somewhat in the types of behavior
regarded as abusive.

Sexual abuse consists of "the employment, use, persuasion, inducement, enticement, or
coercion of any child to engage in, or assist any other person to engage in, any sexually
explicit conduct or any simulation of such conduct for the purpose of producing any
visual depiction of such conduct; or rape, and in cases of caretaker or inter-familial relationships, statutory rape, molestation, prostitution, or other form of sexual exploitation
of children, or incest with children." (Sexual abuse, 2005)

Sexual abuse "is any sexual act with a child that is performed by an adult or an older child.
Such acts include fondling the child's genitals, getting the child to fondle an adult's
genitals, mouth to genital contact, rubbing an adult's genitals on the child, penetrating
the child's vagina or anus . . . showing his or her genitals to a child, showing the child
obscene pictures or videotapes, or using the child to make obscene materials." (Child
sexual abuse, 1990)

In a third definition, sexual abuse includes all of the following:

Molestation—attempting sexual stimulation of a victim's body and genital areas, including penetration.

Rape—in which "power and control is expressed sexually in an attack on a victim that
may or may not include violence and or violent penetration of body openings (oral,
anal, and vaginal)" (Defining sexual abuse, 2005b).

Sexual assault—a rather imprecise term that can refer to a wide array of behaviors
ranging from rape to inappropriate touching.

Self-exposure—flashing, displaying the naked body or sexual organs, or masturbation in
an effort to shock, scare, intimidate, or sexually arouse a victim.

Voyerism—surreptitiously witnessing people who are unclad or engaged in sexual acts.

Pornographic display—exposing minor children to "adult sexual activity, pornographic
movies, magazines and or photographs. May also include having a minor child pose,
undress, or perform in a sexual fashion on film, video, or in person" (Defining sexual
abuse, 2005b).

Harassment—sexual or gendered attention directed at someone but against that person's
wishes; behavior a person considers threatening or intimidating, such as remarking
on the person's appearance, telling sexually suggestive jokes or anecdotes, or touching
the person in unwelcome ways (Defining sexual abuse, 2005a).

Stalking—constantly following a victim out of sexual motives.

It is impossible to know the extent of sexual abuse because definitions
vary and much of the sexual abuse of children goes unreported. There are
several reasons people fail to report maltreatment. Most abuse is committed
by family members—parents, stepparents, siblings, cousins, uncles and aunts,
grandparents—or by friends of the family; and those persons attempt to cover
up their acts. In addition, children often do not realize they are being abused,

for they trust that family members, babysitters, teachers, or priests and ministers are simply doing what is acceptable. And other children don't expose their abusers out of shame or fear of retaliation.

Although no exact figures on the incidence of sexual maltreatment of children are available, it is apparent that abuse is widespread. And as the definitions of abuse add more kinds of behavior as misconduct, the numbers of sexually maltreated children and youths mount.

For convenience of discussion, sexual abuse—whether committed outside the school's jurisdiction or within school settings—can be placed in ten categories: (a) extreme violence, (b) seduction, (c) fondling and groping, (d) harassment, (e) displaying pornography, (f) exhibitionism, (g) voyeurism, (h) producing pornography, (i) child prostitution, and (j) combined offenses.

Extreme Violence

Behavior qualifying as extreme violence includes such acts as rape and inflicting serious physical or psychological injury. The physical struggle involved in a rape attempt can result in serious injury or death for the victim.

For kidnapping, raping, and murdering a 15-year-old East Buchanan (Missouri) high-school girl, one of her male schoolmates was sentenced to two life sentences for forcible rape and murder and to a 15-year prison term for kidnapping. On the day the girl was missing, she had last been seen alighting from the school bus near her home. Her body was discovered two days later in a creek bed (Tripp loses appeal, 2005).

At Royal Palm Elementary School in Lauderhill (Florida), a 10-year-old fourth-grade girl wept and struggled to walk after she had been raped by two boys—ages 11 and 12—in a school bathroom. Her claim that she had been raped was later confirmed by an examination at a rape treatment center. After the boys confessed to police, they were arrested for sexual battery on a juvenile and for lewd/lascivious exhibition, both felonies. An expert on child sexual predators, when questioned about why such an event would occur, said, "There are never quick or easy solutions to determining why this happened. For perpetrators this young—considering their knowledge of sexual activity—there are all sorts of possibilities, including sexual abuse in the home" (Frantz & Deutsch, 2004).

Attempted Rape

Another extremely violent act is attempted rape in which victims can be seriously harmed physically and psychologically.

A pair of 14-year-old high-school football players in Laurel (Maryland) were charged with assault, attempted rape, and false imprisonment after they pulled two 13-year-old girls into a boys' locker room and assaulted them. The girls had been waiting in the hall for a friend after school when the two boys opened the locker-room door, grabbed the girls, and sexually abused them before they could escape. The girls reported the incident to school security officers, who sent the boys to a juvenile detention facility (Klein, 2005).

Date Rape

One subclass of rape is *date rape* that involves a couple going out on a date, which ends up with one member of the pair—almost always the male—forcing unwanted sexual intercourse on the other member. Or a version of date rape called *acquaintance rape* can occur at a party where more than one male takes advantage of a female partygoer, often preparing the attack by first weakening the intended victim's ability to resist by plying her with liquor or drugs.

A government survey reported that 96 percent of date rapes were male-on-female, 2 percent male-on-male, 1 percent female-on-male, and 1 percent female-on-female (Larsen, 2005). Another nationwide survey on college campuses revealed that 52 percent of women students had experienced some form of sexual victimization.

1 in 8 college women had been victims of rape.

1 in 12 college men admitted to sexually abusing women but did not consider themselves rapists. Of the women raped, almost 75 percent didn't identify it as such.

47 percent of rapes were by first or casual dates or by romantic acquaintances.

Over 1/3 of the women didn't discuss the rape with anyone, and over 90 percent didn't report it to the police. (Sexual victimization, 2005)

A study of 81,247 ninth- and twelfth-grade boys and girls in Minnesota public schools showed that nearly one in ten girls and one in twenty boys reported experiencing violence and/or being raped on a date (Ackard & Neumark-Sztainer, 2001).

In brief, date rape or acquaintance rape is widespread and typically involves alcohol and drugs as perpetrators seek to relax their intended victims' inhibitions by serving them conscience-numbing substances.

A 15-year-old girl drank an orange-juice-and-vodka drink given to her by one of the four young males who had organized a small party at a Grosse Ile (Michigan) apartment. Shortly after finishing the drink, the girl lost consciousness, and the young men placed her on the bathroom floor. Another girl also passed out and was placed on the floor next to her friend. When the two girls had failed to recover by 4:00 a.m., the young men—ages 18–26—took the pair to a hospital, where the first girl died. Vomit had entered her lungs and had stopped her breathing. It was then discovered that one of the men had spiked the girls' drinks with the drug GHB (gamma hydroxybutyrate)—an odorless, colorless liquid often referred to as a "party drug." In response to police questioning, one of the youths admitted that "We thought if we put a little into the drinks, maybe they'll liven up a bit." When the four were indicted and tried in court, the jury found three (two age 18, one age 19) guilty of involuntary manslaughter and poisoning charges. The 26-year-old was found guilty of being an accessory to manslaughter after the fact, poisoning, and possession of GHB (A deadly trip, 2000; Cohen, 2000).

GHB is one of several substances that have become known as date-rape drugs, used at an increasing pace to "loosen up" high-school and college girls who would otherwise be unwilling to engage in sex acts. Drug-use experts usually prefer the expression "drug-facilitated sexual assault" to the term "date-rape drugging." Effects that can result from ingesting GHB include relaxation, drowsiness, blurred vision, dizziness, nausea, vomiting, sweating, dream-like feeling, unconsciousness, breathing difficulties, slow heart rate, inability to recall what happened during the drugged state, tremors, seizures, and coma (Date rape drugs, 2005).

Another popular date-rape substance is Rohypnol (flunitrazepam), known on the streets as *roofies, ruffies, roche, R-2, rib,* and *rope.* Rohypnol acts as a very potent tranquilizer, similar to valium (diazepam) but far stronger. It produces amnesia, muscle relaxation, and a slowing of psychomotor responses. Sedation appears from 20 to 30 minutes after administration and lasts for several hours (Staten, 1996).

A third date-rape substance is ketamine (ketamine hydrochloride), a white powder that can cause such reactions as hallucinations, loss of sense of time and identity, distorted vision and hearing, slurred speech, feeling out of control, breathing problems, distorted memory, dreamlike sensations, vomiting, convulsions, loss of coordination, numbness, and violent behavior (Date rape drugs, 2005).

As noted earlier, date rape does not always involve an encounter between a male and a female.

A 24-year-old male teacher at Middleboro (Massachusetts) High School was arrested on a dual charge of rape of a child with force and indecent assault and battery. The victim of the attack was a 15-year-old male student. Earlier suspicions that the teacher was engaged in illicit sexual activity were aroused by his habit of chatting with students over the Internet and having them visit him at his apartment. According to the police, the teacher had taken the boy to a hockey game, and after the game he drove to an empty parking lot where he raped the 15-year-old. A police officer said the boy "tried to get out the door, but it was locked, [and then] he tried to fight the teacher, but he could not get him off" (Former Middleboro teacher, 2004).

Seduction

Seduction consists of an individual seeking to entice others into an illicit sexual encounter. Teenagers can often be lured into a relationship with an adult out of curiosity, a chance to vent their newly discovered sexual drives, and intimidation applied by the adult who, from a position of power, initiated the relationship. Thus, youths may go along with such a relationship for a considerable period of time until they feel too guilty about their actions or until someone else—such as a parent—discovers the liaison and moves to end it.

Sometimes a relationship between a teacher and student begins as platonic friendship and then advances into a sexual attachment that may last for months or years.

A 16-year-old girl came to the Tempe (Arizona) police headquarters to tell about three years of weekly sexual intercourse with a teacher she first met when she was a 12-year-old pupil at McKemy Middle School. Her initial friendship with the 50-year-old man did not involve sexual contact but gradually evolved into a physical love affair. The relationship lasted until one month before she came to report the matter to the police. The couple's assignations had taken place in the teacher's home, the girl's home, and in Tempe parks. The teacher was arrested on suspicion of having sex with a student (Biggs, 2003).

Whereas most cases of seduction involve males enticing females, instances of females serving as the aggressor are not uncommon.

The 29-year-old wife of a former school-board candidate confessed to 29 counts of lewd conduct for her sexual affairs with three 13-year-old boys in the Southern California schools in which she had taught over the period 2003–2005. Among the evidence collected by police at the woman's home were multiple journals in which she had written poetry, drawn sketches, and in other ways referred to the boys. The Orange County charter school in which the woman last taught was censured by school district officials for disregarding repeated complaints about her behavior. As one example, parents objected to her scanty bathing suit and "physical horseplay" with students at a pool party. She was arrested after the boy with whom she was currently involved reported their affair to the police.

At a court hearing, the woman's lawyer argued that her actions had resulted from clinical depression for which she was presently undergoing therapy. He said, "Her life was just much more comfortable with those boys than with her husband at the time. The [boys] demanded nothing. The relationship with them was not something done for strictly sexual reasons."

The defense attorney hoped the judge in the case would impose the minimum sentence of three years in prison. The woman would also be required to register as a sex offender for the rest of her life (Ex-teacher, 2005).

Often a juvenile enjoys a sexual affair with the adult and willingly continues in the relationship until someone discovers the affair and stops it.

The stepmother of a 13-year-old boy found sexually suggestive messages on her son's cell phone and launched a police investigation that exposed a two-year sexual tryst between the boy and his 49-year-old music teacher, a married woman employed at Rolling Green Elementary School in Boynton Beach (Florida). After the boy at age 11 had been in the teacher's music class, she had established a friendly relationship with his family that included inviting the boy and his two younger brothers to sleep overnight at her home. Following the stepmother's recent discovery of the cell-phone messages, the police listened in on a phone call the boy made to the teacher in which she told him to continue lying about their relationship. She was arrested on six charges, including two counts of capital sexual battery on a child under 12 (Teacher charged, 2004).

With the advent of the computer Internet, seduction efforts have spread rapidly, often with members of a chat group displaying pornographic photos and inviting viewers to join in a personal relationship. A survey by the National Center for Missing and Exploited Children reported that 25 percent of children between ages 10 and 17 had been exposed to sexual material on the Internet (Karl & Associates, 2005). As the Internet has so efficiently promoted instant communication among individuals in different parts of the world, coalitions of sexual predators have mushroomed, resulting in greater threats to the safety of children and teenagers who search the World Wide Web.

The Internet allows pedophiles:

Instant access to other predators worldwide;

Open discussion of their sexual desires;

Shared ideas about ways to lure victims;

Mutual support of their adult-child sex philosophies;

Instant access to potential child victims worldwide;

Disguised identities for approaching children, even to the point of presenting themselves as members of teen groups;

Ready access to "teen chat rooms" to find out how and who to target as potential victims;

Means to identify and track down home contact information;

Ability to build a long-term Internet relationship with a potential victim, prior to attempting to engage the child in physical contact. (Mahoney & Faulkner, 1997)

In the most extreme cases of parents' failure—or inability—to supervise youngsters' computer activities, disastrous consequences result.

A 13-year-old sixth-grade girl had come to Danbury (Connecticut) to live with her aunt, because the girl's parents had substance-abuse problems. In Danbury she attended a Catholic school where she earned good grades, was a cheerleader, and served as an altar girl at church. She became an avid computer user, continually visiting chat rooms where she assumed sexually provocative names for herself that attracted admirers with whom she set up sexual trysts. One of her sexual partners was a 25-year-old married man, an undocumented immigrant from Brazil who worked in a local restaurant. During one of the girl's encounters with the man, he strangled her. When apprehended, he confessed the murder to the police and led them to the ravine in which he had dumped her body (Karl & Associates, 2005).

In schools, seduction sometimes involves teachers inviting students to their homes for ostensible counseling, aid with homework, or tutoring.

A 46-year-old Minneapolis (Minnesota) high-school teacher's efforts to entice students to serve as "sex slaves" led to his arrest on a charge of first-degree criminal sexual conduct. The report of the enticement and subsequent sexual abuse came from a 21-year-old who had first been involved with the teacher when, as an eighth-grader, the teacher had invited the boy to his home. There the teacher gave the student alcohol and marijuana and started a sexual relationship that lasted until the youth's sixteenth birthday. When police searched the teacher's house, they found a black-magic altar, books on witchcraft, potions, pornographic photos of men and boys, and a three-page sorcerer's spell designed to make the former student "become sexually obsessed with me. . . . He shall be my sexual slave. . . . He will want me to tie him up and tease him and whip him. . . . He will endure whatever I ask in order to please me." Police also found three Burmese pythons, a king snake, an anaconda, an iguana, a large turtle, a water monitor lizard, and an alligator. The head of the Minneapolis police department's sex-crimes division described the teacher as "a classic pedophilic sexual predator." Following the arrest, another former student came forth with similar claims of abuse (Padilla & Shah, 2003).

Seduction is particularly apt to occur in school classes that provide close contact between teacher and student in informal settings. Thus, sexual abusers are more often music, art, and drama teachers or athletic coaches than ones who conduct formal classes in mathematics, science, language arts, and social studies.

After pleading guilty to two counts of felony child seduction, a popular theater-arts teacher at Broad Ripple High School in Indianapolis (Indiana) received a one-year jail sentence for having oral sex with a 16-year-old girl from his theater class. A yearlong relationship between the two had begun with a kiss in a darkened school auditorium.

Things progressed to fondling in his truck and then sexual encounters at his home. In interviews with detectives, the girl said she was confused several times by the relationship, which included daily phone calls, e-mail, and instant messaging with [the teacher]. Despite assurances that he loved her, eventually she broke off their encounters.

In addition to the jail term, the teacher was required to register as a sex offender and to pay $2,100 for the victim's counseling sessions that had resulted from the victim's need to cope with the distress of guilt and shame from the affair (Corcoran, 2005).

An illicit sexual connection between an adult and child may continue for months or years as the pair maintain a bond of friendship and desire until the relationship is severed, either by others discovering the affair or the child revealing the relationship out of a sense of guilt.

A 15-year-old boy confessed to his father that he had engaged over a five-month period in a sexual affair with a 31-year-old woman, his eighth-grade Spanish teacher at Franklin Middle School in Reisterstown (Maryland). The confession was the result of the youth's friends urging him to reveal the relationship to his parents and thereby clear his conscience. The teacher was arrested for a third degree sex offense. According to papers filed with the court, the teacher and her student had sex nearly every night behind a school in a nearby town, in the woods at a reservoir, and in the teacher's townhouse when her husband was at work. The boy said he was very reluctant to reveal the affair because, "I did not want [the teacher to get] in trouble, nor did I want to see her go to jail" (Barnhardt, 2003).

Between mid-2004 and the close of 2005, at least twenty-five cases nationwide involved female teachers molesting students (Koch, 2005). In nearly all instances, women teachers had sex with boy students, which raised the question of whether men teachers who were charged with sexually abusing girls received more drastic punishment from courts than did women teachers who molested boys. In other words, was there a double standard by which men were treated more harshly than women—and, in particular, more harshly than attractive young women?

News media brought the question of fairness to public attention in late 2005 through reports that a 25-year-old female teacher in Florida, instead of being sentenced to a jail term for her sexual act with a 14-year-old boy, was placed on three years house arrest to be followed by seven years of probation. She had been charged with two counts of lewd and lascivious battery and one count of lewd and lascivious exhibition for engaging in sexual intercourse with the student in the back seat of a sport utility vehicle that another teenager was driving. Critics estimated that if a male teacher had committed the same offense with a girl student, a judge would have sent him to jail (Koch, 2005).

Fondling and Groping

As sexually inappropriate behavior, fondling or groping consists of a person touching someone in unwanted ways. Whether touching should be deemed sexual misconduct worthy of criminal prosecution can sometimes be difficult to determine. Prosecuting attorneys, in lieu of filing a charge, may send a warning letter to the person accused of fondling if an incident had apparently occurred but there is insufficient evidence to support a charge of battery. The letter would not be intended as a threat to file charges, but merely as a request to stop any potentially unlawful acts.

A girl at Custer Baker Middle School in Franklin (Indiana) complained that a 32-year-old male math teacher had tapped her on the buttocks with a piece of rolled paper in the hallway and later touched her on the shoulder and back in the classroom. After her parents reported the incidents to the police, a prosecuting attorney said an investigation would have to be carried out in order to estimate whether the touching was enough to bring charges or, perhaps, would only warrant sending a warning letter to the teacher (Bir, 2004).

Sometimes the touching is obviously quite deliberate, with no pretense that it was accidental. Other times sexual touching is masked by a pretense to help the victim accomplish some task.

A 49-year-old music instructor at Marina (California) High School was arrested on a charge of sexually molesting six girls, ages 14 to 17, by feeling their breasts while, during private singing lessons at the school, he pretended to show them the proper location of their diaphragms. The incidents occurred even after school officials had formally warned the instructor two years earlier against using his so-called "diaphragm technique" when teaching singing (Teacher charged, 2005).

In schools, students are more often accused of groping than are teachers and other staff members.

Several parents filed complaints with Illinois child-welfare authorities and with the Cook County sheriff's office after ten third-grade girls at Sandridge School near Chicago Heights reported being groped and harassed by three third-grade boys. The state Department of Children and Family Services opened an investigation of the complaints to determine if school staff members had been guilty of inadequate supervision (Rozek, 2004).

School buses are among the most likely sites in which pupils will be fondled or groped.

A 6-year-old girl, riding a bus to her gifted-pupil program in Frederick County (Maryland), was fondled by a middle-school boy. She was afraid to tell her mother, so the mother learned of the incident only months later when informed by the bus driver (Williamson & Aratani, 2005).

An 11-year-old girl who attended Roberto Clemente Middle School in Germantown (Pennsylvania) was crying in her bedroom in the evening. When her mother asked what the trouble was, the girl only said her stomach hurt. She was ashamed to tell her mother that on the bus ride home from school that afternoon, six older boys had held her down on the bus floor, had groped her, and had lain on top of her. The next day when she boarded the bus, the boys threatened to "finish what they started." At school, she found an assistant principal and reported what had happened. He phoned the girl's mother, and the mother phoned the police (Williamson & Aratani, 2005).

Harassment

In the somewhat distant past, what is now referred to as *sexual harassment* in schools was often considered to be nothing more than teasing—just a normal part of growing up that children were obliged to bear. However, in recent years, harassment has become recognized as a matter of serious concern. A survey in 1993 found only 26 percent of students reporting that their school had a sexual-harassment policy. By 2001, that number had risen to 69 percent.

Typical behaviors in a school environment that are considered harassment, but are not illegal, are the following actions whenever the intended recipient of the acts finds them offensive or annoying.

Requests for sexual favors

Sexual gossip

Personal comments of a sexual nature

Sexually suggestive or foul language

Sexual jokes

Whistling

Spreading rumors or lies of a sexual nature about someone

Unwanted pressure for dates

Making sexual gestures with hands or body movements

Touching or rubbing oneself sexually in view of others. (Colorado Department of Public Safety, 2003, p. 46)

Of particular note, over the past decade lawsuits filed by students who were badgered for their sexual orientation have forced schools to introduce training programs to promote greater tolerance of people who follow a homosexual life style.

The Morgan Hill (California) Unified School District agreed to pay $1.1 million to six former students who had been abused, humiliated, and beaten by schoolmates over the period 1993 and 1997 for their gay/lesbian sexual orientation. At a court hearing, one student re-called anti-gay obscenities that had been scrawled on the door of her locker: "You don't belong here," "Die, dyke bitch," "We'll kill you." Also, taped to the locker was a porno-graphic picture of a woman bound and gagged with her throat slit. A second student tes-tified that one day when he was a seventh grader, a group of schoolmates at his bus stop kicked and beat him while calling him "faggot." The bus driver saw what happened but did nothing to stop the abuse. Instead, he left the boy on the ground and drove off with the ones who had assaulted the lad. The school district, in addition to paying the $1.1 mil-lion, agreed to establish a mandatory anti-harassment educational program for all students (Finz, 2004).

Displaying Pornography

Pornography typically consists of pictures or descriptions of naked per-sons or of people engaged in sex acts. Individuals who exhibit such material to the young, or who have pornographic material available where children or youths might find it, are guilty of breaching child pornography laws or regulations.

Child pornography—sometimes known as *kiddie porn*—is defined as:

Visual depiction of minors (i.e., under 18) engaged in a sex act such as intercourse, oral sex, or masturbation as well as the lascivious depictions of the genitals. Various federal courts in the 1980s and 1990s concluded that "lewd" or "lascivious" depiction of the genitals does not require the genitals to be uncovered. Thus, for example, a video of underage teenage girls dancing erotically, with multiple close-up shots of their covered genitals, can be considered child porn. (Child pornography, 2005)

The most common form of pornography violations in recent years has in-volved sexually explicit images on computers, particularly images from the Internet.

At Castlemont Elementary School in San Jose (California), a third-grade boy saw pictures of a partially robed girl on his teacher's computer screen. When the boy reported this to his mother, she informed the police, who seized computers from the 44-year-old teacher's home, his classroom, and a relative's home. The police found additional pictures of children in sexual poses on the computers as well as a folder in the classroom containing explicitly sexual photos of children. Authorities arrested the teacher on a charge of possessing child pornography (Buchanan, 2004).

Not only can sexually suggestive pictures qualify as pornography, but written material can also be deemed objectionable.

Love letters and poems sent by a 57-year-old foreign-language teacher at Holliston High School in Bellingham (Massachusetts) to a junior-class girl led to his being barred from the campus and cited for distributing obscene material to a minor. In the letters that the girl's mother submitted to the school principal, the teacher had professed his adoration for the student and his desire "to make love to her with his hands" (Edo, 2004).

Exhibitionism

As a sexual act, exhibitionism consists of persons exposing sexual parts of their bodies in order to gain sexual sensations and/or to entice or shock the people to whom they display themselves. In the most common form of exhibitionism, a male exposes his genitals to unsuspecting strangers and becomes sexually excited when doing so. More intimate sexual contact is almost never attempted, so exhibitionists rarely commit rape. Most exhibitionists are younger than age 40 and may or may not be married. Rarely do females expose themselves in order to gain sexual satisfaction.

There are several subtypes of exhibitionism or indecent exposure. *Streaking* consists of an individual running around naked during such a public event as a football game, school picnic, or graduation ceremony. *Flashing* typically involves a person, clad only in a coat, opening the coat to expose his or her genitals to a startled observer. In *mooning*, the exhibitionist pulls down his pants, turns his back, bends over, and exhibits his buttocks to one or more observers.

As three Cleveland (Ohio) schoolgirls were walking home from St. Joseph Academy, a 44-year-old fireman, wearing only sunglasses, honked his car horn at the girls, stopped, and exposed his naked body to them before driving away. The girls phoned the police, who apprehended the flasher and charged him with disseminating matter harmful to a juvenile, a felony (Baird, 2005).

A male social-studies teacher and coach at East Leyden (Illinois) High School was forced to resign from the school district after he was accused by a girl on the junior-varsity softball team of having "mooned" her. He had been dismissed the previous year as the girls' basketball coach for similar behavior, so this incident represented a second offense. The girl's parents declined to prosecute the coach for criminal misconduct. They said they were satisfied with the way the school district had responded to their complaint (Ihejirika, 2005).

Sometimes exhibitionism leads to an extended sexual relationship between the exhibitionist and his victim.

A series of sexual encounters between a 29-year-old male Phoenixville (Pennsylvania) High School teacher and a 16-year-old girl began with his exposing his genitals to her and her girlfriend. Subsequently, over an eight-month period, the teacher and one of the girls engaged in sex acts in such places as the middle-school boys' locker room, a parking lot, and the teacher's classroom and home. The teacher, a former high-school wrestling champion, was arrested on 30 counts of corrupting minors and two counts of indecent exposure after one of the girls described the encounters to a vice principal at the high school (Shea, 2003).

Voyeurism

Voyeurism is the act of secretly watching or photographically recording the appearance of a person who is in a location that the person could logically expect to be private. A typical definition of photographic voyeurism is the one in Idaho law statutes.

It is unlawful to use any camera, videotape, photo optical, photoelectric, or any other image-recording device for the purpose of secretly observing, viewing, photographing, filming, or videotaping a person present in a residence, place of business, school, or other structure, or any room or particular location within that structure, where that person is in a private area out of public view, has a reasonable expectation of privacy, and has not consented to the observation. A violation of this section is a felony. (Crime of video voyeurism, 2005)

Voyeurs or *peeping toms* usually indulge in their surreptitious spying in order to satisfy sexual urges or to obtain information that could be used in an effort to intimidate the person who had been observed.

Campus police at the University of California, Los Angeles, arrested a 22-year-old youth at 1:40 a.m. as he was on top of a parking garage aiming his video camera at the windows of a house occupied by women students. He was charged with "the intent to invade the privacy of a person or persons inside." One of the house residents said that, until the police notified her, she had been unaware that anyone might be spying on her and her housemates: "The incident has definitely changed me. It made me very edgy the next day. I felt like I was being watched all the time" (Peeping incident, 1999).

Producing Pornography

The creation of child pornography involves photographing minors (under age 18) posing nude or engaging in sex acts. But determining if a photograph or video qualifies as criminal sex abuse can be difficult because states can differ in how they define child pornography and because some such photography is a traditionally acceptable family activity. Should parents be prosecuted for taking pictures of their infant daughter in the bath or of their four-year-old son partially clothed? Is photographing a girl at the beach in a skimpy bra and string thong pornography production? Thus, what qualifies as the punishable creation of child pornography can differ from one state to another and from one court case to another.

Child Prostitution

Child prostitutes are girls and boys, usually between ages 11 and 17, who habitually engage in sex acts for pay—money, gifts, or privileges. Although there are no accurate figures about the extent of child prostitution in the United States, an estimate by International Relief Organizations places the number at around 300,000. More than one million children run away from home each year. Probably one-third of them become involved in prostitution or in the production of pornography. Some engage in prostitution on their own, but many others are controlled by adults—by pimps who manage the teenagers' lives and take a major portion of the money that the youngsters earn from sexual services (Child prostitution, 2004). According to the U.S. Department of Justice (Domestic sex trafficking, 2003), about 75 percent of girl prostitutes work for pimps whose exploitation of children is linked to "escort and massage services, private dancing, drinking and photographic clubs, major sporting and recreational events, major cultural events, conventions, and tourist destinations." The average age at which girls first engage in prostitution is from 12 to 14. For boys and transgender youths, the average age of entry into prostitution is from 11 to 13.

Child prostitutes, even when they live on the streets, may attend school. Therefore, it becomes a responsibility of school personnel to inform the police and social service authorities of the names of adolescents who are apparently engaged in prostitution. The purpose of reporting suspected prostitutes is to enable authorities to free them from the control of pimps and to rehabilitate them. Although no federal or state agencies provide comprehensive rehabilitation services for child prostitutes, over the past three decades a growing number of private organizations have engaged in such work. A typical organization is Children of the Night.

Each child who enters the Children of the Night home is given the individual attention he or she needs. Upon arrival, youngsters are assigned to private bedrooms if possible (each with its own bath) until they get a chance to settle in, and receive fresh clothing and hygiene kits. Each child is designated a Primary Caseworker who coordinates medical care, psychological care, academic assessments, and other social services as needed. Residents follow a highly structured program that includes attending an on-site school where they study a curriculum individually tailored to their specific needs so they can reach age- appropriate grade levels in all subjects before leaving. With the help of caseworkers, each youngster formulates a "life plan" and attends independent-living classes, as well as participating in sports and recreational activities plus evening workshops in crafts, yoga, 12-step meetings, poetry, AIDS education, and more. (Child prostitution, 2004)

Combined Offenses

Sometimes sex offenders are cited for more than one form of sexual abuse.

A 33-year-old fourth-grade male teacher at Empire Elementary School in Folsum (California) was originally arrested on 10 misdemeanor counts of suspicion of possession of child pornography and one count of sexual exploitation of a child. When police investigated the case further, they located four more girls in addition to the one on whose testimony the arrest had been based. In view of evidence gathered from the four, five felony counts of suspicion of lewd acts with a child under 14 and one count of a forcible sex act were added to the charges against the teacher (Gates, 2003).

Over the past two decades, priests and other personnel in schools sponsored by Catholic orders have been particular targets of child-abuse claims, especially claims of child sexual molestation. Offenses have included sadistic beatings, sodomy, oral sex, exhibitionism, and pornographic display. Frequently the reports of abuse have been filed many years after the alleged mistreatment took place, so that determining the validity of the complaints has often been difficult. The likelihood that such claims are true is bolstered whenever the charges are made by a variety of plaintiffs who corroborate each other's account.

In late 2005, eight men filed a lawsuit claiming that they had suffered "horrific" physical and sexual abuse when, as youths, they had been pupils at the Brisco orphanage and day-school operated in Kent (Washington) by a Catholic order, the Congregation of Christian Brothers. The suit followed earlier ones brought by an additional 30 men who also had attended the school. Because the orphanage/school closed in 1970, the eight petitioners could not sue the school itself, so their claim was directed at the two present-day bodies that had been responsible for supervising the Brisco faculty—the Christian Brothers and the Roman Catholic Archdiocese of Seattle. According to the suit, the eight men agreed that at the orphanage they were routinely molested sexually and beaten with sticks, leather straps, and paddles (Clarridge, 2005).

SEXUAL ABUSE OUTSIDE THE SCHOOL'S JURISDICTION

As with other forms of child abuse, school personnel are responsible for reporting evidence that children have been sexually abused by persons beyond the school, such as at children's homes or in the wider community. Failing to report signs of sexual maltreatment is a criminal offense in most states. Thus, it is important that teachers, administrators, and other staff members be able to recognize such signs.

A variety of symptoms are potential indicators that a child or youth suffers from the effects of sexual maltreatment. In general, the more symptoms observed, the more likely the youngster was indeed mistreated and is distressed by the experience. Signs of abuse can include general fearfulness or fear of being left alone with a particular person, withdrawal from social contacts, crying without provocation, recurrent nightmares, bed wetting, over-compliance with others' demands, excessive aggression, and unusual interest in or knowledge about sexual matters. Further potential symptoms are se-ductiveness, avoidance of things related to sexuality, rejection of one's own genitals or body, secretiveness, depression, eating disorders, self-injury, and attempted suicide (Child abuse: Types, 2005; Freeh, 2005).

Treating Abusers

The consequences child molesters may experience for sexually molesting children include (a) a jail or prison term, (b) probation, or (c) required regis-tration as a sex offender.

Jail or Prison

Individuals found guilty of misdemeanors can be sentenced to jail for several months to 1 year. Those found guilty of felonies may draw a term in prison, with sentences ranging from only 2 or 3 years to the offender's entire lifetime. Sometimes a portion of a long sentence will be suspended if the individual commits no further offenses.

A man who coached the Connecticut Express girls' softball team pleaded guilty to sexually molesting three team members during a four-year period. A superior-court judge assigned him 15 years in prison. But after he served 33 months with good behavior, the remainder of the sentence would be suspended and he would be placed on probation for 10 years. He would also be required to register as a sex offender and could no longer be involved in youth sports. Because he had already been in jail 34 months while awaiting a decision on an appeal of an earlier court decision, the ex-coach was immediately released from custody because he had served more than the required 33 months (Former coach, 2005).

Probation

Probation means that a person found guilty of a sex offense will not have to serve jail time if, within a specified period, he or she has not commit-ted further criminal acts. About 60 percent of convicted sex offenders are on probation, subject to criminal-justice supervision (Colorado Bureau of Inves-tigation, 2005). Extenuating conditions in a case can result in child abusers being assigned such a lenient sanction as probation when, under ordinary cir-cumstances, the offense would have drawn harsher punishment.

A 67-year-old Honolulu bank executive was sentenced to five years probation for sexually assaulting a 12-year-old girl who had been hired by the executive's wife to do housework in their condo. In addition to the probation period, the man was required to register as a sex offender, complete a sexual-offender program, and pay $510 to the girl for therapy expenses and $5,000 to an organization that helps sexual-abuse victims. When the executive agreed to confess to the crime so that the girl would not need to testify at a trial, the district attorney reduced the first-degree-assault charge to second-degree assault, thereby permitting the probation sentence. The defense attorney's claim that the girl had been partly to blame for the sexual act may also have contributed to the probation decision (Barayuga, 2003).

Sex-Offender Registration

In recent decades, more states have passed legislation requiring convicted sexual abusers to register with the police as sex offenders. For example, under New York's Sex Offender Registry Act—known as Megan's Law—anyone in prison, on parole, or on probation for a sex crime since 1995 has been required to register with the State Division of Criminal Justice Services. Local police are notified when a moderate or high-level offender moves into their area, and they pass the information on to schools and other agencies.

In 1991, Texas lawmakers passed a similar regulation that has since been revised on several occasions. In 2004, critics complained that the law needed still more refinement to cover such cases as one that arose early that year.

A 27-year-old man, who had served a six-year-probation sentence for having exposed his genitals to a 6-year-old boy, was accompanied by a friend as the two attempted to visit three schools in Fort Bend County (Texas). Authorities confirmed that the man could not be arrested for entering a school because, under state law, a sex offender who had completed his assigned sentence was free to visit anyplace he wished, including schools. In response to news of that incident, the president of Justice for All, a crime-victims advocacy group, said "she was stunned when she heard about the visits and said the law should be changed to make it illegal for sex offenders to go into schools" (Hanson, 2004).

Treating Victims

The treatment of potential and actual victims of sexual abuse can usefully be divided into two stages. Stage one consists of preparing children ahead of time to recognize signs of impending sexual misconduct and to know ways to avoid and ward off abuse. Stage two involves treating students who have already suffered sexual mistreatment.

Preparing Children to Protect Themselves

Equipping children to guard themselves from sexual predators can include teaching them how to act safely in public places, in private settings, and in visiting the computer Internet.

Public Places

Warnings that children can profitably heed about how to act on the street, on public buses, or in buildings can include:

Never talk to strangers—particularly older boys or men.

Never ride in a stranger's car.

Never accept gifts from a stranger—such gifts as an ice-cream cone or toy.

Always try to go places with one or two friends, because sexual predators are then less likely to bother you.

Private Settings

A large amount of sexual maltreatment is suffered at the hands of people the child already knows. That abuse typically occurs in a familiar place, such as the child's own home, a relative's home, or a family acquaintance's car, home, garage, or motel room. Or the assault may take place in a secluded grove or field. Therefore, children can properly (a) be alerted to kinds of behavior that often precede an assault, (b) be shown how to ward off an assailant, and (c) be told what to do following an assault.

To help children recognize the behavior of a relative or acquaintance that is inappropriate, they can be taught it is wrong for anyone to:

Expose that person's genitals to a child.

Touch a boy's or girl's genital area or a girl's breasts, even when the child is fully clothed.

Take a child's clothes off, or to ask the child to disrobe, so that the person can look at the child's genitals or take photographs.

Want to wrestle with, or tickle, a child.

Try to be alone with a child in a secluded place.

To prepare children to ward off attempts at sexual molestation by acquaintances, children can be taught to:

Firmly say "Stop that" or "No, No! Don't do that." Or "I'll tell my parents if you try that." Or if it's a parent who is engaged in the maltreatment, "If you don't stop, I'll tell the police."

Scream and shout if the molestation is in a place in which people outside could hear and come to the child's rescue.

Push the abuser away, fight to get free, and run off.

In case a child's or teenager's efforts to prevent an assault are unsuccessful and an assault does indeed take place, then the victim should know how to immediately describe the assault to a responsible authority, such as a parent, a teacher, a social worker, a medical doctor (as in a hospital emergency room), the local Child Protective Services (whose phone number is in the phone book), or—if the offense has been rape or attempted rape—to people at the local Rape Crisis Center (whose phone number is in the phone book).

Advising children about what to do in the face of potential abuse by relatives or acquaintances is far easier than ensuring that they act on that advice. If a father is abusing a daughter, the girl faces a difficult decision. Should she risk alienating this parent on whom so much of her welfare depends? Should she reveal the episode to her mother, who may not believe the tale? Can she be sure that the disgraceful event will not be announced widespread by persons to whom she might turn for help? Such problems contribute to the fact that much abuse is never exposed, or else it is exposed long after it occurred.

Visiting the Internet

The U.S. Federal Bureau of Investigation has suggested that, when children have access to the computer Internet, their parents and teachers should warn them to:

Never arrange a face-to-face meeting with someone they met on-line.

Never display pictures of themselves onto the Internet to people they do not personally know.

Never give out identifying information such as their name, home address, school name, or telephone number.

Never download pictures from an unknown source, as there is a good chance there could be sexually explicit images.

Never respond to messages or bulletin board postings that are suggestive, obscene, belligerent, or harassing. (Freeh, 2005)

In addition, children need to learn that whatever they are told over the Internet may or may not be true.

Most children that fall victim to computer sex-offenders spend large amounts of time on-line, particularly in chat rooms. They may go on-line after dinner and on the weekends. . . . They go on-line to chat with friends, make new friends, pass time, and sometimes look for sexually explicit information. Children on-line are at the greatest risk during the evening hours . . . [because most sex] offenders work during the day and spend their evenings on-line trying to locate and lure children or seeking pornography. (Freeh, 2005)

Treating Sexually Abused Students

Deciding how best to help victims of sexual abuse can begin with recognizing the kinds and severity of reactions victims display following sexual maltreatment. For example, in the days following a sexual assault, victims may exhibit a variety of symptoms (Colorado Department of Public Safety, 2003, p. 45):

Startled reactions in response to loud noises or to other people's quick movements

Hyper-vigilance [fearful even under nonthreatening circumstances]

Intense mental reviewing of the assault—second-guessing their behavior and asking "what if . . . "

Difficulties with intimacy; damaged ability to trust

Difficulties in concentrating

Heightened interest in personal safety in general

Nightmares or night terrors

Fatigue and a sense of being drained

Moodiness, irritability, and general sensitivity to any criticism

Extreme anxiety and/or excessive crying.

Such symptoms are common and should lessen over time. Therapists have suggested that people who have been victimized recover from their trauma in their own time frames—some earlier than others (Colorado Department of Public Safety, 2003, p. 45).

Methods of helping victims after they have suffered abuse include (a) counseling and therapy, (b) school transfer, and (c) foster care.

Counseling and Therapy

While recognizing that the conditions in each case of child abuse call for a particular way to counsel the victim at hand, experienced therapists are still willing to offer some general advice to parents, teachers, or friends who are trying to help a victim. For example, in counseling children and adolescents who have been sexually molested, it is desirable to:

- Remain calm, because a display of anger or hysterics on the adult's part serves to further disturb a distressed child or teenager.
- Offer positive solace, such as "It wasn't your fault," "I know you couldn't help it," "You did nothing wrong," and "I'm proud of you for telling."
- Listen to what the child has to say without continually interrupting.
- Answer the child's questions honestly.

- Discuss the abuse only with people who really need to know about the incident. In other words, respect the child's right to privacy.
- Seek the help of professionals at an agency that specializes in such matters—Child Abuse and Neglect Service, Child Protective Service, or Department of Social Services whose phone number can be found in the local telephone directory.

It is important to avoid:

- Appearing shocked or disgusted when hearing about the child's experience.
- Appearing to blame the child for what happened.
- Pressuring the child either to talk about the experience or to avoid talking about it. Allow the child to tell about the event at his or her own pace.
- Confronting the child's abuser in the child's presence (Sexual Assault Crises Center, 2005).

For children who suffer a high level of anxiety and perhaps physical ailments following abuse, counseling may be accompanied by medication.

School Transfer

It often seems wise to allow a sexually abused child or teenager to transfer to a different school after being abused, particularly if the molestation occurred at the school or at the hands of a staff member or another student.

Foster Care

Foster care consists of placing children in the homes of adults—called *foster parents*—who are willing to house the youngsters for a period of time. Such care can be ordered by a juvenile court for children who are unable to live in their own homes, usually because their parents have abused or neglected them. Although foster parents have legal responsibility for their foster children, they do not have all the rights of biological parents. For instance, foster parents may be limited in their right to discipline the children, to control their religious education, or to authorize nonemergency medical treatment. Foster parents are rarely encouraged to adopt their foster children permanently, because the aim of foster care is to eventually return children to their own parents. Foster-care settings include individual-family foster homes, homes of children's relatives, group homes, emergency shelters, residential facilities, childcare institutions, and preadoptive homes.

According to the National Clearinghouse on Child Abuse and Neglect (2003), an estimated 542,000 children were in foster care during 2001, with approximately 290,000 entering care that year and 263,000 exiting.

SEXUAL ABUSE WITHIN THE SCHOOL'S JURISDICTION

The expression *within the school's jurisdiction* refers to places and occasions in which the school and its personnel are considered responsible for students' welfare. The places include the school building, the surrounding campus, school buses, and school stadiums. Occasions include such events as school-sponsored dances, athletic contests, concerts, dramas, debates, and excursions. People who sexually mistreat students in such settings may be students, visitors from outside the school, or teachers, administrators, counselors, bus drivers, janitors, teacher-aides, and other staff members.

There are significant differences among states in laws governing sexual abuse that involves school personnel. A 2003 survey by *Education Week* (Hendrie, 2003) reported that:

- Over half the states had laws relating to educators having sex with students.
- Although many states still permitted school employees to legally engage in sex with students as young as 16, more states were amending criminal codes to outlaw such behavior.
- The age of consent for sexual relations with an adult varied among states. The age in thirty-two states was 16, in one state (Colorado) it was 15, in six it was 17, and in eleven it was 18. School personnel in fourteen states usually could not be prosecuted for "consensual" sex with students age 16 or older.
- Applicants for professional certification in forty-two states were required to undergo criminal-background screenings that included fingerprint checks through the Federal Bureau of Investigation and the state police.
- North Carolina in 1999 made it a felony for school employees to have sex with students in the schools in which the employees worked. However, as a school-boards official explained, "There were stories of teachers at middle schools who waited till their previous students were 16, and then engaged in a relationship with them. There was no way you could pursue them criminally. All you could do was dismiss them and try to revoke their license" (Hendrie, 2003).
- In Maryland, because of lenient legislation, teachers having sex outside of school with students who were above the age of consent (age 16 in Maryland for intercourse and 14 for other intimate acts) could not be charged with a felony.

In summary, in past decades, many states neglected to establish regulations governing sexual misconduct by school personnel, but recent years have brought increasingly punitive laws bearing on sexual abuse by school staff members.

As already mentioned, sexual abuse by teachers is more likely to occur in situations that place teachers and students in less formal, more intimate contact than is usual in a typical classroom. Therefore, more teachers of art, music, drama, and sports engage in sexual misconduct than do teachers of history, science, and English. A study in the state of Washington revealed that, over the 1993–2003 decade, 159 male coaches in the state had victimized girls, with their offenses ranging from harassment to rape. More than two-thirds of the discovered abusers continued to teach, usually after transferring to a different school. However, researchers discovered that the number of abusing coaches was actually much larger than reported because:

When faced with complaints against coaches, school officials often failed to investigate them and sometimes ignored a law requiring them to report suspected abuse to police . . . [and] to the state education office. Even after getting caught, many men were allowed to continue coaching because school administrators promised to keep their disciplinary records secret if the coaches simply left. (Wilstein, 2003)

Treating Abusers

Sanctions applied to school personal who are accused of sex offenses can consist of such alternatives as reprimand, suspension, dismissal, jail, psychiatric evaluation, assignment transfer, license revocation, or probation.

Reprimand

The lightest punishment for sexual misbehavior is an oral or written rebuke for a minor infraction. For example, a high-school boy may be warned to stop calling gay classmates *faggots*, *fairies*, or *fruits*. A fifth-grade girl may be chastened for trying to pull down a boy's pants. A school-bus driver may be admonished for failing to stop two middle-school boys from fondling a girl in the back of the bus. A school principal may be reproved for speaking admiringly about a teacher's breasts.

A reprimand, rather than a harsher penalty, is often judged sufficient in the case of a first offense by an individual with a previously unblemished record. An oral warning is the less aversive form of rebuke, because it involves no permanent record of the event. A more detrimental form of rebuke is a note or letter placed in the student's or staff member's personnel file.

Reprimands are sometimes issued to teachers whose instructional method or manner of treating students is disapproved by the author of the rebuke.

During a month-long ninth-grade study-unit on sexuality at Oakton (Virginia) High School, a health-education teacher showed students a movie about a teen-age lesbian couple—*The Coming Out of Heidi Leiter.* The story told of a pair of high-school girls who wanted to attend their high-school prom together in spite of objections from the community. At one point in the story, the girls kissed. Criticism from parents whose children had seen the film resulted in the teacher being warned against showing such material again. To avoid future episodes of a similar kind, the county superintendent of schools sent all school principals a letter that included the directive: "Under no circumstances may a teacher bring any outside materials into the classroom which have not been approved by the School Board" (Teacher rebuked, 1994).

Suspension

It is common practice to suspend a school employee during the period of time that charges of sexual abuse are being investigated.

A gym teacher at Portsmouth (Massachusetts) High School was suspended for two weeks with pay while officials looked into a student's accusation that the man had been viewing pornographic material on a school computer (Teacher suspended, 2005).

Dismissal

School personnel found guilty of sexual abuse are usually fired or urged to resign, particularly if the maltreatment has been of a serious nature or has been habitual—sexual intercourse, fondling, distributing pornography, multiple counts of sexually suggestive comments. And students who severely abused schoolmates are often expelled, either permanently or for the remainder of the school year.

One weakness of expulsion as a way to prevent sexual offences is that dismissed abusers may continue maltreating students in other schools. Teachers, coaches, counselors, and principals often retain their professional credentials after they are dismissed for sex offenses, so they can be hired in other districts. Students who have been expelled can enroll in a different school.

A music teacher, dismissed from West Side High School in Newark (New Jersey) because of reported inappropriate relations with students, was hired as a performing arts instructor at University Middle School in nearby Irvington. Subsequently he was suspended in Irvington while officials investigated an accusation by a former student that the teacher had engaged him in sex acts for two years at West Side High. The Newark school district's attorney said that he did "not know if the Irvington district had sought information on the instructor's background. But even if it had, fear of lawsuits [filed by dismissed employees] would have caused Newark only to release [the music teacher's] dates of employment" (Music instructor, 2005).

Jail or Prison

As noted earlier, people found guilty of misdemeanors can be sentenced to a jail term of several months to one year. Those charged with a felony may draw a term in prison. Offenders who are below age 18 are usually confined in a juvenile detention facility rather than in an adult jail or prison.

Upon pleading guilty to fondling 10 girls when he was a teacher at Captain Strong Elementary School in Vancouver (Oregon), a 54-year-old man was sent to jail for two months and required to register as a sex offender for 10 years, submit to a sexual-deviancy evaluation, and pay court costs (Gilbert, 2005).

In Ohio, a Cuyahoga Falls High School soccer coach and math teacher was assigned six months in jail for having sex with a student, while a Laurel School gym teacher was sentenced to 16 years in prison for sexually abusing a student. However, neither of the offenders had his teaching license cancelled (Dissell, 2004).

Psychiatric Evaluation and Therapy

The belief that socially unacceptable sexual behavior can stem from mental illness or a personality disorder leads to the justice system often ordering sex offenders to undergo psychiatric examination and treatment that includes private or group counseling sessions that are frequently accompanied by medication.

A sentence of two years supervised probation and the requirement that she submit to evaluation and treatment as a sex offender was imposed on a 31-year-old teacher who confessed to disseminating harmful materials to a minor. The teacher was married at the time and the mother of two young children. The minor in the case was a 16-year-old boy from the teacher's English class at Shepherd Hill Regional High School in Dudley (Massachusetts). During their yearlong affair, the couple had engaged in videotaped sexual acts and had e-mailed naked photos and messages to each other. The boy told authorities that rape was not involved, since the sex was consensual. The trysts were finally discovered by the boy's mother when she questioned him about an Internet on-line chat with the teacher. At the time of the teacher's psychiatric evaluation, she told the doctor that her relationship with her husband was "somewhat strained as of late" (Fargen, 2005).

Assignment Transfer

A school employee suspected of minor sexual misconduct is sometimes moved to a place in which such behavior is unlikely to occur.

While school officials investigated charges that a science teacher had made improper sexual advances to girl students, the 54-year-old teacher at Admiral King High School in Lorain (Ohio) was reassigned to the position of resource coordinator of reading programs in two elementary schools. The investigation had been launched by a complaint from a former student that the science teacher had hugged her in class, slapped her buttocks, driven her home in his car, and kissed her neck. Similar complaints came from other girls as well. When parents learned that the teacher was now working in elementary schools, they objected to the reassignment on the grounds that the man would still be in touch with children. In response, school officials moved him to the curriculum center in the school district's administration building, pending the outcome of the investigation of complaints of sexual abuse (Matzelle, 2005).

License Revocation

Some school districts revoke the teaching or administrative licenses of personnel found guilty of sexual offenses with students, but others do not. Thus, abusers who retain their certification can be employed in other districts and continue in close contact with children and adolescents.

Over a two-year period at Admiral King High School in Lorain County (Ohio), three teachers were either dismissed or resigned following allegations of improper sexual relations with students. One of the teachers was committed to prison and the other two left the school, but all three retained their state licenses to teach. During the same period of time, four other Lorain County teachers were found guilty of unacceptable sexual contact with students. Three of them served jail sentences—one for sending sexually explicit e-mails to a student, another for sexual intercourse with a student, and the third for fondling a student. The fourth teacher was discharged from his job for improper sexual advances. Only two of the four had their teaching certification rescinded (Dissell, 2004).

Probation

As explained earlier, extenuating conditions can result in child abusers being assigned such lenient sanctions as probation in cases which, under ordinary circumstances, would draw harsher punishment.

A 31-year-old drama instructor at Granite High School in San Diego (California) received a probation sentence when he confessed to unlawful sexual intercourse with a 17-year-old boy who had been a member of the instructor's theater company. The youth testified that he had engaged in sexual intercourse with the teacher on several occasions over a three-month period. Under the unusually light sentence, the instructor would avoid jail time but would have to surrender his teaching credential, register as a sex offender, and do community service. Several mitigating circumstances influenced the judge to award probation: (a) the student said the sex had been consensual, (b) he also admitted having sex with other adult males, including group sex, (c) a detective reported that the student had said he and the instructor "would go off and 'hook up' with different guys and have sex", and (d) the defendant had no past police record of misconduct (Teacher pleads guilty, 2003).

After pleading guilty to two counts of sexual conduct with a minor, a 25-year-old woman coach of a girls' basketball team at Marcos de Niza High School in Tempe (Arizona) lost her job, and the court sentenced her to probation with the requirement that she register as a sex offender. The victim in the case was a 17-year-old girl to whom the coach had sent love letters and with whom the coach had engaged in sex acts at the coach's apartment. The fact that the student was nearly 18 years old was considered by the judge to be an extenuating circumstance supporting lifetime probation as a suitable punishment (Walsh, 2004).

Suicide

Sometimes accused sexual abusers determine the disposition of the charge against them by committing suicide.

The day after a Brooklyn (New York) 45-year-old high-school basketball coach was cited for statutory rape and endangering the welfare of a child, he parked his car near a football field and shot himself dead. His sexual tryst with a student had begun in late 2001 when a 14-year-old girl gave him her phone number. By early 2002 the pair had started a series of sexual encounters that lasted until April 2005. When the girl later told a friend about the affair, the friend suggested that she report the matter to the police, who then arrested the coach, thereby bringing his 21-year teaching carrier to an end (Fahim, 2005).

Treating Victims

The same methods suggested earlier for treating victims of abuse outside the school's jurisdiction are suitable for treating victims of abuse that has occurred within the school's domain.

THE PROBLEM OF FALSE ACCUSATIONS

The possibility that allegations of sexual abuse are false can affect decisions about which people should be informed of an accusation and about the time when they are informed. This is the problem of weighing (a) the need to take prompt action to apprehend an actual abuser against (b) the damage to an accused individual's reputation in case the charge of abuse has been fictitious.

Parents in Bloomington (Minnesota) demanded to know why the police had waited five days before telling school officials that a janitor at Polar Bridge Elementary School was guilty of sexually molesting children. A police official, in response, explained that the department had no rules about when to notify the school district. In the present case, a 9-year-old girl had complained to her mother that the 62-year-old night janitor had fondled her; the mother reported the incident to the police. When the girl was interviewed at Corner House, an agency that specializes in helping sexually abused kids, she said that she had returned to school to get a book in the late afternoon and it was then that the janitor had touched her breasts, inner highs, and buttocks. The police investigated the janitor's background and inquired about reports of other similar episodes.

A police spokesman said, "Our focus is not to call the district right away. First we do the criminal investigation. We notify the district as soon as is practical. The goal is to keep other kids from being victimized."

The superintendent of schools agreed with police procedures: "I am confident in the police ability to do this in a way that is going be proper. If there is not enough information for them to make a report, I understand that."

The investigation led to the janitor's arrest for second-degree criminal sexual conduct. When interviewed, he confessed to having fondled at least a dozen other girls as well (Adams, 2003).

In attempting to judge the validity of a charge of sexual misconduct, school officials are often faced with deciding which sources of evidence are the most trustworthy.

As a result of two students reporting pictures of naked women on a music teacher's pair of classroom computers, administrators at Torrington (Connecticut) Middle School (a) seized the computers and (b) conducted a survey of students enrolled in the teacher's eight classes, asking whether they had seen anything inappropriate on the machines. Five students reported having seen photos of naked women. When the teacher was suspended and offered the chance to resign in order to avoid charges of sexual misconduct, he refused to resign. He was cleared of all allegations when the State Police Computer Crime Laboratory analyzed the computers' contents and found nothing inappropriate. School officials were obliged to reinstate him as a music teacher and assign him to an elementary school (Kim, 2005).

Claims of sexual maltreatment become especially perplexing when two government agencies arrive at opposite conclusions about a charge of abuse. In the following case, those agencies were a state child-welfare department and a district court.

Fired by from his job at Weaver High School in Connecticut, a 45-year-old special-education teacher was acquitted by a jury of two counts of fourth-degree sexual assault and risk of injury to a minor. The charges against the teacher had resulted from a complaint by a 14-year-old girl who accused him of sexually molesting her in his classroom. According to the police arrest warrant, the girl said she had gone to the classroom to use the telephone and that the teacher had complimented her on her lips and her body, had grabbed her hand and placed it on his crotch, and had asked her to engage in oral sexual intercourse, but she should not tell anyone. The girl testified that she had pulled away from the man and left the classroom.

The teacher's defense attorney rejected the girl's claim as "implausible," because two other girls who were in the classroom at the same time said they saw no evidence of any sexual talk or gestures. In addition, the accuser "didn't cry out" and the teacher wrote hall passes for all three. The attorney told jurors that he suspected the girl's accusations were an attempt at revenge because the teacher had "confronted her days earlier because she had spread a rumor about him. Then this allegation arose a few days later."

Prior to the court trial, the case against the teacher had been complicated by the fact that the girl's original accusation had been turned over to the state Department of Children and Families. That agency investigated the claims and found in favor of the girl. On the grounds of that decision, the teacher—despite his status as a tenured employee—had been discharged from his job (Gottlieb, 2005b).

The danger of destroying an innocent person's career occurs whenever news media publicize an accusation of sexual misconduct before investigators have determined the validity of the allegation.

Police jailed a 53-year-old fourth-grade teacher at Farnsworth Aerospace Elementary Magnet School in St. Paul (Minnesota) after a 9-year-old girl accused him of foundling her during a kickball game and on two other occasions. News of the arrest was spread in newspaper headlines and on television. During the two months between the arrest and the eventual court decision, most teachers at his school avoided him, as did the teachers union and many of the friends he had made over the past 30 years.

The child's accusation was investigated by the police and a social worker, who submitted a report to the judge who would handle the case. At the same time, the teacher's lawyer filed a report with the court, contending that the analysis of the case had been botched by the investigators, who had apparently based their guilty charge solely on the girl's accusation, her parents' word, and the social-worker's impressions. The defense attorney's affidavit noted that the investigators had failed to interview any of the 26 other children who were present at the time of the alleged molestation, nor had the social worker or prosecutors spoken with a substitute teacher who had watched the kickball game and testified that "she never saw [the teacher] push a child to the ground or touch a child in any way inappropriately." The defense report also questioned the wisdom of believing the accusation of a child who was "a special-education student with a history of behavior problems." According to the case file, the girl once had once "accused another teacher of being a spy and once insisted that a football game between the Packers and the Vikings took place in 'outer space.'"

The ultimate disposition of the case did not involve a trial. Rather, both sides agreed to have the judge base her decision on the evidence in the prosecutors' and defense-lawyer's reports. When the reports were presented to the magistrate, she took only five minutes to render a not-guilty verdict. Officially the teacher had been exonerated, but not in the world of everyday living, because the accusation of child molestation would linger in people's minds. The teacher concluded that "My reputation was annihilated." He resigned from the school district and moved to Ireland where he hoped to become a writer (Rosario, 2005).

In view of the damage that a false accusation may cause a teacher's reputation if his or her name is openly announced before the validity of the charge has been determined, an important question becomes: Under what circumstances should school officials or the police reveal to the public the names of teachers who have been accused of a sexual offense? This issue was the focus of a court decision in the state of Washington in late 2005. At the heart of the case was a distinction drawn by an appeals-court judge among three terms: *proven true*, *unsubstantiated*, and *patently false*.

In a series of articles about sexual abuse in schools, *The Seattle Times* had reported that nearly 100 athletic coaches in Washington still held teaching positions after they had been dismissed or censured for sexual misconduct. The *Times* investigators then wanted to know (a) school districts' policies about publicly revealing the names of teachers who had been accused of sexual offenses and (b) what were the names of teachers who had been so accused and were still teaching. In response to the newspaper's request for such information, several teachers who had been accused of sexual misconduct filed injunctions to prevent their districts from identifying their names, contending that such disclosures would invade their privacy. In adjudicating the issue, the appeals court ordered the districts to reveal the names of accused teachers in 15 out of 18 cases that were in dispute. The judges ruled that in 15 cases the accusation had been "unsubstantiated" and in three had been "patently false." In explaining the rationale behind the decision, the presiding judge wrote that:

"School districts must disclose the names of teachers who have been accused of misconduct of a sexual nature, even when the districts have concluded after investigation that the allegations are unsubstantiated or too minor to justify discipline. 'Unsubstantiated' and 'false' are two terms that do not mean the same thing. Unsubstantiated complaints often are two conflicting accounts in which a firm conclusion cannot be made. . . . If a teacher's record includes a number of complaints found to be 'unsubstantiated,' the pattern is more troubling than each individual complaint. Yet, if the teacher's name in each individual complaint is withheld from public disclosure, the public will not be able to see any troubling pattern that might emerge."

In response to the ruling, an attorney for the Washington Education Association said that the decision "will harm and endanger a lot of professionals who are innocent."

The ruling did not involve dispute over cases in which sexual misconduct was clearly proven, since the appropriateness of announcing abusers' names in clearly proven instances was not questioned (Willmsen, 2005).

CONCLUSION

The past three decades have witnessed heightened public concern over the sexual maltreatment of children and adolescents, with the concern reflected in new legislation, more criminal-court cases, more civil lawsuits, additional school regulations, and far greater attention in newspapers and on television and radio programs.

The purpose of this chapter has been to identify types of sexual abuse, to illustrate those types with cases from newspaper accounts, to describe commonly practiced ways of treating offenders and their victims, and to inspect the problem of false accusations of sexual molestation.

CHAPTER 7

Bullying and Hazing

Bullying is the act of tormenting a person in ways the person detests. Hazing is a subtype of bullying that involves someone being forced to submit to humiliating treatment in order to earn membership in the group responsible for the hazing. A distinction sometimes is drawn between bullying and harassing, with *bullying* used to identify any single attempt to frustrate or intimidate an individual and *harassing* used to label repeated attempts to cause a person grief.

In the past, children teasing and harassing schoolmates was usually considered a harmless, natural part of growing up. But in recent times bullying has been taken far more seriously, viewed now as a form of harmful violence that deserves censure. Efforts to curb bullying have particularly been stimulated by the recognition that students' ridiculing and mocking schoolmates can contribute to such violent acts as the deadly shootings at Columbine High School in Littleton (Colorado) in 1999, at Santana High School in Santee (California) in 2001, and at Red Lake (Minnesota) in 2005. In effect, those who are bullied may retaliate against their oppressors in brutal ways. The U.S. Secret Service reported that in about two-thirds of school shootings, the attackers felt threatened or persecuted by peers (Ave, 2003).

Bullying in schools is very common. A survey of 15,686 public and private school students in 2001 revealed that nearly one-third of students in grades six through ten were either bullies or victims of bullies. An estimated 10,000 U.S. schoolchildren stay home from school at least once a week because they have been targets of bullying. However, statistics on the extent of bullying are not very accurate because many children who are tormented never report it. Because of underreported bullying, teachers may be unaware of bullying incidents even when the acts occur in their own classroom. In one study, teachers were found to intervene in only 18 percent of bullying cases. Many adults seem to believe they intervene when children torment, but children often see it differently. In another study, 70 percent of teachers said adults "almost always" act to stop bullying incidents, but only 25 percent of the students agreed (Committee for Children, 2005).

The analysis of bullying in this chapter is presented in four segments: (a) the bullying process, (b) prevention efforts, (c) treating bullies, and (d) treating bullies' victims.

THE BULLYING PROCESS

The process of taunting and tormenting can be viewed from the perspectives of (a) forms of bullying, (b) the nature of bullies, and (c) the nature of bullies' targets.

Forms of Bullying

One way of classifying bullying is to divide it into eight forms—physical abuse, property damage, direct taunting, written messages, rumor spreading, exclusion acts, bystander bullying, and cyberbullying.

Physical Abuse

Physical torment can include pushing, kicking, hitting, biting, pinching, twisting, hair pulling, and the like. Although students of either sex may engage in physical bullying, boys inflict physical damage more often than girls.

A 10-year-old boy was hit and choked repeatedly by a bully, leaving the boy with severe bruising on his neck. The bully's mother, in response to complaints about her son's behavior, said her son was having problems at home and that the injured boy was to blame for having provoked her son (Woolf, 2004).

A news reporter interviewed a Duquesne (Pennsylvania) fifth-grade girl who was hospitalized for a concussion suffered when the girl had been assaulted by schoolmates, despite the presence of security guards.

> Interviewer: "How many girls were there and what were they doing?"
> Student: "There was five girls kicking me in my head."
> Interviewer: "So, you're down on the floor?"
> Student: "Yeah and everybody's on top of me. The security guard's on top of me. Children are on top of the security guard. That's how it was that I couldn't breathe, couldn't move. I passed out like twice" (Welles, 2005).

"A teacher calls two students to the front of the class to complete a math problem on the blackboard. As one of the students walks to the front, a boy sticks out his foot and trips him. The student falls clumsily to the floor as the rest of the class laughs" (Bullying, 2005).

Property Damage and Theft

Bullies often damage, destroy, or steal their victims' belongings. Despoiling property can take many forms. For instance, a second-grade boy was distressed by a classmate's spitting on his lunch. The locker in which a high school band member kept his drumsticks was raided, and the sticks were broken in two before they were returned to the locker. Middle-school bullies stole epilepsy medicine from the book bag of a 13-year-old epileptic schoolmate. When a high school girl put her lunch tray on a table near a group of other girls, one of them picked up the new arrival's milk carton and poured milk over the victim's enchilada. After a middle-school girl hung her jacket on a clothing rack outside the classroom, another girl searched through the jacket pockets and removed a comb, loose change, and a package of gum.

Direct Taunts and Threats

Perhaps the most common form of bullying is that of oral assaults—threats, derogatory name-calling, and insulting remarks about a person's appearance, mental ability, race, religion, habits, family background, mode of speech, lifestyle, friends, sexual orientation, and more.

"My name is Dennis. Kids used to call me Menace when I was young, and I didn't like it at all."

A high-school girl reported that after having an argument with a schoolmate, she thought their differences had been resolved. But the next day the schoolmate arrived with friends who said "they were going to get me after school. They didn't get me, but I was scared for two weeks."

After an 11-year-old girl was told by her family physician that she was overweight, she reported that "Someone found out I'd been to the doctor about my weight and then they started picking on me. They do it when the teachers aren't around—calling me 'earthquake' and 'whale'. Sometimes it makes me cry. I used to play sports but now I don't do that any more because people laugh at me" (Real life, 2005).

A nine-year-old told her school counselor that she was bullied by several girls because of her race. They had called her "Blackie", and now she feared they would beat her up "because that's what happens to Black kids." Although her mother told her to ignore the taunting, the child said she couldn't ignore it. She said she felt ugly and wanted to kill herself (Real life, 2005).

Written Messages

Written threats and insults can assume several forms—notes passed around a classroom or left in a victim's notebook, graffiti on walls, letters sent through the mail, and e-mails sent from a computer.

A 15-year-old girl, whose younger brother suffered from a severe illness, was sent a note saying, "I hope your brother dies". The girl also received threats to beat her up, and she once came home with footprints on her stomach where she had been kicked. Her parents felt school personnel had failed to confront the bullies. The girl was removed from school by her doctor to protect her from future assaults (Woolf, 2004).

Rumor Spreading

Rather than say insulting things directly to a fellow student, bullies often create hurtful rumors about the student and spread the tales through the school's hearsay network. Rumors are apparently the most frequent of the various forms of bullying, especially among teenage girls. Making up vicious gossip can be a particularly attractive means of tormenting schoolmates because (a) it does not require that bullies confront their victims face-to-face and (b) it extends its damaging effect well beyond the creator of the rumor by influencing other people's impression of the rumor's target.

What begins as a rumor often expands into other forms of torment.

A girl at Holmes Junior High School in Davis (California) never did understand why a classmate disliked her and created cruel rumors about her. Nor did she understand why the classmate then convinced other girls to shun her, so that "I would walk around school and no one would talk to me. I just had to go home and I would cry and be all sad about it. You feel so helpless" (Martineau, 2002).

In her second day at school, a new eighth-grader was pushed into the street by a schoolmate. She thought the pushing was just play, so she pushed back. But the instigator of the pushing then started the rumor that the new girl was a violent bully, an accusation that was soon believed by others—students and teachers alike. The rumors were then followed by silent phone calls, threats, and occasional physical abuse—shoving, poking, tripping—that lasted for three years. On one occasion, when a group of girls had cornered their victim against the wall, a teacher approached and, thinking the girl was the aggressor, threatened to punish her if she continued her supposed bullying. "Roughly once every two weeks the girl's parents would meet with the principal to try to convince him that their daughter was the victim. No one in authority admitted that bullying existed at the school. Nothing was done" (Pathway Courses, 2005).

Exclusion Acts

Bullying is not limited to direct assaults or spreading rumors, but can also take the form of preventing a student from joining a group or engaging in attractive activities. This kind of bullying is especially common among girls. Thus, a bully may reject a girl in the lunchroom or on a school outing, encourage basketball teammates to never pass the ball to her, never invite her to a party, and never choose her to be on a committee, and such.

Three girls are talking together on the playground. A fourth girl approaches, but as she gets closer, the others see her and move into a tight circle, their backs to her. She hesitates, then goes to the swing-set to play alone. The other girls giggle loudly at her discomfort (Bullying, 2005).

Bystander Bullying

People who witness a bullying incident may contribute to the damage either by cheering the bully on or by watching in silence without objecting, thereby appearing to give tacit approval to the abuse. However, bystanders may suffer from their failing to openly condemn tormenters' actions. That is, silent witnesses to bullying episodes can (a) feel angry and helpless for not knowing what to do, (b) worry about their becoming a bully's target, and (c) suffer guilt and shame for not having acted to stop the bully.

Cyberbullying

Over the past two decades, students' ability to bully at a distance and to remain anonymous has been greatly enhanced by the advent of the electronic computer and its associated gadgets—cell phones, digital cameras, pagers, hand-held computers, or all of these components in one small instrument. Such devices are the tools of *cyberbullying*, which consists of harassing, humiliating, intimidating, or threatening others on the Internet.

Internet services that can be used for cyberbullying include e-mail, chat groups, Web pages, blogs, opinion polls, and instant messaging that enables users to engage in multiple written conversations simultaneously.

Blogs are sites on the World Wide Web in the form of personal-opinion journals or logs containing entries on any subject of the writer's choice. The opinions are e-mailed to selected recipients or shared with others through links on the Internet. Some blogging sites require users to register personal identifying information and to conform to the site's rules.

Such polling or voting Web sites as www.freevote.com offer users the chance to create online voting booths that enable cyberbullies to encourage Internet users to vote for whichever schoolmates they regard as the ugliest, fattest, dumbest, or the like.

Popular forms of cyberbullying by teenagers include:

Sending cruel, vicious, and sometimes threatening messages.

Creating Web sites that have stories, cartoons, pictures, and jokes ridiculing others.

Breaking into an e-mail account and sending vicious or embarrassing material to others.

Engaging someone in instant messaging, tricking that person into revealing sensitive personal information, and forwarding that information to others.

Posting pictures of classmates online and asking students to rate them on such derogatory features as boring, repulsive, bad smelling, and disgusting.

Using a digital phone camera to take a photo of a person undressed in the locker room and sending that picture to others. (Center for Safe and Responsible Internet Use, 2005)

   The extent of cyberbullying among youths was suggested in a survey of 1,400 adolescents. The researchers reported that over one-third of respondents said they had been victims of cyberbullying. Most victims (56%) had been bullied in a chat room or via computer text messaging (49%). Forty-one percent did not tell anyone about the bullying incident (Patchin & Hinduja, 2005).

   Some typical ways in which cyberbullying operates are illustrated in the following cases.

One of the most widely publicized examples of cyberbullying is the website created by Eric Harris—one of the two Columbine High School killers—where he discussed murdering his fellow students.

Another instance that received worldwide attention was the case of a Canadian teenager who gained notoriety as "the Star Wars Kid." At home one day, he used a video camera to film himself acting out a scene from the *Star Wars* movie. He twirled awkwardly about the room, wielding a golf-ball retriever as his simulated light saber. When some schoolmates illegally got hold of the video, they displayed it on the Internet and passed it around to friends. They then altered videos of three movies—*The Matrix, The Terminator, Chicago*—by splicing into them parts of the antics from the teenager's original video and adding special effects and sounds. The resulting caricatures were posted on the Internet and downloaded by viewers around the world. According to news reports, the youth was so distraught that he had to drop out of school and seek psychiatric help (Paulson, 2003).

As a prank, two 11-year-old Duxbury (Massachusetts) pupils used the name of a 13-year-old neighbor girl when they entered an Internet chat room where they gave an older man the neighbor girl's personal contact information. When the man's Internet request to meet the 13-year-old arrived in her home computer, her parents phoned the police. The girl said, "I didn't know who this guy was. He said he wanted to meet me. It was scary" (Crane, 2005).

A high-school boy, enraged because his girl friend had rejected him, used a photo-editing program on his computer to paste her face on a pornographic photo, which he sent to his entire e-mail list. The girl was emotionally devastated. When the school principal learned of the event, he removed the boy's website. The girl had to seek counseling and was transferred to a different school (Paulson, 2003).

During a school trip to Costa Rica for Milton (Massachusetts) High School students, two girls logged onto the Internet's LiveJournal.com website where users shared journal entries with friends. On the website, the two girls posted a fictitious entry under the name of one of their 16-year-old classmates. Included in their fake entry was the admission of a sexual liaison that their 16-year-old classmate supposedly had with a Costa Rican. The impersonators had written:

"I was in the elevator going to my room last night and it stopped all of a sudden. The only other person in there was this older man named Juan. His hands were so gentle and loving. I thought I could be there all night just stuck in the elevator."

When the 16-year-old victim of the hoax later discovered the false material on the website, she said she fell apart emotionally. "I keep asking myself why they would do such a thing—because there was nothing I had ever done to make them hate me. Anyone in the world could read this stuff. Anyone in the school could say, 'Wow, look at what kind of person she is.' They could judge me by what other people wrote about me."

School authorities responded by reprimanding the two impersonators and eliminating access to the LiveJournal.com website from school computers. But when the victim's mother reported the incident to the police, they told her that there was nothing they could do about it, because there were no laws preventing such behavior (Welles, 2005).

As a reaction to the threat of cyberbullying, some officials have completely banned the use of cell phones, messaging, and computer instant messaging at school. Others have published rules, backed by strict penalties, to prevent cyberbullying via school computers that students use.

The Nature of Bullies

Bullies are not all alike. They can vary in several ways—in their reasons for picking on others, in their bullying techniques, in their family's socioeconomic condition, and in their physical and mental abilities.
Bullies' reasons for tormenting schoolmates can be their

- Feeling inferior to peers; thus, they turn to pestering others in an attempt to compensate for their sense of inadequacy.
- Feeling superior to schoolmates, so they express this feeling by ridiculing others.
- Finding themselves in a difficult situation, and not knowing a reasonable solution for their plight, so they blame and attack others.
- Having been overindulged by their family, so they expect to enjoy special privileges; when those privileges are not forthcoming, they bully others in order to get their way.
- Having been bullied themselves, so they retaliate—not by attacking the bully who has made their own life miserable, but by bullying someone even more vulnerable than they.
- Growing up in a family in which bullying is a normal social-interaction technique, so they follow that model in their social relations outside the family.
- Yearning for acceptance with a particular group of schoolmates, so they adopt the same bullying habits (rumor mongering, name calling, voicing racial slurs) that are common among members of that group.
- Expressing jealousy of schoolmates' success (in wealth, talent, friendships) by tormenting those schoolmates.
- Reacting to an upsetting change in their family circumstances—a parent's loss of employment, loss of home, divorce, death of a family member, imprisonment of a family member, violence in the family, alcoholism, drug abuse, illness of a family member.
- Suffering a disability (deafness, dyslexia, autism, impaired sight) that hampers their academic performance, so their frustration leads them to bully schoolmates.
- Being abused or neglected at home, so they vent their frustration by abusing schoolmates—particularly ones who are physically smaller or psychologically more vulnerable than they.

- Spending time with companions who are bullies, so they adopt their companions' social-interaction habits.

- Suffering an antisocial, psychopathic, or personality disorder.

Studies indicate that bullies often come from homes where physical punishment is used, where the children are taught to strike back physically as a way to handle problems, and where parental involvement and warmth are frequently lacking. Students who regularly display bullying behaviors are generally defiant or oppositional toward adults, antisocial, and apt to break school rules (Banks, 1997). Bullies are often lonely, have difficulty making friends, compile poor academic records, and are prone to smoke and drink (Committee for Children, 2005). Those who continue to torment others invite future troubles of their own. One study revealed that boys identified as bullies in middle school had one criminal conviction by age 24, with 40 percent of bullies accumulating three or more arrests by age 30 (National Education Association, 2005).

The Nature of Bullies' Targets

Like bullies, students who are bullied appear to be at risk of poor success in school and are frequently involved in such problem behaviors as smoking and drinking. Victims of bullying are often lonely, lack social skills, and have difficulty making friends. They are typically anxious, insecure, and cautious, rarely defending themselves or retaliating when confronted by those who bully them. They tend to be physically weaker than their peers. Other physical characteristics such as weight, dress, or wearing eyeglasses do not appear to be significant factors that can be correlated with victimization (Banks, 1997; Committee for Children, 2005).

The act of being bullied tends to increase some students' isolation because their peers do not want to lose status by associating with them or because they do not want to increase the risks of being bullied themselves. Being bullied leads to depression and low self-esteem, problems that can carry into adulthood. Student surveys reveal that a low percentage of students seem to believe that adults will help. Students feel that adult intervention is infrequent and ineffective, and that telling adults will only bring more harassment from bullies. Students report that teachers seldom or never talk to their classes about bullying. (Banks, 1997)

The distress that bullying causes victims can include fear of going to school, of taking a school bus, of using a school bathroom, of walking along a corridor, of eating lunch in the cafeteria, or of going to a playground. Physical effects of bullying can include headaches, indigestion, and eating disorders (anorexia, compulsive overeating).

PREVENTION EFFORTS

As bullying in schools has become a serious concern over the past decade, a rapidly growing number of school systems have adopted bullying-prevention plans. Typical features of prevention programs are

- A written code of conduct posted on bulletin boards, explained to students in their classes, and sent to parents. The code includes examples of bullying acts and explains the penalties to be faced by students who engage in those acts.
- Training sessions for teachers and other school personnel so they recognize bullying and know how to respond to incidents. Experts from outside the school can serve as instructors.
- Training sessions for students so they can identify bullying behavior, can tell why such behavior is unacceptable, and can learn the punishment that bullies will suffer. Such sessions can be conducted by outside experts or by members of the school staff—teachers, counselors, administrators—who have been prepared as trainers.
- Emphasis on the need for students to break the unwritten code that cautions children and youths, "Don't tattle, don't tell." To counteract that code, students are urged to report to designated school personnel any bullying they personally suffer or witness. As the coordinator of a bullying-prevention program in Michigan has suggested, "When we teach children not to keep quiet, that empowers them and breaks the code. Stressing such lessons with all students also works to help prevent bullying because it increases the odds that groups of students will criticize unacceptable behavior. If kids band together, they can stand up to the bully because there's strength in numbers" (Olberliesen, 2005).

Classroom activities used in bullying-prevention programs include brainstorming sessions, role-playing, and story analysis.

Brainstorming involves students describing (a) bullying incidents with which they are acquainted, (b) how the incidents turned out, and (c) what actions victims and others (onlookers, teachers, parents) might have taken to produce a more positive outcome than occurred in those episodes.

During a class, the teacher guides class members in preparing a set of rules that govern bullying behavior, with the rules including consequences to be suffered by perpetrators of different kinds of bullying.

One form of role-playing consists of a class being divided into small groups (three-to-five members) and assigned to write and perform a short skit in which bullying occurs and victims of the bullying display appropriate communication skills—both verbal and nonverbal—to avoid escalating the torment or to get themselves out of the bully's control. In a discussion session following each skit, class members who believe a different solution to the bullying problem can describe their alternative or act it out.

Book or story analysis involves a class reading a story or seeing a drama on a video and discussing the bullying issues depicted in the tale. The discussion can focus on (a) the bully's likely motives, (b) characteristics of victims that contributed to their becoming the bully's target, and (c) constructive ways that victims and onlookers might have acted in order to produce a positive outcome. An example of a book that can serve as the stimulus for such analysis is a novel titled *The Misfits* that was used in middle schools across America during "No Name Calling Week" each spring, beginning in 2004 when more than 4,000 schools in all 50 states and the District of Columbia participated in the campaign. The misfits in the story are a "Gang of Five" friends trying to survive seventh grade in the face of taunts about their weight, height, intelligence, or sexual orientation. The friends create a political party during student-council elections and run on a platform of wiping out name-calling. Middle-school classes that participated in the event read the novel and discussed its implications for the treatment of students who are different from the majority of their agemates in appearance, ethnic background, skills, social-class status, or sexual preference. For the 2005 "No Name Calling Week," 5,100 educators in 36 states registered to participate (Crary, 2005; Johnson, 2004).

An example of a commercially available antibullying plan is one created by Dan Olweus, a professor at the University of Bergen in Norway, and used in at least fifteen nations. The Olweus Bullying Prevention Program is designed for pupils aged 6 to 15 in elementary, middle, and junior-high schools. The plan "attempts to restructure the existing school environment to reduce opportunities and rewards for bullying." Members of the school staff are chiefly responsible for conducting the program to improve peer relations and make the school "a safe and positive place for students to learn and develop" (Olweus bullying, 2005). All students participate in most aspects of the program, while ones identified as bullies or as targets of bullying receive additional individual attention. The program includes activities at three levels—schoolwide, classroom, and individual.

Schoolwide

(a) All students complete a forty-item bully/victim anonymous questionnaire designed to reveal their perception of bullying in their school.
(b) A bullying-prevention coordinating committee is formed as the body responsible for guiding the implementation of the program. Members of the committee participate in an initial all-day training session with a certified trainer and thereafter attend 1- to 2-hour monthly meetings.
(c) A system of training school staff members in antibullying practices features a teacher's handbook that offers detailed advice on how to carry out the plan. Teachers are expected to participate in an initial one-day training session and then engage in periodic teacher discussion groups during the first year of the program.
(d) Schoolwide rules against bullying are developed and publicized.
(e) A system is devised for supervising students between class periods, at recess, and during lunch hour.

Classroom

(a) Teachers conduct weekly 20- to 40-minute classroom sessions that focus on bullying and peer relations, with emphasis on types of unacceptable bullying tactics and on more constructive ways that students can interact.

(b) Teachers introduce parent meetings at which bullying is analyzed and parents learn what they can do to help their children avoid bullying others and avoid being the targets of taunting and abuse.

Individual

Teachers hold individual meetings with (a) children who bully, (b) children who are targets of bullying, and (c) parents of children involved in bullying incidents, either as bullies or victims.

Studies of the effect of the Olweus approach suggest that it has enjoyed significant success in reducing bullying in a variety of school settings. Olweus (2001) reported that

There were marked reductions—by 50 percent or more—in bully/victim problems in 42 schools during the two years following introduction of the intervention program. The results generally applied to both boys and girls and to students from all grades studied (from grade 4 through 9). There were also clear reductions in general antisocial behavior such as vandalism, fighting, pilfering, drunkenness, and truancy. In addition, we could register marked improvement as regards various aspects of the social climate of the class, improved order and discipline, more positive social relationships, and a more positive attitude to schoolwork and the school. At the same time, there was an increase in student satisfaction with school life.

Schools' efforts to prevent bullying have been intensified in recent years by victims filing lawsuits against school systems for failing to take action against bullies.

A federal court mediator arranged a settlement in which the Tonganoxie (Kansas) School District would pay a former high-school youth $440,000 damages for the district's having done nothing to stop classmates from harassing the boy from the time he was in ninth grade until he dropped out of school in eleventh grade. The lawsuit charged that students had constantly accused the youth of being gay, although he contended that he was not gay. At the court trial, the youth's attorney claimed that the Tonganoxie district had enforced its sexual harassment policy when a female student was harassed, but failed to do so when the boy was bullied. The attorney said, "I expect this case will have profound effects nationwide in dealing with schoolyard bullying and harassment. Insurance companies will have a very powerful economic incentive to see that districts' anti-harassment policies are aggressive and effective" (Bullied Kansas teen, 2005).

Treating Bullies

Probably the most frequent response that bullies draw from school personnel and parents is a verbal reprimand. Telling a tormenter to stop harassing schoolmates is often followed by a warning about what other unwelcome consequences can result from future bullying—a phone call to parents, a critical note in the student's personnel file, the removal of privileges, or suspension.

In recent years, as school officials and the police have increasingly viewed bullying as destructive behavior that deserves serious attention, more formal measures have been adopted to curb students' taunting and pestering acts. By 2005, twenty-one states had antibullying laws, and twelve more had proposals for such laws currently before their legislatures (High, 2005). And because schools bear a legal duty to protect their students (*a duty of care*), if they fail to take steps to correct reported cases of bullying and if someone suffers physical or psychological injury as a result of bullying, school personnel risk being sued under civil law for neglecting that duty. In addition to state laws requiring school districts to prohibit bullying, many districts have passed zero-tolerance policies even without state mandates. The threat of legal action has become a stimulus for schools to prepare antibullying programs that include training teachers, administrators, and counselors. Programs usually include suggestions for how staff members should respond to bullies, such as

- Keep clearly in mind the various forms of bullying so that you can recognize an episode of tormenting when it occurs.
- Don't let a bullying episode—however minor—pass without a response. Suitable responses may include cautioning the bully to stop, discussing the incident with class members, penalizing the bully, informing the bully's parents, or reporting the event to authorities.
- If you feel less than competent to confront the bully at the time of the incident, you should describe the event to someone in authority (school principal, coach, security guard, police) who is better equipped to cope with the tormenter.

Treating Bullies' Victims

Students who have suffered from bullying incidents may profit from counseling sessions in which they learn techniques useful for warding off bullies and diminishing abuse. The counseling may include suggestions about how to behave in future encounters with tormenters. For instance, consider the following sorts of advice about potentially helpful ways to act.

- "Don't be an easy target. Walking with your head down makes you look weak. Stand up straight and try to have eye contact. Keep calm. A bully wants to upset you. Avoid places where you are alone and no one could hear you [if you called for help].
- "Try humor. Danny was waiting for Sergio near the bus stop. 'Hey!' Danny yelled. 'You've got a face like a gorilla.' Sergio laughed. 'Tell me something I don't already know.' He kept walking and made it to the bus before Danny could think of a comeback.
- "Ignore the bully and walk away. Keep moving and don't look back. It's hard to bully someone who isn't there." (Donahue, 2004)
- Avoid places in which bullies hang out.

- When you are going someplace in which there is risk of being bullied, go with a group rather than alone.
- Report any tormenting to school authorities or the police. Don't be frightened into keeping silent.
- Learn ways of settling arguments by talking-out problems or by walking away rather than fighting.
- To reduce the chance of being physically intimidated and abused, get training in self-defense techniques.

Antibullying teaching techniques include (a) analyzing stories about bullying episodes that are described in books or depicted in movies and television programs, (b) discussing episodes that have occurred in the school, and (c) having students engage in role-playing dramas that focus on bullying practices. For example, at Hart Middle School in Rochester Hills (Michigan) a student group called Club Pride created skits based on bullying that students may experience. Using the skits as role-playing activities in class enabled students to practice their skills of coping with bullies (Olberliesen, 2005).

THE NATURE OF HAZING

As mentioned earlier, hazing is a form of bullying in which candidates for acceptance into a group or organization are obliged to endure humiliating and sometimes dangerous treatment as a requirement—a rite of passage—for group membership.

Surveys among high school and college students reveal that hazing is very common in American schools and usually results in distressing outcomes for participants. One study of more then 1,500 high school students from various sections of the United States yielded the following figures:

48% of students who belong to groups reported being subjected to hazing activities.

43% reported being subjected to humiliating activities.

30% reported performing potentially illegal acts as part of their initiation.

Both female and male students report high levels of hazing, although male students are at highest risk, especially for dangerous hazing.

Even groups usually considered safe haze new members—24% of students involved in church groups were subjected to hazing activities.

71% of the students subjected to hazing reported negative consequences, such as getting into fights, being injured, fighting with parents, doing poorly in school, hurting other people, having difficulty eating, sleeping, or concentrating, or feeling angry, confused, embarrassed, or guilty. (Hoover & Pollard, 2000)

Sometimes a group's mock initiation activities are defined by written rules, but far more often by unwritten tradition. Other times the bullying is not part of tradition but, instead, is a spontaneous, self-initiated act by a few veteran members of a group.

Ten members of the Coronado High School band in Scottsdale (Arizona) were disciplined for a hazing incident during the band's summer camp. The episode consisted of their duct-taping the hands and feet of five other students, who then complained to their parents upon their return from the camp. Under the school district's zero-tolerance policy toward bullying and hazing, six of the 10 disciplined students were suspended for a period of time but allowed to stay in the band. The other four were expelled from school, and the band director resigned (Madrid, 2005).

The most abusive hazing is frequently inflicted by members of athletic teams. Such torment often includes sexual and scatological affronts to the victims. Consider, for example, the following cases from the *Respect-the-Game* Web site:

For holding down a sophomore teammate and cutting his hair, three high school baseball players were suspended from the team and charged with assault and battery.

A student who suffered learning disabilities had newly joined the high-school wrestling team when he was hazed by teammates in a series of attacks—smashed against the wall, stuffed into a locker, hog-tied, and sodomized with a plastic knife. On one occasion he suffered a serious knee injury and needed counseling for emotional trauma. Eight participants in the assaults were arrested; seven were expelled from school. A team member told police that "both the wrestling and the basketball coaches at the school saw the victim hog-tied and did nothing."

A freshman gymnast reported that 30 upperclassmen had surrounded him and forced him to perform a mock sexual act.

When a junior-varsity football player entered the varsity locker room, he was beaten so badly that he needed medical treatment for fluid in his lungs. He later quit school. Thirteen varsity players who had participated in the assault were suspended.

Fourteen girls were dropped from a high-school field hockey team after they subjected younger team members to sexual simulation acts and other demeaning experiences.

A hazing ritual forced on a new member of a high-school choir included beating him across the buttocks with a two-by-four timber that caused welts. He was then covered with a mixture of human feces, cooking oil, and peanut butter.

When a new 17-year-old member of a high school track team came to the athletic field to appear in team photos, he was attacked by teammates. "A kid grabbed me from behind and held me. Another one ran up and tackled me to the ground. And then two others came and held me down to the ground, and one of them started putting his fingers into my rectum area through my sweats and underwear" (Actual hazing cases, 2005).

In an effort to curb dangerous hazing, more states have adopted antihazing laws. By the opening of the twenty-first century, forty-one states had passed legislation making it a criminal offense to require newcomers to a group to undergo dangerous alcohol consumption, paddlings, or savage beatings (Nuwer, 2000).

The options for treating students guilty of hazing are the same as those for other types of bullying—verbal reprimand, removal of privileges (the opportunity to attend graduation exercises or other school events), suspension (from school or a group's events), expulsion (from school or from a team, choir, band, club), and arrest on criminal charges.

The treatments of hazing victims include counseling, medication, time away from school so as to recover from trauma, and the opportunity to transfer to a different school.

CONCLUSION

The intent of this chapter has been to identify forms of bullying, preventive measures, ways of treating bullies, and ways of treating students who are the victims of torment. The chapter has also addressed the problem of hazing as a special kind of bullying. Over the past two decades, bullying has been seen as a far more serious problem than had traditionally been the case when, during earlier times, taunting and pestering among students were often viewed as rather harmless behaviors and merely a normal part of growing up.

CHAPTER 8

Vandalism

Vandalism is the act of intentionally destroying or damaging property belonging to an institution, to a group, or to an individual other than oneself. Although it is apparent that school vandalism is widespread, the exact amount of destruction and its cost are unknown because many incidents are not reported, particularly when the damage is relatively minor—a few broken windows, slashed bus tires, rude words scrawled on a sidewalk, eggs smashed on a cafeteria wall. However, even though the precise expense of vandalism is not known, it is clear that by the early years of the twenty-first century, the annual cost of school vandalism exceeded $1 billion, a marked increase over the estimated $460 million in 1978 (Vandalism, 2005).

In this chapter, issues of vandalism are addressed under four topics: (a) forms of vandalism, (b) vandalism-protection efforts, (b) treating perpetrators, and (c) treating victims.

FORMS OF VANDALISM

Instances of destruction can be divided among nine classes that identify:

- What has been harmed: (a) structures, (b) equipment, (c) and living things,
- The nature of the harm: (d) disfigurement, (e) graffiti, (f) and computer hacking, and
- Methods or instruments used: (g) arson, (h) noxious substances, (i) and explosives.

Structure Damage

Much of the ruin wrought by vandals is to school buildings, with damage costs ranging from a few hundred dollars to millions.

Four teenagers were caught by police in the early evening at Gibbs High School in St. Petersburg (Florida) where the four had broken into a construction site and started-up three fork lifts and a front-loader tractor with which they smashed a portable classroom. They were charged with trespass and criminal mischief (Four juveniles, 2004).

At night vandals opened a fire hydrant in front of Conant High School in Hoffman Estates (Illinois) and plugged up a storm drain so that a flood of water ran under the school's locked doorways and soaked 40,000 square feet of classroom carpeting and corridor flooring. The damage was estimated at $100,000 (Vandals at Conant, 2005).

Thieves who stole an auto from a garage behind a residence drove the car through the front doors of nearby Southwest High School in Lincoln (Nebraska). The impact damaged 16 glass panels, four heavy metal doors, and railings at a cost of around $25,000 (Vanderford, 2005).

Equipment Damage

Frequent targets of vandals are such items of school equipment as buses, computers, desks, file cabinets, musical instruments, science-laboratory supplies, shelves of books, wall maps, and trophy cases.

Two boys, ages 9 and 10, were caught running away from Danville (New Hampshire) Elementary School after an alarm went off during the pair's Sunday afternoon rampage that caused $100,000 damage to school equipment. When asked why they had attacked the school, the boys said they wanted to "have a little fun."

The demolition began with the pair pelting the school building with eggs and smashing windows with rocks, then forcing open the front door and spending the next two hours moving from room to room, damaging everything in sight. The destruction included:

— Broken classroom and door windows, with shards of glass strewn across floors.
— Chairs and desks smashed beyond repair.
— Phones ripped from the wall.
— A can of soft drink poured into copying machines.
— 50 computers destroyed.
— Paint splattered on walls of an art room.
— Medicine cabinets broken open in the nurse's room.
— The new gymnasium and several classrooms sprayed by fire extinguishers.
— Glass fragments spread across the outside garden that pupils had planted.

School officials said, "Because the offenders are under age, it's not certain what penalty in New Hampshire they may face, if any, other than possibly having do some 'community service.'" The boys' parents "expressed regret" (Perry, 2001).

During the night, vandals slipped through a gap in a chain fence to gain access to the school-bus parking lot in North Royalton (Ohio) where they slashed 50 tires on 25 buses. Because the vandals could only reach the outside tires of the dual-tire rear wheels of the buses, drivers were still able to make their morning round of delivering 3,800 students to school. The slashed tires were replaced at a cost of $14,000 (O'Malley, 2004).

A surveillance camera tape-recorded the activities of six boys, ages 12 to 16, as they spent five hours on a Sunday afternoon breaking into vending machines, smashing windows, upsetting voting machines, and ransacking more than 30 rooms in a Detroit (Michigan) elementary school. The tape enabled police to identify the six and arrest them for breaking and entering and for malicious mischief (Grant, 2004).

Schools in Thompson (Connecticut) were forced to close for a day so that workers could clean the town's 24 school buses whose seats and windows had been sprayed with fire-extinguisher powder during the night. Not only had the vandals emptied the buses' extinguishers during the attack, but they had also broken or stolen onboard security cameras (Stacom, 2005).

Damage to Living Things

Some vandals include animals or plant life among their targets.

Two 15-year-olds, who bragged at their high school about their weekend escapade of destruction at Weibel Elementary School in Fremont (California), were arrested for vandalism that included removing a three-foot-long pet orange-and-black corn snake from its cage and burning it to death in the kindergarten class's microwave oven. The youths had entered the school through an unlatched window, spread paint on walls, and knocked over hundreds of library books, causing an estimated $1,000 damage. The pair were suspended from school for five days and returned to the custody of their parents (Rubenstein, 2001).

Citizens of Valley Center (California) were outraged to learn that 11 graduating seniors had broken into the high school's quadrangle and, using a chainsaw, felled seven ornamental trees. As a result, school authorities banned the 11 from participating in graduation exercises, and plans were laid for obtaining payment for the damage. The school superintended said, "If I could have my way, every one of the kids involved would have to personally get a job and earn every cent it will cost to put things right again. Unfortunately, I have no way of enforcing the manner in which reparations will ultimately be made" (Carr, 2004).

A pair of juveniles broke into JLS Middle School in Palo Alto (California), and killed a pet hamster in addition to scribbling graffiti on the walls, spraying fire extinguisher powder, smashing musical instruments, and altering computer files (Two juveniles, 2004).

Disfigurement

Damage can include disfiguring a building, walkway, bus, auto, billboard, picture, furniture, computer, or other object by scratching it or splattering it with paint, garbage, or staining liquids.

As a prank after a Saturday night dance at Granger High School in Murray (Utah), a group of students threw eggs against the house of the head football coach. When the coach came out of the house, the students drove off in a truck, but the coach was able to see the license number and discover the truck's owner. When school convened the following Monday, the coach confronted the youths and pinned one against the wall. The coach was reprimanded for that act because, as a school official explained, "A district employee is allowed to intervene physically with a student in order to prevent physical harm to another person. Other than that, they shouldn't intervene physically" (Westley, 2005).

Carpets in the library at East Elementary School in Craig (Colorado) needed refurbishing after juveniles doused them with cans of chocolate syrup and fire-extinguisher dust. The two boys who had broken into the school over the weekend were later caught by police who had identified the pair through personal articles they had inadvertently left at the scene of the crime. The boys faced charges of criminal mischief, theft, and burglary. Colorado law required that individuals convicted of criminal mischief have their driver's license revoked. Or, if a teenager did not yet have a driver's license and later applied for one, that license would be suspended for six months to a year after the youth's sixteenth birthday (Currie, 1999).

Graffiti

Graffiti is a special kind of disfigurement consisting of unauthorized inscriptions, words, figures, or designs that are painted, drawn, marked, etched, or scratched onto any surface of public or private sites. Schools are among the favorite targets of graffiti's creators. Tools used for sketching graffiti's illicit phrases and symbols include paint-spray cans, felt-tip markers, paint-and-brush, pens, pencils, chisels, knives, or even a finger on a dirty wall, a window, or a school bus. The most popular instrument in recent years has been the paint-spray can because of its several advantages. It contains the medium (paint) and applicator (spray can) in one relatively small container, making it easily concealed and transported. Spray-paint sticks to most surfaces, and varied effects can be produced (thin lines, wide lines, and large masses) with different sized nozzles.

Graffiti is often employed as a weapon in confrontations between groups or individuals over their ethnic, sex-preference, social-class, or religious differences.

Over a weekend, courtyard windows and walls at San Francisco's A.P. Giannini Middle School were spray-painted with swastikas, racial insults targeting various ethnic groups, and sexual obscenities aimed particularly at women. School-district officials reported that, whereas graffiti at schools was frequent (the district's paint crew spent 40% of its time removing graffiti), racial affronts were uncommon. (The ethnic composition of the middle school's 1,291 students was 59% Asian-American, 10% White, 9% Latino, 6% African-American, and the remaining 16% of mixed or unknown heritage.)

An English teacher who had been at the school for 15 years felt that the swastikas were intended for him. "I happen to be Jewish, so it's personal. I felt like turning around and walking away. This is the most extensive graffiti I've seen. I've been tagged before, but it was nothing with such hateful venom in it. It's very, very disturbing."

The school staff took up a collection to raise $300 as reward money for anyone who would provide information leading to the arrest of the culprits (Marech, 2005).

Students' conflicts over heterosexual versus homosexual orientations were at the center of a graffiti incident at Howell (Michigan) High School where four students, armed with spray-paint canisters, sprayed over the words "God hates fags" that had been written on a rock in front of the school; then they substituted the word "Love." But the four did not stop there. They also spray-painted "Love" 50 times around the flagpole and on nearby sidewalks and benches. In keeping with the school's code of conduct, officials suspended the four from school. But in protest to the suspension, more than 350 students staged a sit-down demonstration in front of the school, claiming that the punishment was too harsh. At the same time, two-dozen counter-protesters, with the word *STRAIGHT* painted on their chests, taunted the crowd of demonstrators. The school principal defended the suspensions by saying, "Although the word 'love' is a beautiful message, instead of using sidewalk chalk that we could wash out, they used spray-paint." The district director of operations estimated that sandblasting the sidewalks to remove the graffiti would cost several thousand dollars because "Concrete is an unforgiving surface" (Howell students, 2005).

Threats against African-Americans and the letters KKK were scrawled alongside smeared feces on the wall of a boys' bathroom at Franklin High School in Elk Grove (California) (Hume, 2005).

Occasionally graffiti is considered to be socially acceptable and of sufficient artistic quality to be retained as a decorative addition to a school.

As a graduation prank, seniors at Montpelier (Vermont) High School sneaked into the school over a holiday weekend to paint a large celestial mural on 170 ceiling tiles in the school's main lobby. When the principal returned to school following the holiday, he was astonished at the sight, then tried to decide how to cope with "a case of vandalism that's really quite beautiful. I think everyone agrees that it's beautiful. We're enjoying it right now, and we don't plan on removing it or eliminating it." School authorities declined to discipline the seniors or press charges against them for entering or for vandalizing school property (School won't erase, 2005).

Computer Hacking

In the world of computers, *hacking* is the act of illegally breaking into computer files by people not authorized to have access to those files. The damage caused by hackers includes (a) obtaining personal information about students or staff members and using that information to cause harm to those individuals (b) stealing tests that are stored in files, (c) transferring funds out of financial accounts, (d) altering information, such as students' grades or records of misconduct, and (e) inserting false information, such as honors, certificates, or degrees supposedly earned by students or staff members.

A 16-year-old sophomore at Harrison High School in Kennesaw (Georgia) was suspended from school for 10 days for having used a school-library computer to illegally enter the school-district's private network and copy students' and staff members' social-security numbers, phone numbers, and addresses (Torres, 2003).

Three students who disliked the grades they had earned in courses at Oak Lawn (Ilinois) High School hacked into the school's record files on several occasions to change their own and others' marks. They entered the school computer system through a program called Parent Portal, designed to enable parents to find information about their own son's or daughter's grades and attendance record. Normally, individuals could only read such information, not alter it. However, the three youths learned how to change the contents of files, then used that knowledge to improve more than 30 grades—raising *failures* to *passings* and *B's* to *A's*. The three operated from computers both at home and at school until a teacher exposed their scheme. Officials suspended the students from school for 10 days and denied them further use of school computers (Napolitano, 2005).

Arson

Arson is the crime of setting fire to property with the intent to do damage. Buildings—including school buildings—are the type of property most often targeted by arsonists. Other types of school property that vandals set afire are books, furniture, file-cabinet contents, office machines, science equipment, and athletic gear. Of the various forms of vandalism, arson usually is the most costly for a school district.

The U.S. Department of Homeland Security reported in 2005 that 61 percent of all school structure fires were the result of arson, with 70 percent of those fires occurring in high schools. "Children under the age of 18 started 41,900 fires, causing an estimated 165 civilian deaths, 1,900 civilian injuries, and $272 million in direct property damage. Seventy-eight percent of fires occur during the school week and 22 percent on weekends. Typically, fires are started in school bathroom trash cans, locations that present children with a place to set a fire and areas that are normally without constant adult supervision" (Brown, 2005).

Two fires at a 370-student Washington, DC, charter school caused $2-million of damage to the main office, two classrooms, and an auditorium. A 15-year-old student at the school was arrested for starting the first fire, while authorities sought to discover who had set the second blaze (Wilbur, 2005).

Clouds of smoke billowing through Harriet Tubman Elementary School in Washington, DC, caused 445 pupils and 87 staff members to evacuate the building while fire fighters extinguished a blaze in a boy's bathroom. The fire had been set by a 10-year-old boy who had ignited rolls of toilet paper that quickly filled the building with smoke. The boy was subsequently enrolled in a juvenile-fire-setters program conducted by the fire department (Wagner, 2005).

Noxious Substances

Both physical and psychological damage can result from vandals using toxic or offensive substances to harm property or people.

A 16-year-old at Cordoza High School (Washington, DC) was arrested for stealing mercury from a science laboratory and releasing it at the school. He was arraigned on five charges— dumping a hazardous material, conspiracy to commit dumping, cruelty to children, theft, and receiving stolen property. A 15-year-old involved in the case was charged with dumping hazardous materials. The Environmental Protection Agency warned that mercury, even in small amounts, can be a health hazard if it is in a confined area. Thus, officials closed the school for four days in order to decontaminate the building (Cauvin & Haynes, 2005).

During a summer training camp for cheerleaders, four girls from Keller (Texas) High School received a pizza from members of a rival team, then covered the pizza with human feces and reported that the pizza had been sent to them in that condition by the rival team. However, investigators discovered that the Keller cheerleaders themselves were responsible for the prank. The camp organizers sent the four home, where the girls faced the prospect of being dropped from the cheerleading team and being enrolled in the school district's disciplinary alternative high school (Cheerleaders, 2005).

Responding to a dare from a schoolmate, a 15-year-old Nicholas County High School fresh-man in Carlisle (Kentucky) urinated into an ice machine in the gymnasium lobby before he reported to gym class. Although several students witnessed the act, no one reported the incident to the school principal until the next day. In the meantime, 33 people had used ice from the machine. The boy was immediately suspended from school pending an expulsion hearing, and authorities contemplated charging him with 33 counts of second-degree wan-ton endangerment and criminal mischief. When questioned about the episode, the youth said that he had been bullied by schoolmates—called names and shoved around—because "They say I dress like a Black person." His tormentors labeled him "wigger," meaning "a White person who acts Black." He said he would "do anything to get out of that school." And by urinating into the ice machine "I knew I wouldn't have to go back."

County health officials, in response to distressed students who had used ice from the machine, said there was no need to worry and no one had to be tested for infection. The boy's act was described as "gross and morally wrong, but not a health risk. . . . Urine is sterile because the body has its own filtering system. If any bacteria did make it through, the ice's temperature would have killed it." Nevertheless, the Nicholas County School Board agreed to pay doctor bills "to ease the minds" of individuals who had used the ice and wanted to undergo a medical examination (Kirby, 2005a, 2005b).

Explosives

Among the most feared instruments that vandals use in their attacks on property and persons are homemade explosive devices such as pipe bombs and Molotov cocktails.

The typical pipe bomb is a metal pipe packed with explosive material—gunpowder, TNT, or a combination of such chemicals as chlorate and sugar. Sometimes the packing includes small, sharp metal objects, such as nails or screws. A fireworks fuse or any military-grade cord is inserted into a hole drilled in the side of the pipe so the bomb can be detonated. Or an electrical timing device can be attached to the pipe to set the bomb off at a predetermined moment. The two ends of the pipe are sealed with steel or brass caps. When the bomb explodes, it splatters metal fragments across the landscape.

A Molotov cocktail or benzene torch consists of a glass or plastic bottle partly filled with a flammable liquid, usually gasoline or alcohol (methanol or ethanol). The mouth of the bottle is plugged tightly shut with a cork or plastic stopper; then a cloth rag is tied tightly around the mouth. "The weapon is used by first soaking the rag in a flammable liquid immediately prior to using it, lighting the rag, and throwing the bottle at the target. The bottle shatters on impact, spilling the flammable liquid over the target, which is then ignited by the burning rag" (Molotov cocktail, 2005).

Incidents of vandals using explosive devices in schools have assumed a variety of forms.

In a Kansas City high school, a bomb that exploded in a locker sent 11 students to the hospital. A California elementary school was closed after ten bombs, in the form of fireworks strapped to aerosol cans, were found in the building. A Nevada middle-school student brought a pound of ammonium nitrate to school. Eight boys placed two homemade bombs in a Minnesota elementary school (Bombs and school security, 2005).

At Sherwood High School in Sandy Spring (Maryland), $10,000 in damage resulted from vandals throwing Molotov cocktails into a computer laboratory (Chellappa, 2004).

Perhaps the most elaborate use of explosives for committing violence in schools occurred in the 1999 Columbine High School episode. Before the two youths started their shooting spree at the school, they had placed two backpacks containing explosive devices at a street intersection some distance from the school. The backpacks were set to go off as a diversionary tactic to draw police and fire personnel away from the school. The diversion did succeed prior to the boys' launching their attack at the school. In addition to the guns they wielded, the two had brought with them a large assortment of homemade bombs which they distributed both inside and outside the school building as their attack progressed. Only after the attackers had killed 13 schoolmates, wounded 23, and shot themselves were the police and bomb experts able to search the premises for explosives. Their task took an entire week during which investigators checked 1,952 student lockers and 700 backpacks for weapons. The search yielded 30 bombs that had exploded during the attack and 46 unexploded devices as well as bombs that the two youths had planted with timing devices in their own autos in the parking lot (Bomb survey, 2000).

In the immediate wake of the Columbine killings, bomb scares in schools rose dramatically. One Maryland school district suffered more than 150 bomb threats and fifty-five associated arrests in a single year. Although the incidence of bomb threats gradually subsided as the years passed, the danger of vandals setting off explosive devices is ever present.

VANDALISM-PROTECTION EFFORTS

Many of the security measures described in previous chapters are useful in protecting schools from vandalism. Would-be vandals are less likely to attempt risky ventures if they know that police officers are patrolling the halls, that teachers keep cell-phones handy, that surveillance cameras are located around the campus, or that students are subject to metal-detector searches when they enter school. Such security efforts are most effective when (a) school officials adopt antiviolence practices that are suited to the types and frequency of vandalism that the particular school is likely to experience, (b) students and staff members are well informed about the school's antivandalism policies and the consequences of violating those policies, and (c) all members of a community feel obligated to support antivandalism efforts.

Appropriate Practices

Kinds of vandalism and their frequency can vary significantly from one school to another. However, some precautionary measures might usefully be adopted by nearly all schools. Those include:

- Banning matches, lighters, or smoking materials from school property.
- Trimming or removing shrubbery that is close to buildings.
- Trimming or removing shrubbery and signs that obstruct the view of the building from the street.
- Ensuring that no combustible items are stored near the outside of buildings.
- Illuminating building exteriors, such as by installing lighting fixtures that are activated by visible motion.
- Installing woven-wire fencing and locked gates.

The recent history of damage to a particular school or to schools within a district can serve as a guide to what additional protection measures are worth the expense and bother to adopt—burglar alarms, extra lighting, window bars or shutters, metal detectors, surveillance cameras, police officers, and restrictions on the use of school facilities after school hours.

The superintendent of schools in Redmond (Oregon) proposed adding 24-hour security personnel to schools after three schools had suffered destructive attacks within a two-week period. At Hugh Hartman Middle School, vandals had caused $10,000 in damage by breaking windows and spraying obscene graffiti messages throughout the building. A soda-pop machine was overturned and torn apart. Bathroom sinks were plugged with paper towels and the faucets turned on, so water spilled into hallways. Officials offered a $500 reward for information leading to the arrest of the perpetrators (Lerten, 2002).

The need for guarding school property from harm can also profitably be balanced against the emotional climate in which children and youths are expected to enjoy learning. Students often complain of feeling oppressed when their school setting resembles that of a prison. Thus, schools in which instances of vandalism are rare can appropriately go light on instituting visibly repressive protection methods.

As computers have become ubiquitous educational tools, an important protective measure that does not involve making the school social atmosphere appear oppressive is the provision of software that blocks hackers' attempts to access confidential or forbidden Web sites and files.

Virus-protection software not only blocked an 18-year-old student's effort to break into the Waubonsie Valley High School (Chicago suburb) computer system, but the program also alerted authorities to the hacker's attempt and led to his arrest for computer tampering. The youth had downloaded a password program from the Internet to use for hacking into the school district's network. However, when he activated the password program, the school's virus-blocker informed school officials of the computer, account number, and password he was using (Cops say teen, 2005).

An Informed Citizenry

On the assumption that potential vandals will often be deterred from carrying out their plans if they know the actual risk involved, officials are well advised to inform students, staff members, and parents of their school's antivandalism provisions—what acts are considered to be vandalism and what penalties vandals can expect. Media for conveying such information include student-conduct handbooks, newsletters to parents, assembly programs for students, classroom discussion sessions, video-illustrated presentations at parent meetings, segments of television and radio news broadcasts, and newspaper articles.

Community Cooperation

Some communities that suffer particularly serious vandalism organize task forces composed of diverse participants.

In British Columbia, the Maple-Ridge/Pitt-Meadows School District assembled a community task force to attack the problem of school vandalism and to reduce vandalism in the community at large. After-hours vandalism was costing the school district "about $300,000 a year in direct costs and much more in indirect costs. School-hours vandalism (i.e., damage to desks, furniture, lockers, and textbooks) costs were in the $150,000 range. In addition to the financial impact, vandalism also had a demoralizing effect on students and staff."

The task force consisted of representatives from "Citizens on Patrol, Principals' and Vice-Principals' Association, District Parent Advisory Council, Canadian Union of Public Employees (Local 703), the Corporation of the District of Maple Ridge, the Corporation of the District of Pitt Meadows, Parks and Leisure Services, the Maple Ridge Pitt Meadows Times Newspaper, the Royal Canadian Mounted Police, the Maple Ridge Fire Department, the Board of School Trustees, and School District Administration."

Steps taken by the task force included:

- Improving school security with window shutters, extra lighting, video cameras, and regular security patrols.
- Providing antivandalism education programs for students.
- Establishing a 24-hour vandalism hotline for people living near schools.
- Creating an evening activity program for youths who loitered around schools (School anti-vandalism, 2005).

Treating Vandals

As with the other types of violence described in earlier chapters, the options available for treating vandals include warning students, conferring with their parents, assigning them to detention, suspending or expelling them, removing privileges, and placing them on probation. For particularly serious or heinous vandalism, students can be sent to jail or prison. An additional penalty especially suitable in cases of vandalism is the requirement that students or their parents pay restitution for the damage done.

Which type of treatment is chosen in a case of vandalism can depend on a variety of variables in the case, including the vandal's age and apparent motives, the type and extent of damage, the potential effect the treatment will have on the student's educational progress, and the estimated likelihood that the treatment will deter the vandal from committing future misdeeds.

Age was an important factor in Salina (Kansas) where police were unable to take two girls into custody because the law prohibited the arrest of anyone under age 10. The girls, ages 6 and 7, had littered the art room in Heusner Elementary School with 34 containers of tempera paint, several jars of glitter glue, and other art supplies. Broken crayons were spread across the floor, and a jar of body lotion was poured on a desk (Girls trash, 2005).

Suspension, Expulsion, and Detention

As in other chapters, the term *suspension* means depriving a student of particular opportunities for a given length of time. *Expulsion* means dismissing a student permanently from school. *Detention* means confining a student to a designated place in which he or she is required to spend time on school assignments—completing homework, taking tests, practicing skills, and the like.

Suspension often consists of sending a student home for a period of time that might range from a day to a year. But from an educational viewpoint, the disadvantage of such a penalty is that it takes the student out of the learning setting. Therefore, officials who wish to punish vandals without endangering their study opportunities will suspend only certain privileges—bus transportation, recess periods, attendance at attractive school functions (athletic contests, dances, parties, and graduation activities), membership in clubs, and participation in sports.

Whereas expulsion has the advantage of removing a troublesome student from the school and serving as a warning to other potential vandals, it may seriously damage the student's future by ending her or his school career.

Detention serves to promote a student's learning progress while, at the same time, providing punishment. However, if detention is to fulfill that dual role, someone must be present to supervise the student's studies.

Probation

Probation consists of assigning a punishment to a vandal, but not implementing the punishment if the individual avoids committing additional offenses within a defined period of time. Probation is most applicable for cases in which the offender does not have a past record of misconduct, is too young or too naïve to have recognized that he or she was doing harm, and appears to be sincere in apologizing for having caused trouble. Probation usually takes the form of the student being supervised by a court officer, and the sentence may include an obligation to contribute service to the school or community—cleaning up around the school, aiding disadvantaged schoolmates or elderly people, or tutoring younger pupils.

An 18-year-old former student of Waubonsie Valley High School in Aurora (Illinois) was sentenced to a year of court supervision and ordered to perform 20 hours of community service for using another student's name and a password-circumventing program in an effort to break into the school's computer system. The attempt failed when the system's break-in protection facilities alerted officials to the attempt and prevented the hacker from downloading any information (Ex-student, 2005).

Jail or Prison

Whenever vandalism involves a crime, the perpetrator faces the possibility of serving a jail or prison sentence. As noted in Chapter 1, a crime designated as a misdemeanor can lead to a jail term up to one year. A felony can warrant a prison term ranging from over a year to life. Jail and prison terms are most often applied to vandals who did extensive damage to property, injured or killed people, acted out of malice, or have a record of crime in the past.

Five Eu Claire (Wisconsin) High-School students, ages 17 and 18, were each sentenced to ten days in jail for shooting mortar fireworks at a teacher's home and causing $11,000 in damage when shells broke through a window into the kitchen. The judge ordered the five to serve their jail terms during the Thanksgiving and Christmas holidays. The youths were also expelled from school. In explaining why they attempted such a deed, they said they were drinking beer and playing cards when they decided to take revenge on a teacher who had reported one of their friends to police for breaking the law. During the court hearing, the five apologized for the attack. One said, "It's probably the stupidest thing any of us will ever do" (Teens get jail, 2005).

A pair of teenagers who had extensively damaged J. H. House Elementary School in Rockdale County (Georgia) in 2001 were sentenced to nine years in prison by a judge who imposed such a stiff penalty because, "Rockdale County and its people have a right to self-defense. They have a right to defend themselves, even against their own children." The two youths had caused $250,000 in damage by spending several hours in the school, smashing television receivers and computers, shattering glass, and spraying fire extinguishers throughout the building, including on 12,000 library books. While in prison, the two compiled records of good behavior and were released in 2005, still obliged be on probation for an additional 11 years (Rockdale school, 2005).

Restitution

Students or their parents can be required by state law, local law, or school policy to pay the costs of intentional damage that students caused to school property. In cases that involve only minor damage, some schools allow restitution in the form of working off the expense by such assignments as cleaning the school, painting over graffiti, or contributing community service in place of paying for the damage.

An example of a state law governing school vandalism is the Alaska statute that requires students or their parents to pay up to $15,000 of school property damage resulting from a student's intentional destruction. The $15,000 limit was imposed so that the cost to families with limited financial means would not be unduly burdensome. Where individual cases warranted charging parents more, a court could exceed the $15,000 limit. When more than one family was involved in a vandalism incident, each family could be liable for as much as $15,000 (Meyer, 2003).

The code-of-conduct for secondary-school students in Beaufort County (South Carolina) informed parents that if their son or daughter destroyed or defaced school property, parents would be required to pay for the damage. In order to render the warning more specific after a Bluffton High School student spray-painted profanity on walls and lockers in a men's bathroom, district officials set prices for different types of damage. The price for the bathroom spray-painting incident was $300. For such minor episodes as students writing on walls with marker pens, students were required to make amends by repainting the walls (Knich, 2005).

Seniors who engaged in vandalism activities at Marshwood High School in Eliot (Maine) were required to pay for damage they had committed in what they said was a graduation-week prank. The amount of the cost that each would bear was adjusted by authorities to the role each had played in the prank. The largest amount—$5,300—was charged to the youth who had sprayed fire-extinguisher powder in the high school gymnasium, which resulted in school officials postponing the senior-class assembly. Twelve other seniors were punished for toilet-papering the gymnasium and lobby. All of them were required to pay $60 to $70 each, and they were banned from senior-class activities except the graduation ceremony (Jacques, 2005).

Treating Vandalism Victims

The victim of vandalism can be either an organization, such as a school, or an individual, such as a teacher whose car was scratched, or a student whose computer files were invaded by a hacker. The most common types of treatment that victims receive are (a) complete or partial restitution for the items damaged or for the cost of those items and (b) the satisfaction of knowing that the vandals have been punished.

Not only may victims be compensated by the vandals themselves or by the vandals' parents, but sometimes other members of the community also reimburse victims for their loss.

During the Christmas holidays, a silent alarm alerted police to a break-in at Rogers Elementary School in Tucson (Arizona). When officers arrived at the school, they caught a 21-year-old in a spree of destruction. The youth had broken light fixtures and flower vases, spread feces in the main office, splashed paint on walls, and smashed seven musical instruments—three violins, two violas, a cello, and a clarinet. After the vandalism had been publicized by the news media, members of the community who were concerned about the fate of the school's instrumental-music program donated even more instruments than those that had been lost. The school received 18 violins, four violas, one cello, three clarinets, and more than $2,000 in cash to replace the destroyed items (Bustamante, 2005).

CONCLUSION

The kinds of vandalism illustrated in this chapter have included intentional (a) destruction or disfigurement of school structures, equipment, or animals, (b) invasion of a school's or an individual's computer files, and (c) spreading noxious substances. The chapter has offered suggestions about ways to suit a school's antivandalism efforts to the types and frequency of destruction experienced by that particular school. The description of ways to treat vandals has featured such options as suspension, expulsion, detention, probation, jail/prison, and restitution. The discussion of how vandalism victims are often treated has focused on providing restitution and the satisfaction of knowing that the culprits have been dealt their just deserts.

CHAPTER 9

Theft

From the perspective of this book, theft qualifies as violence because stealing other people's property (a) is motivated by malevolent, antisocial intent—a conscious willingness to harm others in order to further the thief's ambitions and prosperity—and (b) deprives school staff and students of facilities needed for conducting an efficient learning program. Theft violates the culture's social contract—the expectation that people will behave honestly. Theft can also distract students and staff members from concentrating on their assigned tasks.

The most common crime at school is theft, rather than weapon attacks, fighting, child abuse, or sexual abuse. Four types of theft inspected in this chapter are the stealing of (a) school funds, (b) school equipment and supplies, (c) individuals' property, and (d) reports, tests, and grades. Each type is described in terms of the forms that the type commonly assumes, the treatment of thieves, and the treatment of the victims of theft.

STEALING SCHOOL FUNDS

The greatest damage that theft does to schools results from people misappropriating funds. The thieves who steal large amounts of money are rarely students or teachers. Instead, they are administrators, office-staff members, and their coconspirators.

In what one New York State official described as "the largest, most remarkable, most extraordinary theft" from a school system in American history, members of the Roslyn School District's administrative staff stole over $11-million of school funds over a 6-year period. The five individuals indicted for fraud included the superintendent of schools, a companion with whom he lived, the assistant superintendent of finance, and two other central-office employees. When questioned by prosecuting attorneys, the superintendent admitted embezzling $2-million that he used for "vacations, meals, dry cleaning bills, furniture, dermatology treatments, car loans, real estate investments, and personal expenses averaging about $20,000 a month in some years." Angry members of the community who attended his court hearing believed the superintendent was less than contrite in his statement of apology to the judge in which "he seemed to portray himself as one of his own most deeply wounded victims." He had said, "During the past year and a half I have reflected daily on the mistakes I made in the last few years after a 35-year outstanding career in public education. These egregious errors have irreparably damaged, if not destroyed, my career in public education. I cannot adequately explain the pain my errors have caused me. . . . I only hope and pray that someday the Roslyn community will remember the good I did for the district as well as find it in their hearts to forgive me for my mistakes" (Vitello, 2005a).

Another defendant in the embezzlement scandal was the assistant superintendent for business who, along with relatives to whom she gave school-district credit cards, defrauded the schools of $4-million (Vitello, 2005b).

Sometimes a theft of massive proportions results from school district employees conspiring with suppliers of equipment or services to embezzle funds by means of fake purchase orders or excessive charges for goods. When such a scheme continues over a period of years, the loss to the school system can extend to millions of dollars.

The Wake County (North Carolina) School District was robbed of at least $3.8 million by a gang of five conspirators. Two of the gang were school-district employees—the director of transportation and his "quality-control assistant" responsible for ensuring that all purchase orders were genuine. Two others were officials of the auto-parts company that provided services and equipment for the district's buses and other vehicles. The fifth member was the boyfriend of one of the auto-company officials.

The main devices the conspirators used to defraud the schools were false purchase orders sent to the auto-supply company. Investigators discovered that near the end of the fiscal year in 2003 and 2004, the school district's transportation department had issued to the auto-parts company 2,535 false invoices totaling more than $3.8 million. Each invoice was for less than $2,500, which was the maximum amount allowed for orders that would not require competitive bids.

The largest amount of stolen money was banked by the auto company. Lesser amounts were used by members of the gang to buy luxury items for their own use—trucks, campers, motorboats, golf carts, automobiles, wide screen television sets, computers, exercise equipment, storage units, and more (Hui, 2005).

Whenever auditors, financial control officers, or security personnel have been part of a plot to defraud schools, members of school boards are obliged to consider the question of "Who was watching the watchman?" Such incidents draw attention to improvements needed in school security and oversight practices. For instance, the Wake-District episode prompted the board of education to require every employee who ordered supplies or services to sign a form verifying that on a given date he or she had personally received the requested items.

Some school employees who have the authority to spend funds take advantage of their position of trust and write bogus checks or use cash for their own purposes. If the amounts they misappropriate at any one time are small and if the system for monitoring expenditures is lax, then over a period of time substantial amounts of the school's money can be lost.

A 51-year-old secretary at Folly Quarter Middle School in Ellicott City (Maryland) was arrested for theft, counterfeiting, and embezzling more than $10,000. Over a two-year period, she had written checks to "cash" or to fictitious vendors and companies. The checks had required two authorization signatures, so she had signed her own name and had forged the principal's signature. The special account on which she had written the checks contained money for fundraising, booster clubs, and student activities. In her periodic raids on the account, she had taken only small amounts, so the losses were not readily apparent until the principal noticed a significant decline in the fund and ordered the audit that revealed the fraud (Cadiz, 2005).

The 54-year-old mother who served as president of the Parent/Teachers Association at Sessums Elementary School in Riverview (Florida) was charged with grand theft for defrauding the school of nearly $13,000 collected from the sale of T-shirts, books, and snowcones. She had misappropriated the funds by means of false billing charges and forgery (Amrhein, 2004).

Treating Thieves

Punishment for their ill-deeds can include thieves being fined, sent to jail or prison, required to return goods purchased with stolen funds, dismissed from their jobs, forced to relinquish their administrative credentials, and placed on probation.

In the $11-million Roslyn (New York) case described earlier, the superintendent of schools agreed to cooperate with justice-system authorities by admitting his part in the embezzlement, repaying the $2-million that was his part of the theft, and testifying against the other defendants. Consequently, the prosecuting attorney reduced the superintendent's prison term from 25 years for multiple counts of grand larceny and fraud to a maximum of four to 12 years (Vitello, 2005a).

In the Wake-School-District $3.8-million theft, the five individuals arrested for fraud were required to relinquish items they had bought with the stolen money. The auto-supply company was forced to return $1.3 million to the school district that the company had labeled "a prepayment for future parts" and to return $100,000 in supplies belonging to the school system. The five defendants faced charges of conspiracy and obtaining property by false pretenses, felonies that could result in prison sentences of 3 to 5 years (Hui, 2005).

The operator of a small electric company pleaded guilty to overcharging two Macomb County (Michigan) school systems for work performed, for submitting false invoices, and for writing checks to a construction company as a way to launder $370,000 of embezzled funds. He was sentenced to a maximum of 24 months in prison and three years in supervised probation upon release from prison. He was also assessed a $125,000 fine and required to make restitution for the amounts he had overcharged. The electric-company owner was not alone in the $3-million embezzlement scheme. A superintendent of schools, a school-board member, and a maintenance supervisor were also part of the plot (Trela, 2004).

Treating Victims

Schools that are targets of embezzlement receive a measure of compensation for their loss whenever courts require repayment of stolen funds. Schools also profit in the future when instances of fraud motivate school boards and administrators to improve their system of handling funds and of monitoring the activities of personnel who are authorized to order goods and services. Furthermore, the publicity accompanying the successful prosecution of embezzlers may deter other potential swindlers from trying to defraud a school system.

The Wake School District, which was the direct victim in the fraud case described earlier, was partially recompensed by funds received from the auto-supply company and from the auction of the confiscated goods that the defendants had bought with their share of the stolen funds (Hui, 2005).

STEALING SCHOOL SUPPLIES OR SERVICES

School equipment and services are stolen by various sorts of individuals, including students, students' family members, school personnel, and outsiders.

Three boys—ages 13, 15, and 16—confessed to taking over $1,000-worth of equipment from the Mt. Hermon (Louisiana) High School athletic department's field house. The pilfered items included uniform jerseys, gloves, mitts, bats, caps, 30 baseballs, and bases. The boys were arrested for burglary and theft (Hanemann, 2004).

A mother and her two sons, along with one son's teenage friend, were arrested for the theft of electronic equipment valued at over $8,000 from schools in Corvallis (Oregon). The 16-year-old son and his 16-year-old companion were charged with burglarizing Gubser Elementary School. The 21-year-old son was cited for receiving stolen goods, while the mother was arrested for hindering prosecution and tampering with evidence (Day, 2005).

A part-time custodian at Eastside Community High School in New York City was arrested for making more than $13,000 in long-distance phone calls that were charged to the school over an eight-month period. After school officials were alerted to the series of calls by the phone company's security department, they questioned the custodian, who told them he had periodically called relatives in the Dominican Republic. According to an agent who investigated the case, the custodian said that "after making several calls to the Dominican Republic without being questioned, he thought that the school must have had 'some kind of unlimited-use plan.'" Officials dismissed him from his position (Herszenhorn, 2005).

As the rising price of gasoline was straining school-bus budgets, two men were arrested in the middle of the night in Avilla (Missouri) while siphoning over 250 gallons of fuel from the school district's gasoline-storage tanks. The pair were charged with a Class-A misdemeanor (stealing motor fuel) that carried a penalty of one year in jail (Douglas, 2005).

The most damaging consequence of school-property theft is that the loss of items cripples the staff's ability to conduct the educational program. As a result, students' learning opportunities are impaired.

The theft of three cameras from the Waialua (Hawaii) High School news-writing room left the award-winning school newspaper without photographs in its upcoming scaled-down issues. During the same week, burglars had taken a digital video camera, a laptop computer, and a printer from a social-studies classroom. The social-studies teacher was particularly distressed at the loss of hours of lessons she had video-taped as part of her application for national-board teacher certification (Essoyan, 2004).

During the night, robbers had crawled through ceiling passageways to avoid locked doors at Tomales High School in Point Reyes (California) and had stolen seven band instruments from the music room. They left broken ceiling tiles and unscrewed wooden panels above empty instrument cabinets that had been pried open with a crowbar (Baker, 1996).

Sometimes school officials and the police have difficulty deciding whether a regulation or law has been broken whenever school personnel take equipment home or charge the school district for services. Should teachers be commended for using a school computer to do school work at home on their own time? Or should they be censured for keeping a school computer at home on "long-term loan"? And how can officials determine the extent to which "borrowed" equipment or supplies have actually been used for school purposes rather than for a staff member's personal interests?

The principal of National City (California) Middle School became the object of a police investigation to determine whether she had breached school policies by permanently keeping a school computer, other office equipment, and an exercise treadmill in her home. The investigation also focused on additional items in her home that had been reported stolen during burglaries at the school over the previous two years.

The principal, speaking in defense of her actions, said she had been working with the equipment and was planning to return it to the school.

"Everyone at National knows you have to take things home because things get stolen from the school. The treadmill was only housed here until we could figure out where to put it. One of my teachers who is a writer has two computers at home. I know she's going to give them back when she leaves National" (Sierra, 2005).

Several facts unearthed during the investigation raised questions about why the principal could not afford to buy a computer of her own to use at home and why the exercise treadmill was kept there. Her annual salary was $112,179. She and her husband had recently bought a $1.2-million home, and they owned one condominium in Hawaii and another in San Diego. She was a fitness enthusiast who taught kickboxing in her spare time at a health club. And, contrary to the district's nepotism policy, she had employed her son and her mother at the middle school. These revelations were included among the information to be considered by authorities when resolving the case (Sierra, 2005).

Treating Thieves

The punishment that a thief is assigned can range from probation to an extended prison sentence, with the decision in a given case depending on a combination of conditions, such as the value of the stolen goods as well as and the thief's age, record of past misdeeds, admission of guilt, and expressed attitude toward the theft.

A 38-year-old mother and her 20-year-old son admitted conspiring to steal 32 computers valued at $56,000 from a Hattfield County (Pennsylvania) elementary school. The son and a friend had stolen the equipment while the son was working on a building-renovation job at Oak Park Elementary School. During the court trial, the son blamed his mother for the crime by pleading that "I don't think it would have happened if she didn't keep hounding me for money. I basically did what my mother told me to do." The judge, in response, scolded the son for blaming others for his deed, contending that a 20-year-old was "not some innocent baby being led down the path by the evil mother. [You] had free will . . . the ability at any time to say no. You chose to commit these crimes. This is about you, not about your mother" (Hessler, 2004).

The judge sentenced the son to between 4-to-23 months in the county jail, two years' probation, 20 hours of community service, and a $7,000 fine. The mother was assigned 3-to-23 months in jail followed by three years probation and 100 hours of community service. She was also required to pay $14,484 restitution to the school's insurance carrier. Perhaps the son's punishment would have been lighter if he had accepted responsibility for his part in the theft (Hessler, 2004).

Treating Victims

The victims of the stealing of school property are students, the school staff, and the general public whose tax dollars are wasted in theft. The treatment of actual and potential school-property-theft victims can be divided into two stages: (a) the prevention stage that is intended to avert future thefts and (b) the post-theft stage, whose purpose is to compensate victims who have already suffered loss.

The Prevention Stage

The same security measures useful for reducing other sorts of violence—deadly weapons, fighting, child abuse, and sexual abuse—are also useful for combating theft. Such measures include school guards, surveillance cameras, metal detectors, and limited access routes to school buildings and grounds. In addition, newer devices can be adopted for restricting who can open locked doors, such devices as *smart cards* that replace conventional door keys, which are easy to duplicate. Two types of smart cards are (a) *swipe cards* that can be swished through a slot on the door and (b) *proximity cards* that are held close to an electronic reader. To adopt a smart-card system, a school needs to pay for the electronic entry (about $500 per door), card production, a computer, a card-printer, and scanning equipment. Such costs "exceed those of conventional keys in the short run, but the security options are far better" (Schneider, 2001).

Smart cards have a number of advantages for a school. They can be:

- Instantly cancelled if a card is lost or stolen, so anyone using them will no longer be able to open doors. Thus, cards eliminate the need to change keys and locks.
- Coded so that a particular person has access to only those places for which that individual deserves entry. Therefore, a vendor who supplies food products can enter the school's kitchen but cannot enter administrative offices, classrooms, or the gym.
- Coded to provide entry only on certain days or at specified hours.
- Used also as identity and debit cards.
- Used to control who enters particular parking lots.

The Post-Theft Stage

The same measures adopted for compensating schools in cases of loss of funds are applicable as well for instances of property loss. That is, thieves can be required to return stolen goods and pay fines for their misdeeds. A loss can also reduce the likelihood of future thefts by alerting authorities to needed changes in their security practices; and the publicity about the prosecution of thieves may dissuade other potential thieves from taking school property.

STEALING INDIVIDUAL'S PROPERTY

Students, rather than staff members, are usually the ones who take personal belongings from schoolmates, teachers, counselors, secretaries and other school personnel. Popular targets of theft include money, cell phones, articles of clothing, jewelry, laptop computers, books, I-pod music players, digital cameras, bicycles, musical instruments, and notebooks containing students' written assignments. In recent years, new electronic items on the market have become highly popular with students, leading to a rash of thefts, particularly when the items are small and are carried by students in their book bags, backpacks, purses, and pockets or are left in lockers and cars.

Treating Thieves

Depending on the circumstances in the case at hand, people caught stealing others' property can be subject to any of a wide array of consequences, such as:

- The return of the stolen goods.
- A stern reprimand.
- The assignment to write an essay of repentance.
- An apology to the person whose property was taken.

- A note of censure placed in the thief's personnel file.
- Personal counseling.
- Attendance at classes on responsible behavior.
- Suspension from school for a stated time period.
- Dismissal from the school.
- Required school or community service.
- A monetary fine.
- A term in a juvenile-detention facility, jail, or prison.

Circumstances that can affect which consequences a thief is assigned include not only the value of the stolen property, but also the thief's age, past record of misdeeds, apparent awareness of right and wrong, family condition, and expressed attitude toward the theft.

Treating Victims

As in cases of school-property theft, the treatment of actual and potential victims of personal-property theft can be divided into two stages— prevention and post-theft.

The Prevention Stage

The best method of theft prevention is for people to be alert to the circumstances under which thefts are most likely to occur. For example, students and staff members should never leave:

- Valuables in a locker that does not have a lock. Even if there is a lock, it is still a mistake to leave such items as cell phones, music players, cameras, jewelry, or money in school lockers.
- Objects in physical education dressing rooms. Anything of value should be entrusted to the instructor.
- Musical instruments unprotected.
- A watch or ring that is removed to wash one's hands in a washroom.
- A briefcase, book bag, or purse unattended.
- Anything of value on a desk while going to the rest room, an assembly program, the library, or out during recess.

The Post-Theft Stage

Students may be compensated for the loss of their property by (a) the return of the stolen items, (b) monetary damages paid by the thief, and (c) the satisfaction of knowing the thief has been punished. Victims may also be aided by advice on how to keep their property safe in the future.

STEALING REPORTS, TESTS, OR GRADES

Academic cheating involves a person's seeking the symbols of intellectual accomplishment without having acquired the knowledge and skill that the symbols are supposed to signify. Those symbols can be of various sorts—diplomas, certificates, degrees, high marks on school assignments, letters of recommendation, scholarships, job opportunities, public acclaim, and the phrase *magna cum laude* appended to a diploma.

Cheating in schools is nothing new. There always have been students willing to "borrow" classmates' homework, have other people write term papers for them, copy material verbatim from sources without crediting the original authors, peek at other students' tests, or improve their own marks in teachers' grade-books. But the methods of cheating have improved substantially over the past three decades. As a result of technological advances in recent years, cheating has become more sophisticated. Not only has technology increased students' opportunities to cheat, but the ability of school personnel to catch cheaters has also been enhanced. The inventions contributing to such progress include photocopying equipment, computers, the Internet, scanners, optical-character-recognition software, language-translation programs, cell phones, pagers, and more.

The three forms of school cheating inspected in the following paragraphs are plagiarism, unauthorized test assistance, and grade changing.

Plagiarism

Plagiarism is the act of claiming to be the author of material that someone else actually wrote. Students may plagiarize book reports, term papers, essays, projects, and graduate-degree theses. Teachers—including college professors—may plagiarize journal articles, course materials, and textbooks. Researchers may plagiarize reports, articles, and book chapters.

Academic plagiarism is nothing new. But what has been new since the latter years of the twentieth century is the ease with which writings on virtually any topic can be misappropriated with little risk of detection. The principal instrument responsible for the recent rapid rise in academic plagiarism has been the computer Internet, which John Barrie (a developer of software for detecting Web plagiarism) calls "a 1.5 billion-page searchable, cut-and-pasteable encyclopedia" (Barrie in Thomas, 2003).

Especially popular are the online *paper mills, cheatsites,* or *essay banks,* which are companies that sell students completed essays, book reports, projects, or theses that can be submitted in school under students' own names. By mid-2005, there were at least 780 paper mills worldwide, a 10 percent increase over 2004. Those available on the World Wide Web bear such names as *Evil House of Cheat* (more than 8,000 essays), *Genius Papers, Research Assistance, Cheat Factory Essay Warehouse, School Sucks, Superior Term Papers,* and *12,000 Papers.com.* In Germany, *Cheatwebsite* has advertised high-scoring essays, term papers, stories, interpretations, book reports, and other types of homework. The site reported having between 3,000 and 5,000 high school and college users a day. "One site charges $19.95 per page for seven-day delivery, and will cater to the worst student procrastinators by providing 'same day service' at $44.95 per page" (Secure Computing, 2005).

The extent of cyber plagiarism was suggested in the results of a 2003 survey of 11,000 high school students by the Rutgers' University Center for Academic Integrity in which 58 percent of respondents admitted copying unaccredited material from the Internet for school assignments (Secure Computing, 2005).

Unauthorized Test Assistance

Cheating on tests consists of a person receiving illicit help in answering test questions when that person has failed to master the field of knowledge that the test has been designed to sample. Such help usually assumes one or both of two forms: (a) students study the test questions prior to the test session or (b) students receive unauthorized aid during the test session.

As teachers and test makers have developed computer skills, they have increasingly stored test items in computers rather than in traditional file cabinets. However, the convenience of storing items in computers has been accompanied by the danger that hackers can break into test-question files and distribute the questions to students prior to the test period. Educators' attempts to guard test items now involve devising complex passwords needed to access computer files, strictly limiting the number of people who know those passwords, and equipping computers with firewall software.

During test sessions, present-day students continue to use a variety of traditional ploys to gain advantage—crib notes hidden in a shoe, mathematical formulas written on an arm, and notes passed to neighboring test takers. Those ruses have now been joined by schemes made possible with wireless communication devices known as *personal digital assistants* or *PDAs*, which include cell phones, pagers, and handheld computers. From inside or outside the classroom, students can communicate with each other during a test session by means of PDAs. Thus, it is becoming common practice for teachers to confiscate all such devices prior to administering tests (Thomas, 2003).

The high-stakes-testing movement that began in the 1980s and accelerated into the twenty-first century increased the pressure on school personnel to ensure that their students score well on standardized achievement tests. This pressure reached a high point in 2002 with the introduction of the federal government's nationwide No-Child-Left-Behind program. If, on the once-a-year test, schools failed to reach a state-wide test-score standard, they were liable for such punitive measures as exposure in the public press, elimination of staff members, school closures, or take over by state or private managers. Thus, the temptation for school personnel to engage in test-cheating became greater than ever. Those who succumbed to temptation adopted several methods of manipulating the assessment system to produce high test scores—giving students help during test sessions, changing students' answers after a test session, or providing students with pilfered test items prior to the test period.

In White Hall (Illinois), a high-school principal was dismissed and a guidance counselor suspended for 90 days without pay for their having opened packets of the Prairie State Achievement Test and distributed copies to 65 high school juniors prior to the test session. Not only were the two staff members censured, but the school suffered as well because the results of the tainted testing were never recorded. Consequently, the school was unable to remove itself from the state's "academic-early-warning" list (Principal resigns, 2003).

Grade-Changing

Although teachers still keep grade books in which they record the scores students earn on tests, essays, and projects, schools today store semester-end grades in master computer files whose access is available only to authorized personnel. However, students with a sophisticated knowledge of computer programming are sometimes able to hack into such files by circumventing the system's security walls. Hackers can then change students' grades in the files—raise an *F* to a respectable *C* or elevate a *B* to an *A*.

Treating Thieves

The treatment of thieves can be divided into prevention and rehabilitation stages.

The Prevention Stage

An effective way to treat potential Internet plagiarizers is to erect barriers to their accessing and using unauthorized material from the World Wide Web. Just as the Internet has greatly expanded students' opportunities to plagiarize, so also have software programs and Internet services increased the school's ability to block access to cheatsites and to help teachers discover sources from which students have lifted material.

SmartFilter Bess is an example of a software program that gives school personnel control over which Web sites students can reach on school computers. The program not only allows administrators to block online plagiarism sites, but also displays on the computer screen the school's policy on plagiarism each time a student attempts to visit a cheatsite (Secure Computing, 2005).

The most valuable tools for discovering cyber plagiarism are Web checkers or verifiers. The typical Web checker is an Internet service that works the following way. A student's paper is entered into the checker's Web site. That Web site is programmed to compare the contents of the paper with the contents of thousands of documents on the Word Wide Web. A report is sent back to the teacher, showing how much of the student's paper is identical to, or highly similar to, documents on the Web; and the report identifies what those original documents were.

Web checkers usually charge for their services, either a flat annual fee or a stated amount for each paper processed. One popular plagiarism checker is titled *Turn It In*. In 2001, the operators of *Turn It In* claimed 20,000 subscribers around the world. Another much-used checker has been *Essay Verification Engine* or EVE, which conducted 28,166,483 assessments between February 2000 and February 2002.

Safeguards teachers can adopt at the outset of a writing assignment include (a) illustrating the difference between plagiarism and the honest identification of sources used in a paper, (b) explaining that written assignments will be Web-checked, (c) requiring students to document the sources used throughout their entire paper, and (d) requiring students to incorporate material from their class in their writing, with the teacher discussing their paper's intended structure and sources ahead of time. Educators who have used Web-plagiarism checkers report that telling students that their papers will be Web-checked reduces the incidence of Internet plagiarism.

The Rehabilitation Stage

The treatment of plagiarizers, test thieves, and grade changers can focus on rehabilitation, in the sense of both deterring students from similar offenses in the future and equipping them with skills that can render thievery unnecessary.

Methods that may serve to discourage students from plagiarizing in the future can include (a) lowering their grade on an assignment that includes plagiarized passages, (b) assigning a failing mark in the class for multiple instances of plagiarism, (c) a verbal reprimand, (d) informing the student's parents of the act, (e) posting plagiarized papers on a classroom bulletin board for all to see, or (f) placing a note of censure in a student's record file.

Attempts to dissuade students from again stealing tests or receiving unauthorized aid in taking tests can include (a) requiring them to retake an alternate version of a test on which they cheated, (b) awarding them a failing grade for the test, (c) publicly posting the names of students who have cheated, or (d) suspending them from school.

Students caught thwarting the school's computer-security system in order to gain access to grade records may be (a) reprimanded, (b) counseled, (c) suspended, (d) dismissed from school, or (e) assigned to school or community service duty.

Thirteen high-school students in Kutztown (Pennsylvania) pled guilty to hacking around their security system on their school-issued laptop computers in order to gain access to administrative files. Although they did not lift test materials or change grade reports, their action did threaten the privacy of school records. After they were charged with felony computer trespass that could lead to incarceration in a juvenile detention facility, school authorities responded to criticism from the community for such harsh punishment and reduced the students' penalty to requiring that they (a) write letters of apology, (b) enroll in a class on personal responsibility, (c) perform 15 hours of community service, and (d) remain on probation for several months (Kutztown, 2005).

The second half of the rehabilitation process consists of furnishing students counseling, tutoring, or course-work that equips them with skills and attitudes which make cheating unnecessary. Because students often cheat when they feel they are not "up-to-the-task" of writing a report or taking a test, special help in bringing them up-to-the-task can reduce their temptation to cheat. It is true, of course, that frequently the motivation to cheat is not a lack of skill but, rather, not wanting to bother to do the thinking, research, or study necessary for writing a paper or passing a test. In those cases, the punishments for cheating must appear sufficiently frightening to make cheating seem unwise.

Treating Victims

The immediate victim of cyber-plagiarism and test-cheating is the school's educational program. Success in teaching students is compromised when methods of teaching and of assessment are distorted by false evidence of what students have learned. But the ultimate victims are the students themselves, who end up displaying badges of accomplishment (grade promotion, diplomas, and high marks) founded on fake term papers and stolen tests.

The treatment of the school's learning program involves improving both the ways of foiling cheaters and the ways of teaching that prepare students so well that they find cheating unappealing and unnecessary.

CONCLUSION

Throughout this chapter, four sorts of theft have been viewed as types of violence because they intentionally damage the school's learning program and violate the culture's social contract regarding honesty. Those four have included stealing (a) school funds, (b) school equipment and supplies, (c) individuals' property, and (d) reports, tests, and grades.

CHAPTER 10

Disruptive Behavior

Over the years, students' classroom antics that disturb the efficient conduct of schooling have been referred to by such expressions as *acting up, fooling around, messing around, monkeying around, horseplay,* and *goofing around.* Students who habitually indulge in such disruptive behavior are often known as troublemakers and discipline problems.

Within the broad meaning assigned to *violence* in this book, classroom behavior that intentionally disrupts the systematic conduct of the learning program qualifies as violence. Hence, acting up and messing around are instances of violence, albeit in a very mild form.

The three sections of this chapter concern (a) forms of disruptive behavior, (b) ways of treating disrupters, and (c) techniques of classroom management.

FORMS OF DISRUPTIVE BEHAVIOR

For convenience of analysis, disruptive behavior can be divided between two classes—typical antics and unusual disturbances.

Typical Antics

Typical antics are ways in which students frequently disturb a class—ways that teachers face so often that they are already prepared with coping techniques, so they can respond almost automatically. Three forms of typical antics are (a) talking out of turn, (b) offensive speech, (c) written insults, and (d) unacceptable actions.

Talking Out of Turn

There are two main forms of talking out of turn. In one form, a student speaks out during a class discussion without permission to speak, thereby interrupting the teacher or a fellow class member who is speaking at the time. The traditional way of getting permission is to raise one's hand and then be called on by the teacher. The second form—far more frequent than the first—consists of students chatting with each other during a lesson without permission to do so.

Teachers use various techniques in their attempts to alter students' talking-out-of-turn habits. The techniques typically begin with a mild verbal remonstrance—cautioning class members to stop interrupting and to cease chatting with classmates. Then, if talking-out-of-turn continues, teachers usually adopt the more demanding measures described in the treatments section of this chapter.

Offensive Speech

Several kinds of language can be regarded as unacceptable in school—cursing, rude speech, sexual and scatological references, ethnic or religious epithets, and personal insults. When students use objectionable language in class, the smooth operation of the learning program is usually interrupted. Class members typically react with either shock or gales of laughter, and the teacher is obliged to stop the lesson and take action, perhaps at length.

It is sometimes difficult to decide which expressions are sufficiently offensive to be banned from the classroom, because cultural expectations can change with the times. What is socially proper or politically correct at one time or place may be considered improper at another time or place.

For example, consider swearing. Unless a school's behavior rules illustrate precisely which expressions qualify as objectionable cursing, teachers may have a difficult time distinguishing between acceptable and unacceptable oaths. Will uttering *heck* be permitted but *hell* not allowed? Will *gosh darn* pass without objection but *God damn* draw remonstrance? Will the oath *Jesus Christ* warrant censure but *geez* not? And how are students to know ahead of time which utterances they can get away with and which will draw punishment?

The expressions *sassing* and *talking back* have traditionally described students' rude, imprudent, impolite retorts to someone in authority, such as a parent, teacher, or school principal. As with cursing, the line between permissible replies and objectionable ones can be difficult for both students and teachers to determine. A remark that one teacher finds impertinent may be accepted without question by another. Particularly when a student and a teacher are from contrasting cultural backgrounds in which social-interaction customs differ, conflicts can arise about the distinction between rude and proper speech.

In like manner, certain words that refer to sexual and eliminative behavior (urinating, defecating) are deemed unsuitable in the classroom. Hence, learners who wish to be considered "good school citizens" are typically expected to avoid in class such terms of ancient Germanic origin as *fuck, fart, shit*, and *piss*, and also to shun the more modern equivalents—*screw, let-a-gasser, crap*, and *pee*. Some pupils—especially young ones—come to school without acceptable terms for bodily functions and thereby find themselves in trouble until they are taught to substitute the school's permissible expressions—*coitus* or *sexual intercourse; break wind; void* or *bowel movement* or *number two;* and *urinate* or *micturate* or *tinkle* or *number one*. The unacceptable terms often serve as habitual curse words, uttered spontaneously by a student during a fit of frustration or anger.

Ethnic and religious epithets furnish a good example of the effect that changing social attitudes exert on the sort of language permitted in schools. During the nineteenth century and well into the twentieth, slang words commonly used in American society to identify different ethnic and religious groups included such labels as *dago, wop, polak, greaser, nigger, chink, jap, hebe, sheenie, redskin*, and far more. Often these terms would be used by students or teachers without censure. But during the twentieth century, and particularly in the later decades, ethnic and religious groups were successful in convincing others—including legislators and the general populace—that those terms were hurtful and violated people's right to be respected. As a result, many traditional nicknames were outlawed in schools. Punitive measures were taken against students or staff members who used those now-forbidden expressions. But the process of finding acceptable substitutes for banned terms has sometimes proved difficult. For instance, individuals of African ancestry, who traditionally had been referred to as *colored people*, were then called *Negroes*, followed by *Afro-Americans, Blacks*, and finally *people of color*, which was a designator sometimes applied to anyone not identified as *White*. Furthermore, conflicts have risen over which identifier should be applied to the descendents of the earliest inhabitants of the Americas. Should they be called *Indians* or *Native Americans*? Or should such folks be referred to solely by the traditional titles of their nations or tribes—Apache, Cherokee, Cree, Lakota, Navajo, and the like?

The issue of politically correct speech has extended beyond ethnic and religious domains into the realm of individuals who are different from the average in physical and mental abilities. Hence, the term *sight-impaired* in some school districts replaces the word *blind, auditorily limited* replaces *deaf, movement-disadvantaged* replaces *lame*, and *intellectually challenged* replaces *mentally retarded*.

At an increasing pace, school districts have established written policies that define the type of speech that is prohibited and the penalties to be suffered by people who violate the policies. However, policies are sometimes contested on the grounds that they prohibit far too many kinds of speech and therefore breach the freedom-of-speech provision in the First Amendment to the U.S. Constitution. By way of illustration, the following is the statement about language usage (verbal harassment) issued by the State College Area School District (Pennsylvania) to carry out the district's intent to furnish "all students a safe, secure, and nurturing school environment ... Disrespect among members of the school community is unacceptable behavior which threatens to disrupt the school environment and well-being of the individual" (Alito, 2001).

Harassment means verbal or physical conduct based on one's actual or perceived race, religion, color, national origin, gender, sexual orientation, disability, or other personal characteristics, and which has the purpose or effect of substantially interfering with a student's educational performance or creating an intimidating, hostile, or offensive environment. Harassment can include any unwelcome verbal, written or physical conduct which offends, denigrates, or belittles an individual because of any of the characteristics described above. Such conduct includes, but is not limited to, unsolicited derogatory remarks, jokes, demeaning comments or behaviors, slurs, mimicking, name calling, graffiti, innuendo, gestures, physical contact, stalking, threatening, bullying, extorting, or the display or circulation of written material or pictures. (Alito, 2001)

The policy declared that "any harassment of a student by a member of the school community is a violation. . . . " and that violators could be subject to "a warning, exclusion, suspension, expulsion, transfer, termination, discharge . . . training, education, or counseling." (Alito, 2001)

When that school district was challenged in court for ostensibly overextending the free-speech guarantee by outlawing so many kinds of language, the presiding judge ruled that the district's policy was well within the limits of the Constitution's First Amendment, so the school's statement could remain unchanged. However, when plaintiffs took the case to a court of appeals, the lower court's verdict was overturned by the appeals-court magistrates who declared

Although [the school district] correctly asserts that it has a compelling interest in promoting an educational environment that is safe and conducive to learning, it fails to provide any particularized reason as to why it anticipates substantial disruption [of the conduct of schooling] from the broad swath of student speech prohibited under the policy. The policy, then, appears to cover substantially more speech than could be prohibited under [the law's] substantial-disruption test. Accordingly, we hold that the policy is unconstitutionally overbroad. (Alito, 2001)

In a similar fashion, some schools have forbidden students to display political opinions on their garments, a restriction that has raised questions about whether students' free-speech rights are thereby being abridged.

At Century High School in Carroll County (Maryland), a senior complained that he had been detained in the principal's office because he refused to remove his T-shirt. The youth, in protesting America's waging war in Iraq, had written on the front of the shirt "They misunderestimated me," a quotation attributed to President George W. Bush. On the back of the shirt he had written "Bush . . . the American terrorist." In response to lawmakers saying the student had acted within his rights, county school officials regretted the detention and said they were newly stressing to school personnel that students did have First Amendment rights. But they added that school personnel also reserved the right to require a student to remove a piece of apparel when it could cause "a disruption" in the school day (Bowie, 2005).

As the foregoing examples illustrate, disagreements persist over what sort of language can legally be forbidden in schools, thereby leaving teachers and administrators puzzled over which words and phrases they can permit students to utter. It seems apparent that, under present-day circumstances, conflicts will continue to arise in the classroom and on the playfield over how to distinguish between violent and nonviolent speech.

Written Insults

Students may not only disrupt classes by what they say but also by what they write about each other. Written insults usually assume one of four forms— (a) graffiti scribbled on walls, sidewalks, windows, or desktops; (b) notes passed among students; (c) e-mail or chat-room comments over the Internet; and (d) slam books.

A *slam book* is a collection of obscene and disparaging remarks students write about each other and pass among themselves. Each recipient of the circulating book adds his or her own vicious comments to the collection.

Two 16-year-old girls and one 14-year-old at Dillard High School in Fort Lauderdale (Florida) were arrested for fighting with knives as the result of comments in a slam book—a series of electronic messages cut out and pasted onto a page. The comments ridiculed certain girls for their body build, hair, and style of dress, with one girl calling another a "stripper." The fact that girls took such insults seriously had been illustrated a few weeks earlier when a 17-year-old on a school bus was so angry over comments about her in a slam book that she shot the author of the comments in the shoulder (Fantz, 2005).

Unacceptable Actions

Perhaps the most common disruptive actions are those of students poking their neighbors or getting out of their seats to walk around the classroom, often tapping classmates on the head or snatching their pencils or cell phones. Another common type of unacceptable behavior involves students' appearance, particularly their mode of dress and cosmetic adornment. To encourage pupils to keep their appearance within the limits of "good taste" and thereby not upset the learning environment, schools typically issue a dress code. For instance, here is the dress code at Highview Elementary School in Nanuet (New York).

No tube tops, net tops, halter tops, pajamas, plunging necklines (front and/or back), see-through garments, extremely brief garments, spaghetti straps, and/or bare midriffs. Hats (except for medical or religious purpose) may not be worn in classrooms. Underwear should not be visible. Clothing should not include words or images that are vulgar, obscene, libelous, or denigrating to others on account of race, color, religion, creed, national origin, gender, sexual orientation, or disability. Clothing should not promote and/or endorse the use of alcohol, tobacco, or illegal drugs and/or encourage other illegal or violent activities. Footwear that is a safety hazard will also not be allowed. . . . In the event of a dress-code violation, parents may be asked to provide a change of clothing. (Highview Elementary School, 2005)

The task of deciding whether a particular case of appearance does, indeed, violate a school's code of conduct can lead to disagreements between school administrators and parents.

A 14-year-old was suspended from Bob Edwards Junior High School in Calgary (Canada) for drawing what looked like black tears running down his cheeks. He said he was simply imitating members of the punk-rock band Good Charlotte. The suspension was imposed by the school principal who objected to the boy's gothic-style face painting. The boy, in defense of his appearance, said, "This is me. It's how I like to express myself. I was just told [by the principal] that it was inappropriate. No one said it was offensive." The student's mother objected to the suspension: "It's not like he's slashing tires or skipping school. The school preaches diversity and to not judge people on how they look, and then they do something like this. If it's the eyeliner, then nobody should be able to wear it. Fair is fair" (Calgary boy, 2004).

A judge in Atlanta (Georgia) ruled that a school district's policy governing the sort of garments students should wear was "fatally vague." The court thereby exonerated an academically excellent high school youth who had been punished for so-called "gang-related activity" based on the color and style of his apparel. The accouterments that school officials considered indicative of gang affiliation were a pocket watch, a rolled-up pant leg, and a shirt with the student's nickname on the back (Judge rules, 2005).

In recent decades, government regulations have required schools to mainstream pupils who are judged to be physically or psychologically disadvantaged. The term *mainstreaming* means placing such pupils in regular classrooms rather than in special-education classes. Therefore, students who, in the more distant past, would be taught in special classes for the hard-of-hearing, sight-impaired, mentally slow, or behaviorally difficult are now in the same classrooms as their age mates who do not suffer such disabilities. This policy of providing the "least restrictive environment" for all students has placed an increased classroom-management burden on regular classroom teachers who are obliged to accommodate students whose habits often disturb a class's study climate. For instance, children with attention-deficit-hyperactivity-disorder (ADHD) are prone to fidget, speak out, get out of their seats, and distract classmates because their ADHD causes them difficulty in concentrating on school tasks.

In summary, a variety of types of student behavior can be deemed *violent*, in the sense of infringing on others' rights and disrupting the process of schooling.

Unusual Disturbances

In contrast to ordinary disruptive acts, other antics sometimes border on the bizarre and challenge teachers' ingenuity for deciding on how best to react.

While walking to school, a sixth-grade boy at Warsaw Middle School in Pittsfield (Maine) found a dead skunk, which he picked up by the tail. When he entered the schoolyard, he whirled the skunk through the air as he chased screaming schoolmates. Later in the classroom, the boy's teacher could not bear the stench and sent the boy to the principal's office where a security officer reported that "His clothes were ruined. He stunk. The school reeked." The officer speculated that the boy had become desensitized to the smell. The principal sent the boy home on a "medical discharge" and suspended him from school for three days (Pupil suspended, 2005).

On the last day of classes at Olathe (Kansas) Northwest High School, a 16-year-old student vomited on the teacher as the youth handed his Spanish-class textbook to the teacher. Later, in court on a misdemeanor charge of battery, the student claimed that the vomiting was unintentional, caused by his nervousness over his final exams. But two schoolmates testified that the boy, upon learning that he was earning a failing grade in Spanish, had told them ahead of time that he planned to retch onto the teacher. The judge who heard the case sentenced the youth to spend the next four months cleaning up after people who had vomited in police cars, a penalty which eventually proved impractical because nearby police departments immediately hosed out a car in which someone had thrown up, and they then sent the car out for professional biohazard treatment (Teen sentenced, 2005).

Two East Leyden (Illinois) High School seniors—in what they described as no more than a prank—dressed themselves in camouflage suits and ski masks to goosestep across the roof of a school building and give a Nazi salute while their schoolmates watched. Authorities were not amused by the stunt and arrested the pair for disorderly conduct. After pipe bombs were found in the home of one of the youths, police added the charge of felony possession of explosives (Patterson, 2005).

An eighth-grade girl at East Alton (Illinois) Middle School was expelled for the remainder of the school year for offering to sell OxyContin painkiller pills to schoolmates. A high-school friend had given the girl the pills to peddle to middle-school students (Eighth-grader, 2005).

TREATING OFFENDERS

The treatment of classroom disrupters can be divided into two phases: (a) ways to respond immediately to a disturbance and (b) ways to treat a student following the disruptive act.

Immediate Responses

Suggestions about how personnel can constructively react to an ongoing classroom disturbance are sometimes offered by teachers, administrators, and psychologists who are well versed in handling such crises. Here are some typical suggestions:

- Don't raise your voice, but try to stay calm and rational.
- Don't touch an agitated or angry student, unless the incident involves young children fighting and one or both are being injured.
- Try to keep the student seated. Although this is often impossible, at least you can suggest that the student remain seated so that he or she might explain to you what is wrong.
- Suggest ways for resolving the problem, other than by fighting or shouting insults, that the student can consider.
- If the situation is quite out of control, phone for help or send another student to summon help from a nearby classroom or from the principal's office.

After-the-Incident Treatments

Options available for treating disrupters following a disturbance include a warning, schoolwork assignments, counseling, fines, suspension and detention, and expulsion.

Warning

Several conditions may warrant teachers or administrators responding to student misconduct with no more than a warning.

For example, a pupil may not have known ahead of time that the kind of language he was using or the garment he wore was unacceptable. Either there had been no published school rule forbidding that precise kind of behavior or else the student had been unaware of such a policy. Hence, a first-time violation can suitably draw only a warning not to do the same thing again. The warning serves as a learning experience in which the teacher specifies the rule, explains the reason for it, and tells the exact consequences that will result from breaking the rule in the future.

Another condition is the presence of concerned parents. The teacher may consult the parents of the recalcitrant pupil and judge that they will take appropriate action to discourage their child from repeating the disruptive act. Hence, the treatment applied by the teacher can be limited to a warning.

Sometimes the warning is best issued to the disruptive student in private. Other times it is usefully presented to an entire class. Warning a student privately can avoid shaming the disrupter in front of classmates. On the other hand, addressing the matter in front of the entire class enables the teacher to caution everyone about that particular type of misconduct and about its consequences. The potential embarrassment to the disrupter might be minimized if the teacher prefaces the discussion in some such fashion as this:

"You see that I objected after Jack used the word *redskins* when he spoke about the Indian tribe that first settled this area where we all live. Now, I don't blame Jack, because we've never talked before about the word *redskin* being considered an insult by most Native Americans. They have a right not to be insulted. So from now on, using *redskin* in this class—just like saying *nigger* or *jap*—will get you suspended."

Schoolwork Assignments

Various kinds of schoolwork may be assigned for disrupters to complete.

The simplest is a written note or letter of apology to the victims of the student's offense—to the classmate who was harassed, to the teacher who was insulted, or to the entire class that was disturbed.

A second kind is a *behavior essay* in which the student writes an explanation of (a) what she had done that was considered wrong, (b) why she believes she did it, (c) what consequences for herself and others resulted from her actions, and (d) how, under similar circumstances in the future, she could act more constructively.

Students are often assigned to perform community service as recompense for misconduct. Typical kinds of service include cleaning up the school grounds, tutoring younger pupils, shelving books in the library, distributing health-practices pamphlets in the neighborhood, and aiding elderly persons in retirement homes.

A traditional practice that is pedagogically questionable is that of penalizing disobedient students by assigning them additional homework beyond the amount required of their classmates. But if teachers want students to view school studies as a desirable contribution to their welfare, using learning tasks as punishment seems counterproductive. Disciplining students for misconduct by adding an extra page of math problems or another chapter in a history book sends the wrong message. Would it not be better pedagogical logic to forbid misbehaving students to do the class's regular homework, thereby implying that learning is a privilege and thus to be valued? If the disobedient are prevented from doing the assignment, their immediate punishment is that of losing the credit (points or grade) to be earned for completing it and of also being deprived of the knowledge the assignment was designed to provide.

Removal of Privileges

The practice of taking away privileges is founded on the assumption that the penalty will cause the disobedient to mend their ways. Many sorts of privileges may serve that purpose. Thus, students may be denied

- Freedom of movement at recess time
- The opportunity to leave the campus at lunchtime

- Membership in a club or on a team
- The chance to hold a student-government office
- Admission to school affairs—parties, dances, athletic events
- Attendance at graduation exercises

The effectiveness of removing privileges obviously depends on how much a student values the privilege in question. Therefore, in any given case, it is important for a teacher to estimate which activity the particular student values. If the disrupter doesn't mind being ousted from the school choir or the chess club, then removing that privilege is not likely to effect the behavior-reform that such a penalty is supposed to promote.

Counseling

The act of counseling students to improve their behavior typically includes (a) allowing them to vent their feelings about their disruptive acts, (b) encouraging them to explain why they acted in such a fashion, (c) having them consider how their behavior affected other people, and (d) generating more productive ways in which the student might have acted.

Sometimes a counseling session is conducted with the student's parents or with the parents and the student together. Other times a student's peers can act as counselors, either by themselves or along with a staff member, such as a teacher, psychologist, principal, or coach.

Monetary Fines

When students breach behavior rules that are also official laws, they, or their parents, may be required to pay a fine.

In an effort to curb students' habit of cursing school personnel, police officers assigned to high schools in Hartford and Bulkeley (Connecticut) began charging cursers with creating a public disturbance, an infraction carrying a $103 fine. The anti-swearing campaign was not aimed at "casual cursers" but, rather, at students who swore while defying a teacher or administrator. A school official reported, "While the idea of $103 fines bothers some parents and students, it seems to be working. In the weeks since officers wrote up 15 to 20 tickets at Hartford Public and another eight or so at Bulkeley, they said a rare hush has settled into the hallways and classrooms" (Gottlieb, 2005a).

Suspension and Detention

Students who persistently "act up" or use forbidden language are often suspended from class or from school for a specified period of time.

The mildest form of suspension is often called *time out*. The offender is required to spend time away from the regular class activity (stand in the hallway, go to another room, go to the principal's office) to think about what he or she did that disturbed the class and to decide not to repeat it. Similar to time out, keeping students in the classroom during recess, at lunchtime, or after school is intended to make them think about reforming.

In suspension's more punitive form, the offender is sent home for a number of days or weeks. The advantages of home suspension are that disrupters are no longer available to upset the class and, it is hoped, they will be sufficiently distressed by their isolation that they plan to avoid disturbing the class in the future. The main disadvantage of home suspension is that the student misses what classmates are learning during the disrupter's absence.

Suspension has frequently been applied to pupils accused of using unaccept-able language. However, critics of that practice have charged that American language usage has been in a state of transition so that formerly disreputable speech has become less objectionable and should not result in excluding of-fenders from learning opportunities.

Boca Raton (Florida) Community High School relaxed its language-usage policies when some of its best students were being suspended from school for cursing, thereby "sullying otherwise clean records." As a result, officials reduced the severity of the penalty for swear-ing. As the school's principal explained, "If a bad word is not used to threaten, but rather to emphasize a point . . . the student would receive [only] an in-school suspension on the first offense. Societal standards have changed dramatically regarding acceptable language. If our policies do not change with societal standards, we set up our students [for unreasonable punishment]" (Boca Raton, 2005).

Because children who are sent home miss out on their studies and thereby fall behind their classmates, detention—in the sense of requiring an unruly pupil to do schoolwork under supervision in a separate room—is sometimes substituted for suspension.

The Pike Township (Indiana) school board authorized the creation of the Pike Support Academy, consisting of a special classroom in the same building as the district superin-tendent's office. Pupils in second-through-eighth-grade who disrupted classes would be sent to the academy for one or more days rather than being suspended from school. The academy would give them the chance to earn full credit for doing their regular schoolwork under supervision. Repeat offenders could get a second or third chance at the academy, but eventually recidivists would be suspended. The classroom would not be an option for violent and severe offenders (Smulevitz, 2005).

Expulsion

Pupils whose disruptive antics continue, despite warnings and suspen-sions, are in danger of being expelled from school. Expulsion is particularly frequent in the lowest grades. Toddlers—ages 2 to 4—are dismissed three times more often than are pupils in the elementary and secondary grades. An estimated 5,000 preschoolers in the United States are being expelled each year (Chute, 2005). Analysts suggest several reasons for such a high incidence of dismissals, including (a) increased emphasis in school systems on academic topics (prereading, premath) for the young, (b) less attention to teaching children social skills, such as ways of coping with frustration that do not involve hitting or biting classmates, (c) large classes that allow teachers insufficient time to help individuals, (d) more younger children (ages 2 and 3) enrolling in nursery schools, and (e) teachers who lack effective techniques for guiding the young.

Like home suspension, expulsion has the advantage of removing disrupters from class. However, expulsion—particularly at the high school level—can terminate students' formal education and thus damage their chance for a successful future.

CLASSROOM MANAGEMENT

The expressions *classroom management* and *classroom discipline* refer to the teacher's task of conducting class in a manner which ensures that students learn in an orderly, uninterrupted fashion. Obviously there is no one way that task can be performed satisfactorily, because diverse factors influence how efficiently a classroom operates. Those factors include

- *Pupils' levels of mental and social maturity.* Managing preschoolers requires different techniques than managing high schoolers.
- *Teacher–pupil ratio.* A class of fifteen pupils poses simpler management problems than does a class of forty.
- *Teacher personality.* Some teachers' appearance and social-interaction manner command more respect from students than do others' appearance and manner.
- *Length of teacher experience.* Veteran teachers are more likely to have securely established class-control methods than are neophytes.
- *Pupils' social-interaction habits.* Some pupils are more biddable than others, in that they readily obey directions and accept suggestions from people in authority—teachers, counselors, principals. Students' willingness to obey rules and follow directions is often affected by the child-raising methods they experience at home. Ones from families in which rancor and violence are common may act unusually boisterous and abusive at school or else quite the opposite—unduly cowed and meek.
- *School policies.* Teachers' management techniques are constrained by the school's rules about which discipline methods are acceptable.
- *Community attitudes.* Teachers' classroom practices can be affected by beliefs of influential members of the community about such matters as corporal punishment, criticizing students in front of their peers, publicizing students' breaches of school rules, and assigning community service as punishment for misconduct.

Despite the fact that there is no formula for classroom management that will succeed in every classroom with every episode of disruptive behavior, experienced teachers are often willing to offer hints—rules of thumb—as guides toward keeping a classroom in order. For example, consider the following eight suggestions (Gaustad, 1997; Kelley, 2005; Manual of rules, 2005)

- *Making learning interesting.* Research supports the commonsense observation that if a class is boring, students will probably be disruptive. Thus, making school attractive by suiting instructional methods to students' learning styles and interests can reduce unruly behavior.

- *Being pleasant.* Research also shows that such social rewards as smiling, inserting humor, and praising students are effective for eliciting desirable classroom behavior.

- *Announcing rules.* At the beginning of the school year, teachers are wise to inform students of the behavior expected in class, including why those rules are appropriate and what consequences will result if students violate the rules. There are several ways of providing such information. The most obvious is by class discussion, with the teacher describing each expectation, then giving the students the chance to respond—ask for clarification, seek examples of cases, offer suggestions for improvements. Particularly in the lower grades, a list of the rules most often broken can be posted on a bulletin board. At all grade levels, student-conduct policies can profitably be described in information sheets or booklets distributed to students and their parents. Rules can also be posted on the school's Internet Web site.

- *Reacting to a first offense.* It is not feasible to identify ahead of time all possible forms of unacceptable disruptive behavior, such as every offensive spoken word or every intolerable gesture. Consequently, some kinds of objectionable behavior will occur that students had not been warned about. Thus, the first mention of such an infraction arises only the first time a student displays that kind of behavior in class. So unless serious harm resulted from the misbehavior and the perpetrator apparently had not acted out of malice, the teacher might reasonably choose not to penalize the perpetrator. Instead, the teacher's response could be a warning against such acts in the future, with the advice in the form of an explanation to the class why such actions are unacceptable and what penalties will be imposed on anyone acting in such a manner in the months ahead.

- *Specifying consequences.* Some teachers are vague about what will happen to disrupters who violate the rules. The vagueness is reflected in such threats as "Anyone using curse words will have reason to be sorry" or "You won't get away with doing those things in this class." Consequently, students cannot easily judge if a particular prohibited act is worth the risk. Some schools avoid this problem by specifying the consequences of different kinds of misconduct.

  The code of conduct at LaSalle (Ontario, Canada) Elementary School states that

[T]he following kinds of behavior will result in after-school detention or, where the case warrants, suspension from school. Each time the behavior occurs it will be noted in the student's file.

- Theft
- Fighting with another student
- Foul or abusive language or gestures
- Verbal or physical harassment of another student
- Insolence toward an adult
- Vandalism
- Possession of dangerous objects such as knives or pellet gun
- Possession of cigarettes, alcohol or drugs. (Code of conduct, 2005)

According to the published discipline policy at Jacobs High School in Cincinnati (Ohio), students are not permitted to:

- Bring pacifiers, stuffed animals, dolls, toys or games to school.
- Wear hairstyles or clothing inside the school building that disrupts the educational environment, such as hats, sunglasses, earmuffs, headbands, rolled-up pants legs, bandannas, or accessories that are drug, alcohol, or gang related, obscene/profane, or sexual in nature.

Students who fail to comply with such rules will be suspended from school—a 3-day suspension for a first offense, 5 days for a second, 7 days for a third, 10 days for a fourth, and permanent expulsion for a fifth offense. Fighting draws a 10-day suspension. (Discipline policy, 2005)

- *Bluffing.* Some teachers ignore *The Law of the West* which warns, "Don't pull your gun from the holster unless you are going to shoot." In effect, don't try to bluff, because threatening students with a consequence but failing to apply that consequence when an infraction occurs only encourages future infractions. It takes students only a short time to learn if they can trust their teachers to keep their word. The message for teachers becomes " 'Tis folly to issue threats and promises that you either cannot or will not carry out."

- *Providing a learning experience.* Discipline methods whose chief purpose is to wreak vengeance or cause pain make less sense than methods designed to teach disrupters nondisruptive ways to act. Hence, teachers can profitably select treatments that equip students to behave more constructively on future occasions. For example, having a boy, by participating in role-playing, practice different ways to respond to provocative name-calling can be a more positive treatment than requiring him to write 500 times "I won't punch a name-caller again."

- *Starting strict.* In an effort to establish a friendly classroom climate at the beginning of the school year, a teacher may start by being very tolerant of students' behavior. Then, when it becomes apparent that much of that behavior seriously interferes with efficient learning, the teacher is obliged to "toughen up"—to set new limits on how to act in class. But this effort to "put the genie back in the bottle" can be a most difficult task. It is usually more prudent to start the school year with rather strict expectations for behavior and then, if conditions permit, ease up later.

CONCLUSION

The intent of this chapter has been to identify kinds of student behavior that disrupt classrooms and to suggest (a) types of treatments that can be applied to students who violate classroom rules and (b) guides to classroom management that should help reduce the incidence of disruptive acts.

CHAPTER 11

Planning Treatments

For many acts of violence, teachers and other school personnel have ready responses. They already know what treatments they will apply, because they have often faced similar acts before. This is particularly true with routine classroom disruptions, bullying, and scuffling. However, in other instances of violence, the matter of how best to react is unclear. Those occasions require more thought and analysis for generating promising treatments. This chapter is intended to serve as a guide on such occasions. The chapter is cast in the form of a combined catalogue, glossary, and shopping list that can be searched for ways to respond to puzzling acts of violence.

As proposed in Chapter 1, behind all reactions to violent behavior there is a mode of thought that leads people to choose the treatments they will adopt. The purpose of Chapter 11 is to suggest such a mode of thought—a planning strategy. It's an approach that involves answering the question: "How can I best respond to this particular violent act?"

A WAY OF THINKING ABOUT TREATMENT

I propose that, when confronted with violence, the person who is planning treatment can profitably be guided by a question composed of the following six underlined variables:

In light of the type of violence in this case, what treatment will best accomplish the purpose I hope to achieve with the kind of person who is to be treated under a particular set of environmental conditions, and without generating undesirable side effects (collateral damage)?

I believe that people are best equipped to answer this question when they are well acquainted with many types of violence, kinds of treatment, potential purposes, sorts of students, varieties of environments, and undesirable side effects. The following sections are designed to promote such acquaintance by describing these six variables in considerable detail. Each variable and its subcategories are presented in two steps. At the first step, the variable is cast in terms of a diversity of options from which school personnel may choose. The second step suggests, in the form of questions to ask oneself, decisions that school personnel can usefully make about each variable.

Thus, the chapter is a compilation of options for each of the six variables. The way I think teachers, principals, and counselors might profitably use the chapter is to skim through the options under each variable to see which one or more of the alternatives might be well suited to the case of violence currently at hand. To show how such a decision-making process might work in practice, the final section of the chapter describes a pair of treatment plans that could result from using the chapter's catalogue of options in two hypothetical cases.

The sections of the chapter are arranged in the following sequence: (a) types of violence, (b) kinds of treatments for offenders, (c) kinds of treatments for victims, (d) purposes/desired outcomes for offenders, (e) purposes/desired outcomes for victims, (f) kinds of persons, (g) environmental conditions, (h) collateral damage, and (i) two sample cases.

Types of Violence

The kinds of violence of concern in this book are those illustrated in Chapter 1 and inspected in detail in Chapters 2 through 10. When a person is deciding how to respond to an act of violence, two aspects of types that are useful to consider are the seriousness of consequences and permissible treatments.

The Seriousness of Consequences

The phrase *seriousness of consequences* refers to the severity of the pain, trouble, or expense that results from a violent act. In most cases, the more serious the effect of an act, the stronger the treatment.

The act of shooting classmates with a revolver warrants a more drastic response than does the act of bringing a revolver to school and showing it to friends. Smashing furniture and windows in several classrooms calls for a more severe reaction than does spray-painting a single desk. Disrupting a class by slapping both the teacher and classmates invites a stronger response than does shooting rubber bands at a wall map. Starting multiple fights is more serious than starting just one.

This notion of applying stronger treatments for more serious consequences is reflected in society's criminal-justice system. Crimes are defined as legally prohibited acts injurious to the public welfare or morals, or to the interests of the state. Crimes are commonly divided into three broad categories—felony, misdemeanor, and infraction. The most injurious crimes are felonies, commonly punished by one or more years in prison or by death. Less serious crimes are classified as misdemeanors that involve minor offences usually leading to less than 1 year in jail and/or a fine of no more than $1,000. Infractions are even less serious violations, with offenders not jailed but required to appear in court and perhaps pay a fine (Thomas, 1995, pp. 50–51).

Permissible Treatments

Frequently, the people responsible for selecting how to respond to violent acts are restricted in the kinds of treatments from which they can choose. For instance, rules that teachers and principals are constrained to follow will often limit treatment choices; sometimes such restrictions are specified and other times they are merely assumed.

Specified rules are usually in the form of written mandates or bans. A mandate identifies the treatment—or treatments—allowable for a particular offense. Treatments other than the listed ones are not acceptable.

In the Colorado Springs School District, an obligatory three-day suspension from school is imposed on any student who damages the personal property of a district employee (Colorado Springs School District, 2003).

State regulations in Kansas require that any pupil who is continually disorderly on a school bus will be refused further bus transportation (Basehor-Linwood Public Schools, 2005).

Student-behavior rules at Barry Goldwater High School in Phoenix (Arizona) state that "No student shall go onto the school's premises with a firearm, explosive, weapon, chains, knife, any other dangerous or illegal instrument, or any instrument represented as such. No student shall interfere with normal activities, occupancy, or use of any building or portion of the campus by exhibiting, using, or threatening to exhibit or use a firearm, explosive weapon, knife, other dangerous or illegal instrument, or any instrument represented as such. Any student violating this policy may be suspended or expelled" (Barry Goldwater High School, 2005).

A ban identifies treatments not permitted for the offense at hand, so school personnel are obliged to choose a type of response not on the banned list.

The following are among America's largest school districts that do not permit corporal punishment (paddling, caning, spanking, slapping) for violent behavior: New York City, Los Angeles, Chicago, Houston, Philadelphia, Detroit, Boston, Palm Beach, Portland, and Sacramento. Large districts that do permit corporal punishment include: Duval County, Hillsborough County, and Polk County in Florida; Caddo Parish in Louisiana; Aldine, Garland, and Plano in Texas; and Shelby County in Tennessee (Center for Effective Discipline, 2005).

In addition to specified rules, there are commonsense or cultural expectations about permissible ways of reacting to violence. Questions of reasonableness often arise when people object to the way regulations have been applied in particular cases.

At an elementary school in Kensington (Pennsylvania), three girls—one age 10, two age 9—were handcuffed and suspended from school for five days for spraying a can of Mace on the playground. According to the police, the Mace injured three other girls, including one who was briefly hospitalized. The handcuffing was in keeping with the police department's written policies about coping with pupils who are caught with dangerous weapons, and Mace was considered such a weapon. But the incident drew criticism from parents who believed that treating young children in such a manner was unreasonable. They urged the school district and police to reconsider their policies. In response, a police spokesman said, "Once we take somebody into custody, we are responsible for their well-being, regardless of their age. I know it's controversial, but we have to handcuff everybody—for their safety and everyone else's" (Dean, 2005a).

In Meridian (Mississippi) the principal of Carver Middle School ordered the assistant principal to paddle a sixth-grade student who had acted up in class. But the assistant principal objected and resigned from the school. He explained, "The idea of a big white guy hitting an 80-pound black girl because she talked back to the teacher did not sit well with me. I decided I did not get my master's degree in education to spend my time paddling students" (Dobbs, 2004).

Questions to Ask Oneself

For the violent act that was committed in the case that I am now considering:

- What kind of treatment is appropriate for the degree of harm the violence caused?
- Are there either specified or assumed restrictions (mandates or bans) on the sorts of treatment that can be used?

Kinds of Treatments for Offenders

As explained in Chapter 1, the term *treatment* is used throughout this book to identify any sort of intentional response that a person—such as a teacher, principal, psychologist, social worker, or student—makes to either a perpetrator or a victim of violence. There are so many possible specific treatments that it is impractical to try describing all of them in this chapter. Therefore, the following analysis is limited to twenty-two kinds, along with examples of each kind.

In many cases, it is easy to recognize who was responsible for a violent act— such as who bullied a classmate, who set a fire, who threatened to spray-paint a teacher's car. Other times, finding the doer of a violent deed is difficult— such as who phoned to take credit for planting a bomb in the gymnasium, who smashed computers during a midnight raid, who scribbled a hate list of students on the history-class chalkboard. In still other instances, it is difficult to distinguish a violent act's perpetrator from its victim. Such is often the case with fights, with the question of fault typically settled by blaming the person or group that apparently started the fight.

But once the perpetrator has been identified, the kind of treatment that might best be attempted can be chosen from such a collection as the following twenty-two kinds: (a) inflicting bodily harm, (b) imprisoning or detaining, (c) suspending or expelling, (d) physically restraining, (e) transferring, (f) restricting or altering rights, privileges, or opportunities, (g) censuring and exposing, (h) confiscating or damaging possessions, (i) assigning labor, (j) threatening and warning, (k) imposing adverse appraisals, (l) requiring penance, apology, or compensation, (m) monitoring, (n) offering rewards, (o) offering personal counseling, (p) educating, (q) applying medical interventions, (r) postponing sanctions, (s) maintaining a record, (t) forgiving, (u) removing an offender's targets, and (v) delegating treatment responsibility.

Inflicting Bodily Harm

Either (a) killing the offender or (b) administering corporal punishment that causes a level of physical pain, discomfort, and/or injury that does not result in death.

An 18-year-old youth is executed by lethal injection in a state prison for having raped and murdered three middle-school girls.

A sixth-grader who smashed a wall mirror in a lavatory is given ten swats on the buttocks with a bamboo cane.

Imprisoning or Detaining

Requiring an offender to remain in a place of confinement.

A seventh-grader was kept in the classroom for an hour after school for disrupting a social studies lesson with a series of rude comments.

A high school student who threw acid on a classmate in a general science class was sentenced to 60 days in a juvenile detention facility.

Suspending or Expelling

Removing an offender from a place or from a position of opportunity. Suspending is temporary removal. Expelling is permanent discharge.

A junior-high girl was barred from attending school for 2 weeks for bringing sleeping pills to school and forcing a classmate to swallow them.

After being caught with a switchblade in his pocket on three occasions, a 16-year-old was permanently expelled from school.

Restraining

Curtailing a violent person's freedom of movement.

When the teacher of a 5-year-old girl was unable to stop the child from screaming, ripping papers off a bulletin board, and kicking other children, the school's security guard handcuffed the girl and removed her from the classroom.

Transferring

Moving an offender to a different location.

After four incidents of verbally and physically attacking girls who were members of a rival gang, a high school girl was transferred to the district's alternative school that served students who seemed unable to cope with a normal school program.

Restricting or Altering Rights, Privileges, or Opportunities

Movement limitations. Confining a student to a given location or declaring that particular sites are off-limits.

For molesting primary-grade children on the playground before school and during recess, a fifth-grade boy was banned from being on the playground at any time.

Curtailment of opportunities. Taking away rights or privileges.

One month before the end of the school year, three middle-school boys—ages 13, 14, and 15—groped a 14-year-old girl on a school bus. School authorities responded by barring the boys from riding school buses and by suspending all three from attending school for the remainder of the term.

Social-contact restrictions. Forbidding certain social relationships.

At the suggestion of the school principal, the parents of a high school girl no longer let her spend time with a boy who had been cited several times by the police for recklessly driving his car around the school grounds.

Activity limitations. Proscribing specified activities.

For drinking beer at the junior prom, a girl was prevented from coming to any more dances during the school year.

A high school senior was denied the chance to participate in graduation activities as punishment for fighting on the school grounds.

Demotion. Reducing rights, responsibilities, status, and perquisites.

The editor of the school newspaper was removed from his position for writing an editorial that denigrated Latinos.

Assignment bypass. Permitting individuals to retain their title, status, and perquisites, but their positions' traditional responsibilities and powers are delegated to others.

A school counselor who slapped a sixth-grader for calling the counselor a "bitch" was allowed to keep her title of counselor but was assigned to clerical duties in the school office and prevented from having any contact with pupils.

Promotion denial. Refusing to promote the offender to a position of higher status, responsibility, or privilege.

A running-back on the high-school football team, chosen by the players to be their team captain, was prevented from accepting that position because he had organized the hazing of three freshmen on the team.

Censuring and Exposing, As in

Private censure. Admonishing the wrongdoer in private (orally reproving the offender face-to-face or over the phone with no witness present, or sending the offender a written note or e-mail message of censure).

A third-grade teacher kept a boy in the classroom during recess to lecture him about his disruptive behavior in that morning's reading group and to describe the consequences he could expect if he continued to act in such a manner.

Limited exposure. Informing certain others of the misdeed.

Both the school principal and the parents of a 13-year-old girl were told by an English teacher that the girl wrote notes threatening a classmate with "deadly harm if you don't stop talking to my boy friend."

Public exposure. Publicizing the wrongdoer's misdeed to the general populace.

Two 17-year-old boys were named in the city newspaper as the vandals who had spray-painted ethnic slurs on the sidewalk leading to the high school's main entrance.

Confiscating or Damaging Possessions

Forfeiture of possessions. Seizing certain of the transgressor's belongings.

School authorities confiscated the cell phone a girl had used to send anonymous threatening messages to a teacher.

Damage of possessions. Impairing or destroying certain of the transgressor's belongings.

The police broke into pieces a dagger a 15-year-old had used in a gang fight in the high school gymnasium after a basketball game.

Assigning Labor

Requiring the offender to perform designated work.

For cursing her math teacher, a 13-year-old girl was ordered to spend 4 hours on Saturday cleaning up the middle-school campus.

Threatening and Warning

Informing offenders of unpleasant consequences they can expect if they commit unacceptable acts in the future.

In response to a ninth-grade boy's trying to pull down a girl's pants at lunchtime, the assistant principal cautioned him that the next time he tried such a stunt he would be suspended from school.

Imposing Adverse Appraisals

Evaluating a wrongdoer unfavorably.

A brief report of a sixth-grade girl's throwing stones at classmates during lunch hour was placed in the girl's cumulative-record folder.

Requiring Penance, Apology, or Compensation

Penance. Offenders are obliged to act in ways that signify regret, sorrow, contrition, and self-reproach for their misdeed (profess remorse, accept blame, engage in self-punitive behavior).

On an Internet Web site, a high school girl falsely accused a schoolmate of engaging in oral sex with several boys. When school authorities discovered who had posted the accusation, they gave the girl the option of publicly admitting her misdeed and of sincerely expressing remorse. Otherwise, she would be expelled from school.

Apology. Offenders offer their expressions of self-reproach and remorse to individuals or groups that were victims of the misdeed; apology may include a plea for the offenders to be forgiven.

A third-grader was told that if he apologized for tearing up a classmate's picture folder, he would not have to stay after school for a week.

Compensation. Offenders endeavor to repay victims in some measure for the damage caused by the violent act (repayment in money, labor, services, goods, property).

The third-grader who tore up the picture folder was required to replace the folder with one of equal worth.

Monitoring

Keeping track of the transgressor's behavior.

A high school boy who had beaten a schoolmate with a baseball bat—thereby sending the schoolmate to the hospital for several weeks—was suspended from school, confined to his home, and required by the district court to wear an electronic ankle bracelet that enabled the police to discover if he left his house.

Offering Rewarsds

Describing to offenders the desirable consequences they can expect if they refrain from future misdeeds.

A first-grade teacher told a chronically aggressive pupil, "If you go through today without hitting anyone or calling them names, tomorrow you can lead the flag salute in the morning and have your name on the chalkboard as the leader for the day."

Offering Personal Counseling

Conferring with wrongdoers during either group or individual sessions in order to discuss factors associated with their violent act and to guide them toward more acceptable behavior.

A school psychologist estimated that a 14-year-old girl who had transferred recently into the middle school might be fighting with schoolmates because she lacked more suitable skills for getting along with peers. Thus, the psychologist planned a series of counseling sessions in which the psychologist might (a) learn the newcomer's perception of her school situation and (b) have the girl practice—in simulated encounters with agemates—more productive ways of responding to the situations that were confronting her at the school.

Educating

Explanation. A teacher or counselor explains to the wrongdoer (a) why the wrongdoer's offense was harmful and (b) how the wrongdoer could act more acceptably on future occasions. Explanation is most suitable when the wrongdoer had been unaware of the harm that would result from his or her act or else had not known a more suitable way to behave under such circumstances.

A seventh-grade boy shouted "Keep away from me, you filthy slut" at a girl who knocked a notebook off his desk as she walked past. The teacher ordered the boy to come to her room after school to discuss the incident. When he appeared, the teacher asked him if he knew what *slut* meant. When he said it meant "somebody really rotten," the teacher replied that *slut* meant a girl or woman who went to bed with lots of boys or men, usually for pay. She asked what evidence the boy had that the girl actually behaved in such a manner. He admitted that he had no such evidence. The teacher also asked him how his name-calling might influence how the girl felt and what other students might think of him for what he had shouted. Then she asked him to suggest other ways he might have responded to the notebook-knocking incident. After the youth proposed other options and the teacher added her own suggestions, she said she would let him off with only a warning this time. But similar behavior in the future would result in his being assigned to clean up the school campus during two Saturday-morning detention sessions.

Demonstration. Rather than merely telling an offender how to behave, the teacher specifically demonstrates what the offender could have done instead of acting violently. In other words, the teacher models actions the offender can copy.

When a 16-year-old girl made an offensive remark about a 15-year-old schoolmate's appearance, the 15-year-old retaliated by attacking the older girl—ripping her jacket, scratching her face, and pulling her hair. The school counselor who spoke with the 15-year-old after the incident suggested several verbal retorts the girl could have used instead of fighting and thereby drawing a 5-day suspension from school. The aim of the suggested retorts would be to brush off the insult by showing it had failed to make its intended anger-generating impression on the 15-year-old. The counselor's proposed options included such responses as:

"Everybody seems to have an opinion these days."

"I suppose that's an example of free speech?"

"Maybe we could all vote on that remark in the next election."

Role-playing. The teacher creates a dramatic situation that simulates conditions of the incident in which the offender acted violently. The teacher and/or classmates assume the roles of the other people who were present at the incident. Role-playing may follow explanation and demonstration, giving an offender a chance to try nonviolent ways to act.

A sixth-grade teacher explains to the pupils that they are going to have a chance to be actors—to try their hand at short plays in which she will assign them roles, will describe a social situation, supply them their first few lines of dialogue, and then let them play out the scenes the way they think their assumed characters might act in real life. There are six pupils in the first playlet. One is portrayed as a bully who taunts a newcomer to the school. Another is that newcomer. The remaining four are bystanders who witness the bully's assaults. Three of the bystanders do nothing to interfere, but seem to rather enjoy the event. In contrast, the fourth tries to defend the victim and stop the taunting. When the teacher appoints pupils to roles, she assigns the class's most active bully to the role of the helpful bystander. The teacher's purpose is to give that pupil a chance to try constructive ways to reduce bullying behavior. Following the role-playing scene, the teacher leads a discussion during which class members comment about how the bullying incident was resolved.

Another variation of antibullying role-playing can involve a class bully being assigned the role of a victim in an incident so as to give him a chance to experience how it might feel to be tormented.

Behavior modification. The expression *behavior modification* identifies an approach to improving offenders' conduct by a training program that involves the teacher taking four steps.

1. Identifying the specific actions that the teacher hopes the student will substitute for the violent act that the student had committed.
2. Arranging for the student to try out this new, desirable behavior. There are several ways to do this—simply wait for it to occur spontaneously, verbally explain what the desired behavior is, or demonstrate the behavior by acting it out.
3. Determining what sorts of consequences will be strongly rewarding to the student and what sorts will be strongly punishing.
4. Manipulating consequences so that the desired new actions, when the student performs them, yield greater reward and less punishment than did the student's previous violent actions. In other words, arrange a schedule of reward and punishment that makes it profitable for the student to give up the old behavior in favor of the new.

Applying Medical Interventions

Using medicinal or surgical procedures to ameliorate physical and psychological factors that ostensibly contributed to individuals' wrongdoing.

A second-grader who constantly disrupted the class by shouting, walking around the room, and teasing neighbors was diagnosed as suffering from attention-deficit disorder with hyperactivity. A physician prescribed the administration of Ritalin to calm the boy and enable him to attend school without disrupting the class.

Postponing Sanctions

Delaying the identification or announcement of a treatment.

A high school principal felt he had insufficient evidence on which to base a decision about who was responsible for throwing a cherry bomb in a toilet in one of the school's bathrooms. Thus, he held back his report of sanctions to impose until he had more decisive information.

Because a gun-wielding high school student was still in critical condition in the hospital after having been shot by a school security guard, the police withheld the announcement of charges against the shooter.

The disposition of a case of sexual abuse, lodged against a coach of a high school girls' volleyball team, was delayed because the school board was unable to reach a decision about the matter.

Maintaining a Record

Keeping a report of the incident for future reference.

In the computer file that a high school chemistry teacher kept about each student in his classes, he recorded that a particular junior girl had broken a shelf of beakers as an angry reaction to the low grade she had earned on a mid-semester test.

Forgiving

Unconditional forgiveness. Assessing no penalty for the offense and issuing no warning that sanctions might be applied for future misdeeds.

When a fifth-grade girl lied about taking a classmate's I-pod music player, her teacher spoke to the girl in private, asking her, "What do you think you should have done when I asked you if you knew what had happened to the I-pod?" The girl answered, "Well, I shouldn't have stole it. And when you asked me, I should have said I took it and I should give it back." The teacher responded, "I think you've learned your lesson. I believe you'll not do something like that again. You're a good person. I have confidence in you."

Pardoning. Excusing the individual from penalties for the present offense, but making no commitment about what consequences could be imposed for future misconduct.

A sixth-grade boy, assigned to help tutor second-graders during their math period, jerked a chair out from under a second-grade girl as she was about to sit down at a table. As the girl fell to the floor, she banged her head on the chair. When the teacher took the boy aside to speak with him about the incident, the boy claimed it had been just a joke. He said he was sorry and would apologize to the girl. The teacher agreed: "We'll let it pass this time, but no more funny business."

Second chance/probation. Assessing no penalty for the first offense, then applying sanctions for subsequent misdeeds.

A high school student who had zipped open his pants to expose his penis before two girls in the school library was arrested for lewd and lascivious conduct. A juvenile-court judge sentenced the youth to a month in juvenile hall, but agreed not to carry out the sentence if the boy would commit no misdeeds over the next 12 months. In other words, the youth would be on probation throughout the coming year.

Removing Offender's Targets

Not restricting the transgressor's freedom of movement, but rendering inaccessible the people or goods that have been the objects of the wrongdoer's misdeed.

In an effort to prevent several high school students from tormenting a girl classmate, the school principal recommended that the victim's parents transfer their daughter to another school.

Delegating Treatment Responsibility

Transferring to some other person, group, or agency the tasks of proposing and implementing treatment.

As a reaction to a high school girl's smashing a classmate's cell phone, a history-class teacher escorted the disruptive student to the office of the dean of girls.

Questions to Ask Oneself

- Which treatment, or combination of treatments, will likely be the most effective in controlling the offender's future behavior and, at the same time, is feasible to use in view of (a) the law and school rules, (b) available personnel, (c) cost, (d) time constraints, and (e) parental cooperation.
- If the preferred treatment option proves unworkable, what alternative treatment might then be appropriate?

Kinds of Treatment for Victims

Victims of violence may profit from consolation, trauma therapy, compensation, or training.

Consolation

Offering victims sympathy and a chance to vent their feelings about the episode of violence.

Following a fight in which a fourth-grade girl was scratched and slapped by a fifth-grade girl, the school nurse met with the sobbing fourth-grader and listened sympathetically to the girl's account of the event.

Trauma Therapy

Beyond simple consolation, helping victims cope with the shock, fears, and distress that resulted from a violent encounter.

The day after an enraged high school student, wielding a semiautomatic rifle, had shot three schoolmates and had killed himself, a team of four crisis counselors met with students—individually and in groups—to hear their concerns and to suggest ways they might constructively deal with their memories of the frightening events they had witnessed.

Compensation

Arranging reparations for losses that victims suffered as the result of violence.

Three students arrested for vandalizing the art classroom at their middle school were expelled from school and required by the court to pay $4,000 to repair the damage. Because the teenagers themselves lacked the money to pay the cost, the responsibility for payment fell to their parents.

Training

Preparing victims to cope with potential future violence.

In an effort to help a junior-high-school boy defend himself against tormentors who shoved and hit him on the way to school and on the playground, the school principal advised the student's parents to have their son enroll in a self-defense class offered by the local YMCA.

A Question to Ask Oneself

In view of the kind of violence in this case, the kind of person who committed the misdeed, the environment surrounding the misdeed, and the kind of person that the victim seems to be, which treatment of the victim is most likely to produce the outcome I desire?

Purposes/Desired Outcomes for Offenders

I believe that sometimes—perhaps often—people who are responsible for proposing treatments do not thoroughly consider the purposes they hope a selected treatment will serve. As a result, they may choose methods that are not the most appropriate for the results they desire. The intent of the following section is to illustrate this point by identifying a variety of purposes of treatments. Two treatment examples are described under each aim or purpose. The examples illustrate my estimate of which of the pair is more likely to achieve the stated purpose and which is less likely to achieve that aim.

Preventing the Disruption of Schooling

Nearly all kinds of treatment are intended to promote the peaceful conduct of the school program.

More likely to achieve aim. Suspend student from school.

Less likely to achieve aim. Orally reprimand the student during a private interview session.

Preventing Offenders from Further Violence

The purpose of prevention can be either specific or general. It is specific whenever the aim is to stop the wrongdoer from repeating the same unacceptable act in the future. The aim is general whenever the intent is to reduce the likelihood that the offender will commit any violent deeds in the years ahead.

More likely to achieve aim. Expel the student from school.

Less likely to achieve aim. Send the student to a detention room to work on school assignments under supervision.

Imposing Just Deserts

Oblige offenders to suffer the same treatment as did the victims of their violence. This "eye-for-an-eye and tooth-for-a-tooth" response is based on the *lex talionis* principle which proposes that justice is served when wrongdoers "get what they deserve" by experiencing the same pain and inconvenience that their victims were obliged to suffer.

More likely to achieve aim. For a student who has sketched graffiti on a wall, require the offender to clean or repaint the wall.

Less likely to achieve aim. For a student who has sketched graffiti on a wall, caution the offender not to do such a thing again.

Diagnosing Causes

Discovering the causes behind a misdeed so that steps might be taken to correct the cause as a way of reducing the probability of the misdeed being committed again.

More likely to achieve aim. In the case of a third grader who habitually disrupts the class, the teacher speaks at length with the child, the child's parents, and the family's physician to learn probable reasons behind the disruptive behavior.

Less likely to achieve aim. In the case of a third grader who habitually disrupts the class, the teacher sends the child to sit in the principal's office periodically.

Teaching Right from Wrong

Helping offenders distinguish between acceptable and unacceptable behavior.

More likely to achieve aim. Telling offenders why what they did was wrong, explaining what would be proper behavior in such a situation, and having them practice distinguishing right from wrong by analyzing cases that illustrate children engaging in acceptable versus unacceptable behavior.

Less likely to achieve aim. Warning offenders not to misbehave again.

Fostering Alternative Behavior

Obliging offenders to adopt acceptable ways of fulfilling their needs and desires.

More likely to achieve aim. (a) Telling offenders why what they did was wrong, (b) explaining what would be proper behavior in such a situation, (c) having them practice distinguishing right from wrong by analyzing cases that illustrate children engaging in acceptable versus unacceptable behavior, (d) rewarding them each time they display proper behavior, and (e) withholding rewards or applying punishments when offenders revert to their previous unacceptable behavior.

Less likely to achieve aim. Berate offenders in the presence of their classmates.

Reforming Wrongdoers

Changing offenders' motives and the values on which their behavior is founded.

More likely to achieve aim. Enroll offenders in a peer discussion group that meets periodically to analyze participants' life goals and ways of successfully pursuing those goals in daily settings.

Less likely to achieve aim. Assign students to read passages from books that focus on moral behavior, such as passages from Aesop's Fables, the Jewish Torah, the Christian Bible, the Islamic Quran, the Confucian Analects, or the Hindu Laws of Manu.

Accommodating for Physical and Psychological Disabilities

Adjusting treatment to recognize physical and mental handicaps that offenders display.

More likely to achieve aim. For a 12-year-old girl of well-below-average mental ability who has physically attacked schoolmates who have teased her, two measures are adopted. First, the teacher engages the teasers in a discussion session during which the group's members suggest answers to five questions: (a) Why did kids tease the girl? (b) In what ways is she similar to and different from the teasers, and why are there such differences? (c) Are those differences something the girl is responsible for and can do something about? (d) Are there ways that her schoolmates could help her get along more adequately with life in school? (e) How would you feel being teased in the way she has been teased?

Second, the teacher meets with the girl on several occasions and demonstrates ways—other than physical and verbal attacks—that a person can react to the sorts of teasing the girl has suffered. The girl is then guided to practice those ways a number of times as the teacher plays the role of teaser.

Less likely to achieve aim. After the incident of violence, the 12-year-old is sent to the detention room for the remainder of the school day to contemplate her attack on her schoolmates.

Enhancing Knowledge, Skills, and Habits

Offering educational opportunities that prepare offenders for a socially constructive future.

More likely to achieve aim. A ninth-grade math teacher is surprised at the high grade earned on a state math test by a boy who had been doing below average work in class. Then the teacher discovers that, prior to the testing session, the youth has stolen a copy of the test from her desk. In response to this discovery, she changes his grade of *A* on the test to an *F* and assigns him to meet three times each week with a competent tenth-grade math student for tutoring. The purpose of the assignment is to enhance the test-thief's math skills so he will not need to resort to stealing to succeed on future tests. The boy is given the option of later taking an equivalent state test, with the score from that exam replacing the *F* that had been recorded.

Less likely to achieve aim. The test-thief is given a two-week suspension from school.

Questions to Ask Oneself

- What is my intent in selecting a treatment? In other words, how do I expect the treatment will affect the offender?
- Do I have single purpose or intended outcome, or do I envision more than one kind, such as preventing further violence as well as reforming the offender's general behavior?

Purposes/Desired Outcomes for Victims

Compensating

Making amends for the damage done by recompensing victims for their losses.

More likely to achieve aim. A tenth-grade boy who deliberately smashed a girl's I-pod music player by stomping on it is required to buy her a new I-pod.

Less likely to achieve aim. A tenth-grade boy who deliberately smashed a girl's I-pod music player by stomping on it is required to apologize to the girl in front of the class.

Developing Defensive Skills

Enhancing victims' ability to defend themselves against future violent acts.

More likely to achieve aim. A sixth-grade boy who has been incessantly tormented by classmates pushing, hitting, and tripping him is enrolled in a self-defense class.

Less likely to achieve aim. A sixth-grade boy who has been incessantly tormented by class-mates pushing, hitting, and tripping him is transferred to a different elementary school.

Avenging Wrongdoing

Gaining satisfaction from punishing offenders.

More likely to achieve aim. A pupil who bullied younger schoolmates by slapping and punching them is sent to juvenile hall for a month.

Less likely to achieve aim. A student who bullied younger schoolmates by slapping or punching them is warned to stop such behavior.

Offering Therapy

Furnishing victims physical and/or psychological treatment designed to correct damage caused by violent acts.

More likely to achieve aim. A 14-year-old girl whose father sexually abused her over the past two years is placed in a foster home with sympathetic foster-parents and engaged in weekly counseling sessions with a psychiatric social worker.

Less likely to achieve aim. A 14-year-old girl whose father sexually abused her over the past 2 years is placed in a juvenile detention center to protect her from her father.

Questions to Ask Oneself

- What is the intent of the treatment I propose for the victim? In other words, how do I expect treatment to affect the victim?
- Do I have single purpose or intended outcome, or do I envision more than one kind, such as providing compensation and offering therapy?

Kinds of Persons

The expression *kinds of persons* refers to characteristics of individuals who have been engaged in violent events, either as perpetrators or as victims. The characteristics of significance are ones that are part of the person (not part of the person's environment) that can influence decisions about the treatments that will be suitable. The following discussion does not include all influential personal traits but, rather, is limited to eight of the more salient ones—age, intent/motivation, character, physical appearance, physical ability, mental ability, emotional stability, and cultural characteristics.

Age

Some treatments are more suitable for young children than for older children or adolescents, and vice versa.

A 4-year-old who hit a teacher with a stick will likely be treated differently than a 16-year-old who did the same. The preschool teacher would probably disarm the 4-year-old and then (a) explain why such behavior is not tolerated, (b) demonstrate what behavior the child could properly substitute for hitting, and (c) have the child practice the suggested substitute. In contrast, the 16-year-old would probably be expelled from school or at least assigned a long-term suspension.

However, the variable of significance here is not age itself but, instead, is something else that tends to be highly correlated with age. In other words, age is merely an indicator—a proxy or surrogate variable—of a physical or mental condition that influences the suitability of a treatment. In many cases, that variable is "knowledge of right and wrong" or "knowledge of likely consequences." Young children are thought to lack such knowledge because they are deemed "below the age of reason," therefore prone to faulty judgment. Hence, they are either forgiven an act of violence or else assigned less aversive consequences than would be applied to an adolescent or adult.

Intent/Motivation

Before people propose a treatment for a wrongdoer, they usually want to know "Why did he do it?" "What was her motive?" "Was it an accident?" "Was it self-defense?" "Was it revenge?" "Was it greed?" "Was it to vent anger and frustration?"

Traditionally, a violent act warrants a more drastic penalty if committed out of deep-seated malevolence and a lack of concern for others' welfare (particularly if an attack was planned ahead of time *with malice aforethought*) than if it occurred on the spur of the moment and might be blamed on a sudden fit of temper or thoughtlessness (a lack of awareness of undesired consequences).

Character

The word *character* refers to what people mean when they say of a student who is accused of violent behavior—"She's not that kind of person" or "It's just what you'd expect of him" or "I can't imagine his acting that way" or "I'm not at all surprised." In effect, character is the impression people hold of the behavior to be expected of student as based on their knowledge of how the student has acted in the past. Thus, *good character* is a composite of traits attributed to a student, such as honesty, courage, forthrightness, and kindheartedness. Traits of *bad character* include mendacity, cowardice, deceit, and cruelty. Even though judges in criminal courts tell jurors they are to weigh only the "facts" in the case at hand and not pay attention to the defendant's past history, in daily-life situations people typically do take into consideration wrong-doers' characters as reflected in reports of their past behavior.

In the early evening, a security guard caught a 17-year-old girl using colored marker pens to sketch drawings and print phrases on classroom windows, with the phrases condemning the high school's recently adopted dress code. Because the girl had no previous record of misconduct and because she was on the school's academic honor roll, the principal—rather than suspending her from school—let her off with a reprimand and the task of cleaning the windows.

When a 16-year-old boy was told by the librarian to quiet down in the library, the youth shouted, "Screw yourself, you silly bitch." The high school principal—rather than simply reprimanding the boy—transferred him to an alternative school for chronic troublemakers because of the boy's extensive past record of breaking school rules.

Physical Appearance

The role a person's appearance played in a violent act often affects the kind of treatment applied to either an offender or a victim. The term *appearance* can refer to a variety of physical characteristics, including

- Facial features—pretty, ordinary, distorted
- Stature—tall, short, skinny, husky, fat
- Complexion—pale, dark, swarthy, smooth, pock-marked
- Mobility—agile, clumsy, halting
- Clothing—stylish, old-fashioned, clean, soiled, quaint, foreign
- Adornments—ear rings, nose gems, tattoos, face paint, gold teeth

A high school girl who pummeled a classmate who continually taunted her about her facial acne may be assigned a less aversive treatment than is applied to the girl who did the taunting.

Physical Ability

A student's physical limitations can influence the consequences assigned for wrongdoing. Requiring a fifth-grade girl to pull weeds in the schoolyard because she painted graffiti on sidewalks could be considered unduly cruel if the girl is highly allergic to weeds. Assigning a middle-school boy to run twenty times around the gymnasium for pummeling a classmate will be inappropriate if the boy is partially lame.

Mental Ability

Whether students will act violently can be affected by such intellectual skills as their (a) knowing which sorts of behavior at school are forbidden and which are acceptable, (b) knowing how to perform the acceptable behaviors, and (c) accurately predicting the likely consequences of their actions. How well students master these skills depends both on their genetic endowment (the quality of their inherited brain-cell structures) and on the life experiences that have produced the contents of their memories. Those skills are less developed in young children who are still mentally immature and in older youths whose neural structures have been impaired by flawed genetic endowment or by disease or injury. Thus, the young and the intellectually disadvantaged can lack mental skills that equip them to act in ways considered proper in school. Also, students will act in unacceptable ways if their neural endowment is adequate but they have not had the experiences that would teach them the difference between suitable and unsuitable behavior. These factors may be taken into consideration by school personnel and members of the criminal-justice system when they propose treatments for offenders.

A mentally disabled girl who cursed the junior-high-school principal deserves a different response than a mentally gifted student who swore at her volleyball coach.

Emotional Stability

It is apparent that children can differ markedly from each other in emotional control—in how they express anger, delight, fear, humor, embarrassment, shame, and more. A teacher's or counselor's estimate of the nature of a given student's emotional control can affect the treatment attempted after the student's emotional outburst has disrupted a classroom or resulted in a fight, bullying, or a threat of violence.

Late in the school day, during recreational-reading period, a fifth-grade girl screamed at the boy in the desk behind her, and she flung the boy's books on the floor because he had continued to hum the same tune over and over. The teacher was surprised at the girl's drastic reaction, because the girl was habitually mild-mannered, polite, and tolerant of her classmates. Since such behavior was so out of character, the teacher imagined that the outburst was the result of fatigue and perhaps current worries in the girl's life. Thus, the teacher felt that a mild sanction—moving the girl to a seat in a rear corner of the classroom for the remaining class time—would be sufficient punishment to discourage a repeat of such behavior in the future.

A third-grade boy, diagnosed as suffering from attention-deficit hyperactivity disorder, began disturbing the third-grade class by interrupting the teacher and pupils who were speaking and by wandering around the room, often poking classmates. When the teacher phoned the boy's home, she learned that the family's supply of the boy's medication (Ritalin) was depleted and his parents had not yet renewed the prescription, so their son had not been taking the medicine recently. Thus, the treatment of the boy's disruptive behavior consisted of the teacher's urging the pupil's mother to resume giving her son his medication.

Asperger's syndrome is a developmental disorder that impairs a person's social-interaction skills. Children and adolescents who suffer from the ailment have trouble empathizing with other people's feelings and understanding such nonverbal modes of expression as facial expressions. They often display odd speech patterns—repeating words or phrases and speaking in a flat, emotionless voice. They appear to lack "common sense" as they engage in such repetitive behaviors as hand wringing, finger tapping, or incessantly watching spinning objects. Although Asperger's syndrome is related to autism, it is not marked by the language and learning problems of autism. Instead, Aperger's victims are usually of average or above-average intelligence, so they appear to others to be both "bright enough" and "pretty weird."

During lunch hour at a junior high school, a teacher ordered three boys to stop taunting a schoolmate who sat at a table in the corner of the cafeteria. The schoolmate was a 13-year-old boy who suffered from Asperger's syndrome. In his distress over the taunting, the boy was rubbing his palms back and forth on the table and seemed near tears. The teacher took him to her classroom to relax until the end of the lunch period. She later asked the school psychologist what might be done to help the youth. The psychologist suggested counseling sessions, because Asperger's-syndrome youths often profit from either individual or small-group psychotherapy designed to help them understand and cope with the sorts of social situations which, to them, seem incomprehensible.

Cultural Traits

For present purposes, *culture* can be defined as a collection of attitudes and habits held in common by members of a group. In popular parlance, such groups are often identified by ethnic, social-class, religious, locality, or gender labels, or by some combination of designators—Muslim women, Latino Catholics, Chinese Buddhists, Laotian men, small-town Bible-belt Whites, inner-city Blacks, reservation Navajos. Cultural habits can become part of a student's personality. Among a group's cultural traits are beliefs about proper and improper social behavior, including behavior at school. In America's multicultural society, those beliefs can differ significantly from one group to another, resulting in conflicts about what sorts of behavior at school qualify as violence and about what treatments are appropriate for offenders.

A fifth-grade girl whose family had recently immigrated from the Samoan Islands was accused of stealing three textbooks. After the books were missing from the classroom shelf, a schoolmate reported seeing the Samoan girl carrying the texts home. When the principal learned of the episode, she said that her acquaintance with Samoan culture suggested that the apparent theft might well be a case of cultural misunderstanding. She explained that traditional Samoa had been a communal society in which people were free to use items that belonged to the village as a whole. After the islands had been taken over as an American colony at the beginning of the twentieth century, many of the original traditions remained. Thus, the principal asked the girl's parents to visit the school along with their daughter so they could learn the school rule that forbade pupils from taking classroom books home without permission.

A Question to Ask Oneself

Which characteristics of the offender should influence the choice of treatment, and why are such characteristics important in this case?

Environmental Conditions

Environmental conditions are ones that surround a violent episode or its participants. Thus, the response chosen as appropriate for an episode can be affected by a participant's family background or companions, by the place in which the episode occurred, by the composition of the school population, and by mass-communication media.

Family Influences

Families can differ markedly in their ability and willingness to play a consistent, constructive role in guiding the school behavior of their children and youths. A teacher's, administrator's, or judge's estimate of family members' child-rearing skills and dedication can influence the choice of a treatment that shows promise of success.

For instance, consider how two 16-year-olds—Students A and B who sprayed a high school library with fire extinguisher dust—might be treated differently because of their family situations.

Student A's parents are married and have three children. The father is an insurance agent and the mother a nurse and vice president of an elementary school PTA. Both are appalled at their son's library prank. They immediately confiscate his driver's license and order him to be home every night for the next month instead of out with friends. The juvenile court judge who handles the case orders the 16-year-old to pay half the cost of cleaning up the library and also sentences him to 2 months in juvenile hall. But instead of implementing the sentence, the judge places the boy on probation and turns him over to his parents. If the youth is involved in no misdeeds for a period of 1 year, he will not be required to serve the 2 months in juvenile hall.

Not only were Student B's parents never married, but Student B has never known his father. Instead, he has been living with his mother whose live-in male friend has been in and out of jail on drug charges. Student B and his mother's male friend have fought on numerous occasions, with the result that Student B has spent much of his time on the streets. He is often absent from school. The juvenile court judge, informed about such family conditions, sends the youth to a juvenile detention facility hall for 2 months, with the sentence to begin immediately and to include counseling sessions.

Companions' Influence

Particularly during the teenage years, the nature of students' companions can influence the treatments suggested for offenders. Judging the role that companions played in an act of violence is especially important when a teacher, administrator, or court assigns blame for the act, because a decision about who-was-to-blame can affect the choice of treatment.

"She probably wouldn't even have started the fight if the crowd hadn't urged her on."

As six members of a high school football team were crossing the parking lot of a shopping mall, they exchanged insults with a member of a rival team who had just alighted from a car.

The six challenged the lad from the rival team to a "fair fight," with the youngest of the six assigned the task of battling the rival. The assigned youth was reluctant to fight, but he was urged on by the older players taunting him, charging that he would be "chicken" if he failed to fight. The resulting battle brought the police, who arrested the two combatants. At the juvenile court trial hearing, the judge listened to witnesses' versions of the event, then let the youth from the rival team go free and recommended that the local high school football coach deny the youngest team member as well as his five teammates the chance to play in the school's next three football games.

On the playground during a middle-school's lunch period, an eighth-grade boy continued poking a smaller seventh-grader until another seventh-grader intervened and punched the eighth-grader until he fell to the ground. A teacher, drawn to the fight by the sight of students clustered around the combatants, stopped the fight and marched the pair to the principal's office. The principal listened to the antagonists' versions of the episode and to the opinions of students who had witnessed to the event. He then (a) briefly admonished the boy who had come to his bullied classmate's rescue and suggested that the boy try more peaceful means of settling disputes in the future; and (b) assigned the eighth-grader 2 days of after-school detention for bullying the younger schoolmate.

Setting of the Violence

The location of a violent act may influence the treatment of offenders because of how misbehavior in such a place may violate school rules or how the setting relates to the school's jurisdiction.

When a high school history teacher left the classroom to usher a cursing student to the principal's office, two girls in the class started fighting, pushing each other over desks, pulling hair, scratching, and tearing clothes as several classmates cheered them on and two others ran from the room to find a security guard. When the guard entered the room, he separated the combatants and escorted them to the dean of girls' office. The dean suspended the pair from school for 2 weeks, pending a hearing at which they would likely be expelled.

After school let out in the afternoon, two ninth-grade girls injured a classmate by attacking her at a city bus stop half a block from the junior high school. The injured girl was taken to the school nurse to be treated for abrasions on her knees, which had been scraped when her assailants knocked her down and dragged her across the sidewalk. The girl's parents demanded that the school punish the attackers. However, school officials said the bus stop was out of their jurisdiction, so the school could not legally punish the pair. The parents would need to take their complaint to the police, who might charge the attackers with battery.

School Population

Student populations can vary in significant ways. A school may be ethnically homogeneous—enrolling mostly Latinos or Blacks or Whites. Or it may be highly heterogeneous—a mixture of Asians, Latinos, Blacks, Pacific Islanders, and Whites. The school may draw the majority of its students from (a) a socially deteriorated, crime-ridden inner city, (b) a rural village, (c) an upper-class suburb, (c) a vacation-resort community, (d) an Indian reservation, or some other sort of locality.

Any particular student may either "fit in well" (or at least "moderately well") with the majority of schoolmates or may be "a misfit." How well a student melds into the mix can affect both (a) the likelihood that he or she will act violently and (b) the type of violence committed.

In high-crime-rate section of a large city, a teenager was caught trying to steal the radio from a faculty member's car in the school parking lot. When asked his reason for the attempted theft, he said the leaders of the street gang that he belonged to had told him to steal the radio. When asked why he had joined the gang in the first place, he said that being in a gang was the only protection he had from being tormented by members of other gangs.

At a rural village public high school, a girl who had torn down posters from corridor walls was charged with vandalism by school officials. The posters had advertised a school-assembly character-development program to be presented by an evangelical Christian group sponsored by a local church. When officials informed the girl's parents of the incident, the parents said that they not only approved of their daughter's action but that they had encouraged her to remove the posters. The parents contended that the planned assembly program violated the first amendment to the U.S. Constitution that required the separation of church and state. They complained that students at the school had taunted their daughter because she, like her parents, was not a Christian but, rather, was an atheist whom schoolmates called "devil worshipper" and "hell cat."

Communication Media

A large body of evidence supports the contention that the great quantity of violence on television, in movies, in video games, and on Internet Web sites contributes to violent behavior by children and youths.

The three major effects of seeing violence on television are:

- Children may become less sensitive to the pain and suffering of others.
- Children may be more fearful of the world around them.
- Children may be more likely to behave aggressively toward others.

The average American child will have watched 100,000 acts of televised violence, including 8,000 depictions of murder, by the time he or she finishes sixth grade. (Children and television violence, 2005)

School and juvenile court personnel may be influenced by such evidence when they propose treatments for students found guilty of violent acts.

In the case of a 10-year-old boy who was arrested for trying to garrote a schoolmate with a leather thong in a fashion he had seen in a video game, a juvenile court social worker recommended that boy's parents confiscate his collection of violent video games and monitor what he watched on television.

A Question to Ask Oneself

Which features of the environment are important to consider when selecting a treatment, and why are those features important in this case?

Collateral Damage

The expressions *collateral damage* and *undesired side effects* refer to unintended, unwanted harm that can result from a particular treatment. Such damage can occur to the perpetrator of violence, to direct victims, or to individuals and groups incidentally associated with the violence episode. People who plan treatments are wise to attempt, as far as possible, to avoid collateral damage or at least reduce it to a minimum. If such damage seems inevitable, then the positive influence of the treatment should outweigh the undesired side effects.

Perpetrators of Violence

A high school girl is suspended from school for fighting, so she misses class sessions that prepare students for statewide tests.

A seventh-grade boy is sent to an alternative middle school for stealing classmates' goods on three occasions. At the alternative school he is enticed into using marijuana and cocaine by companions he meets there.

A 10-year-old who set a fire in the elementary school office during a Sunday morning vandalism escapade is expelled from school, which means he returns to the care of his family—a family in which the father is in prison for robbery, the mother is a drug addict, and an older brother is on parole after being in jail for sexual assault.

Direct Victims of Violence

To relieve a sixth-grade girl from constant bullying, the middle school principal transfers her to a distant school. However, the transfer means that the girl is separated from school friends, must adjust to different teachers, and must travel to the new school on a city bus each day.

Associated Individuals and Groups

Frequently, punishment imposed on offenders is intended not only to discourage them from committing the same offense in the future but is also meant to deter other people from trying the same violent act. However, the hoped-for deterrent effect can fail if the punishment is not consistently applied.

A newly hired fifth-grade teacher, after having difficulty maintaining order in her class, warned the pupils that anyone who disrupted the class with silly or rude remarks, or anyone who interrupted her when she was speaking, would be sent to the principal's office. After mid-morning recess, six students in quick succession interrupted the teacher or made ridiculous comments. Because the teacher feared that it would look strange to the office staff to have six disobedient pupils appear all at once, she warned the class that the next time they disobeyed, she really would send them to the office. Several pupils giggled. The teacher pretended not to hear the giggles.

Questions to Ask Oneself

- For different potential treatments of offenders, their victims, or other people, what undesired consequences might result?
- How might such collateral damage be avoided or at least minimized?

Two Sample Cases

With the contents of the foregoing section in mind, consider the following pair of hypothetical cases of violence that are intended to illustrate a suggested thought process that leads to the choice of a treatment. The description of each case is divided into three phases: (a) the type of violence, (b) conditions influencing the selection of a treatment, and (c) the treatment that is chosen. For convenience of presentation, the influential conditions bear the labels (in *italics*) of the categories used for organizing the present chapter. I am not assuming that a teacher, administrator, or counselor would necessarily think of conditions in the order in which they are listed in the three cases. Instead, I believe the process of weighing conditions is likely to involve considering the various conditions in a rather random order. But what is important, I believe, is that all potentially influential circumstances be taken into account.

Internet Hit List

Type of Violence

A 15-year-old girl was arrested for anonymously posting a hit list of eight schoolmates and one teacher on an Internet Web site. The message warned, "Beware! You die for your sins." The author of the threat was discovered by a computer technician identifying which school computer had been used for sending the message and by discovering the time the threat had been composed—a time when the girl was scheduled to use the computer. A file in the computer held a copy of the threat. The police took the girl into custody on a charge of endangering others.

Likely Influential Conditions

Seriousness of consequences. The degree of harm from the threat would depend on whether the girl had formulated a specific plan and had prepared the means (skills, equipment) for carrying out the intended attack.

Permissible treatment options. Confinement in a juvenile detention facility, suspension (at home or in a detention room at school), expulsion from school, transfer to a different school, probation, counseling, work assignment, or a reprimand.

Treatment purpose. The dual aim would be to (a) prevent the girl from issuing threats in the future and (b) dissuade other students from making cyber threats.

Offender's characteristics.

Age. At age 15, the girl should have been old enough to know that what she had done was seriously wrong.

Motive. When police first accused the girl of posting the threat, she denied being the author. But after the evidence against her was laid out in detail, she confessed. When asked why she had threatened those particular eight schoolmates, she said the eight girls had never let her join any of their activities. "And I know they whispered things about me." She said she had included the teacher because "She's real mean. She gave me low grades I didn't deserve." When the girl was asked how she planned to harm the intended victims, she said that she didn't actually mean to do anything. "I just wanted to scare them. They deserved it."

Character. Two teachers—including the one on the hit list—reported that the girl occasionally offered hard-to-believe excuses for not handing in homework. One teacher described the girl as "morose and uncooperative." However, the girl's record of behavior at school was essentially clean. She was not a truant, she had not disrupted classes, and there was no evidence that she was a thief. The cyber threat was the only instance of serious misconduct.

Appearance. The girl had quite noticeable facial acne, and she dressed in a less stylish fashion than the girls on her hit list.

Mental ability. Both of the teachers judged the girl to be of average ability, although prone to put minimal effort into class assignments—"just enough to barely get by."

Environmental conditions.

Family. The girl's father was an auto mechanic of Irish heritage, and her mother a housewife of Korean ancestry. Their two sons were a few years older than their daughter. All members of the family were Catholics, though they rarely attended church. When a police officer first told the parents about the hit list, they said they couldn't believe their daughter would do such a thing, so the school must have made a mistake. But when informed that the girl had confessed, the parents said they would agree to whatever reasonable punishment the school or juvenile court would propose.

The parents gave the police permission to search the girl's room for evidence bearing on the cyber threat. The police found nothing related to the threat. There were no journals with plans for an attack and no equipment useful for harming to others, such as a gun, knife, poison, or bomb-making materials.

Companions. According to her teachers, the girl was "a loner," seldom seen spending time with schoolmates.

School population. Ethnically, the great majority of the school's pupils were second- or third-generation Latinos. The rest of the student body was made up of Whites, Blacks, Asians, and youths of mixed ethnic heritage. Seven of the eight girls on the hit list were Latinos. The eighth was of combined Black/White parentage. The school drew most of its enrollment from middle-class families.

The Selected Treatment

The line of reasoning—including collateral damage. The following is an estimate of the way that a juvenile court judge, with the concurrence of school officials, might arrive at a disposition of the cyber-threat case.

Because the girl apparently did not intend to carry out the implied attack, the treatment should not be as punitive or as drastic as if she had prepared an attack plan and the means to implement it. In addition, she had no record of serious misconduct in the past, so she would not be regarded as having a chronically "bad character." The girl's father and mother appeared to be responsible, caring parents, so removing the girl from their home and placing her either in a foster home or in a juvenile detention center did not seem appropriate. Still, the girl would need to face consequences sufficiently aversive to dissuade her from sending cyber threats again. Expelling her from school, an action inevitably accompanied by embarrassing disgrace, might well serve as such a deterrent. The troubles she faced upon her arrest could also serve as a restraint. However, expulsion would defeat the essential purpose of schooling—that of giving each young person a fair chance to succeed in life. Thus, the expulsion could appropriately take the form of transferring the offender to another high school.

If she were transferred to an alternative school designed for students who were "misfits" in regular schools, then the girl might be enticed into further delinquency by some of the "misfits" there. Hence, sending her to a regular high school might be a better choice. However, simply transferring her would likely not be sufficient for solving some of the underlying problems that apparently motivated her to launch the threat—such problems as her unsuccessful attempt to be included in admired schoolmates' activities, her lack of friends, and her failure to complete class assignments promptly. Therefore, the transfer should be accompanied by counseling that would address those problems. Her parents could be advised to consult a dermatologist about the girl's acne, and a counselor could provide the girl an opportunity to vent her concerns, to discuss how personal attire can affect teenage friendships, to consider ways of attracting and maintaining friends, and to establish a better system for completing class assignments. The counseling could start as once-a-week sessions and continue as long as the girl and her counselor believed the sessions were productive.

Leaving the girl in her present school and offering her counseling there would not be a viable option. The disgrace and embarrassment resulting from her arrest would simply increase rejection and taunting by schoolmates.

The aim of deterring other students from posting cyber threats would likely be furthered by news of the expulsion in (a) an article in the city newspaper about the incident (with the offender's name omitted because she was a minor) and (b) gossip spread through the school's informal rumor network.

Computer Theft

Type of Violence

A man walking his dog late at night past a middle school thought he saw the beam of a flashlight moving about in a classroom. He called the police on his cell phone. When the police arrived, they entered the school by a side door that was ajar and caught two boys removing laptop computers from classrooms. The thieves were 16-year-old high school youths who had been loading computers into a car they had parked behind the school. They already had twelve computers in the car and were in the process of collecting several more. The computers were valued at about $1,000 each.

Likely Influential Conditions

For the purpose of analyzing this case, the two 16-years-olds will be referred to as Youth-A and Youth-B.

Seriousness of consequences. If the theft had succeeded, the school would have lost more than $12,000, and the educational program for students who needed the computers for their school assignments would have been disrupted.

Permissible treatment options. In the criminal-justice system, the treatment options for the juvenile court judge who would rule in the case would include (a) sending the youths to a juvenile detention center for up to a year because the value of the computers made the crime grand theft rather than petty theft, (b) assessing a fine up to $1,000, (c) placing the youths on probation, or (d) requiring the youths to undergo counseling. In addition to the court's treatment, the school could also impose such sanctions as (a) suspending the pair from school for a period of time, (b) expelling them, (c) requiring that they perform tasks (clean up the school grounds, work in the cafeteria, or the like), (d) removing privileges (drive cars to school, attend parties, dances, or athletic events), or (e) requiring that the pair attend counseling sessions.

Treatment purpose. The three-part goal would be to (a) prevent the youths from stealing school property, (b) encourage them to avoid other sorts of misbehavior at schools, and (c) warn other students of the dire consequences of attempting to steal school property.

Offenders' characteristics.

Age. Sixteen-year-olds would know that stealing school property was against the law. Thus, their act would qualify as malicious behavior rather than innocently uninformed behavior.

Motive. The two teenagers were questioned separately by the police who asked them why they tried to steal the computers. What was their intent?

Youth-A said, "I don't know." When the interrogator told him he could save himself from serious consequences if he answered the question truthfully the boy persisted in saying, "I don't know."

In contrast, when Youth-B was questioned in the same way, he broke down and said Youth-A had planned the theft so they could sell the computers and get money for drugs and "to date girls." When asked what kind of drugs, he answered, "Marijuana, angel dust, and LSD." Youth-B claimed he had never broken the law before, but he said Youth-A had often stolen in order to buy drugs. Youth-B added that Youth-A had called him a coward if he wouldn't go along with the computer-theft plan; he had agreed to participate so as not to lose Youth-A's friendship.

After Youth-A was told what Youth-B had reported, Youth-A said, "He's a liar. Taking the computers was his idea. Maybe he uses drugs; I don't."

Character. When a social worker from the juvenile court inspected the two students' academic and behavior records at the high school and spoke with several teachers, she learned that:

Youth-A earned average marks in his studies. He was known for playing practical jokes and ridiculing classmates and staff members. He was often absent from classes.

Youth-B earned average marks in his studies. He was "polite and respectful around teachers."

Appearance. The social worker noted that the boys were both "rather ordinary looking white kids, dressed much the same as most of their schoolmates."

Mental ability. Youth-A's aptitude-test scores and his witty comments during class discussions suggested that his mental abilities were well above average. His marginally acceptable academic marks appeared to result from a lack of diligence in completing school assignments.

Youth-B's aptitude-test scores and his typical performance in class suggested that he was average in academic potential so that average school marks were what would be expected if he was working industriously.

Cultural traits. Both boys' home language was "middle-class American English." Their ancestors had come from Western Europe and were Christians, at least nominally.

Environmental conditions.

Family. Youth-A was the only child of a real-estate broker and his wife. The wife spent much of her time as a volunteer at the regional history museum and the city's rape-crisis center. The social worker reported that the parents were "financially very well off." When the son turned age 16, his parents gave him a new sports car as a birthday present. When the police told the father about his son's arrest, the father said, "I knew something like this would happen. With all the stuff he's been doing, I knew he would end up getting caught in some stunt." The mother said of her son, "I don't understand him at all anymore. We've done everything we could for him."

Youth-B was the youngest son of a restaurant chef and his wife. The wife worked at the restaurant as a waitress and accountant. The couple had an older daughter and older son, both living away from home. On weekends, Youth-B often worked at the restaurant as a busboy. In response to the news of his son's arrest, Youth-B's father said, "That's not the kind of boy he is. It's hanging around with that smart-ass rich kid that's done it. There'll be no more of that. After school's he'll come to the restaurant to work." Youth-B's mother wept and shook her head when told of the theft attempt.

The social worker reported that both of the 16-year-olds were what sociologists describe as "latch-key children"—ones whose parents were away from home at the end of the school day so there was no after-school parental supervision.

Companions. Youth-A had many acquaintances but few close friends. Over the past 2 months, he and Youth-B had spent much of their leisure time together, usually riding around in Youth-A's car, often with a girl or two.

School population. In terms of ethnicity and socioeconomic status, the students who attended the high school were predominantly White and, in terms of social class, were of middle-class and upper-middle-class status. Thus, the two computer thieves were part of the school's ethnic and socioeconomic majority.

The Selected Treatment

The line of reasoning—including collateral damage. The following is my speculation about how a juvenile court judge and school principal might decide what to do about the two 16-year-olds.

First, the judge's thought sequence. In view of the parents' comments about their sons, Youth-B's version of how and why the theft was planned seems believable. But because there's no corroborating evidence, we really don't know that Youth-A deserves the chief blame for the incident. However, the fact that Youth-A is frequently truant at school but Youth-B has a clean attendance record suggests that Youth-A has less regard for living by official rules than does Youth-B. Neither boy has been in trouble with the police before, so they aren't recidivists.

One thing the treatment needs to do is to punish the two enough to make them realize they made a very serious mistake in stealing the computers. In effect, they need to be frightened out of trying such a deed again. And it appears that the parents need some help in monitoring and guiding the sons' behavior. Youth-B's father offered a constructive suggestion—having the boy work at the restaurant after school. But Youth-A's parents were perhaps at a loss in deciding how to handle their son. The treatment should recognize that it's important for the boys to continue their schooling.

In light of the above considerations, here is what I plan. To make the pair realize the seriousness of their crime, they will be sentenced to a full year at a juvenile detention center. However, in order to give them a chance to continue their schooling and earn reduced time for good behavior, they will actually need to spend only 1 month in juvenile hall, then be free on probation for the remaining 11 months of the sentence. The 1 month in detention will demonstrate what life is like in a juvenile facility—a warning of what they will experience for an entire year if they fail to abide by the law during the 11-month probation period. Throughout that period, they will need to report to a probation officer once every 2 weeks. After the month in juvenile hall, they will return to school, either to their original school or to another of their choice. Because students and teachers in their original school will know—at least via rumors—that the two had been arrested, the boys may feel sufficiently uncomfortable there that they will want to transfer to a different high school. That will be allowed, if they so choose. The disposition of the case will also provide for a court social worker to confer with the boys' parents about what measures they intend to adopt in correcting their sons' behavior. The social worker will be expected to establish a verbal contract with the parents regarding those measures and to offer whatever advice or aid the parents seem to need to accomplish the goal of rehabilitating the youths.

Next, the high school principal's thought sequence. The court's required 1 month in juvenile hall will serve as an automatic 1-month suspension from school. When the boys return to school, they will be told that any unexcused absences or any infractions of other school rules will be reported to their probation officer and could result in their having to serve the entire year locked up in a detention center.

CONCLUSION

The purpose of this chapter has been to suggest a pattern of thought that might guide school personnel, juvenile justice personnel, or parents in their search for how to treat the perpetrators and victims of violence in schools. That pattern is founded on the conviction that treatments should be adjusted to accommodate for significant variables that make one case of violence different from another, such variables as (a) the available treatment options, (b) the seriousness of the violent act, (c) the treatment's aim, (d) an offender's personal characteristics, (e) victims of the act, and (f) the environment surrounding the particular case.

References

Abelard. (2005). *Children and television violence*. Available online: http://www.abelard. org/tv/tv.htm.

Abuse charges against ex-teacher are upgraded. (2003, November 12). *Miami Herald*. Available online: http://www.miami.com/mld/miamiherald/news/state/ 7238443.htm.

Accuser in notorious case of preschool abuse admits lying. (2005, November 3). *San Luis Obispo Tribune*, B4.

Ackard, D., & Neumark-Sztainer, D. (2001, August 26). One out of ten female adolescents experience date violence or rape. *American Psychological Association online*. Available online: http://www.apa.org/releases/dateviolence.html.

Actual hazing cases. (2005). *Respect the game—RTG*. Available online: http://www. ohsaa.org/RTG/Resources/hazing/Cases.htm.

Adams, J. (2005, October 21). More abuse reports at Bloomington school. *Minneapolis Star Tribune*. Available online: http://www.startribune.com/stories/ 462/4165844.html.

Adams, J., & Wascoe, D. (2005, May 19). Waconia suspect, 17, was angry, data show. *Minneapolis Star Tribune*. Available online: http://www.startribune.com/ stories/462/5411592.html.

A deadly trip. (2000, April 11). *PBS News Hour*. Available online: http://www.pbs. org/newshour/extra/features/jan-june00/ghb.html.

Aguilar, A. (2003, October 31). Fighting students will face police in Venice schools. *St. Louis Post-Dispatch*. Available online: http://www.stltoday.com/ stltday/news/stories.nsf/News/St.+Louis+City+%2F+County/ A630B3DB4DC5CDE286256DD0004A6541?OpenDocment&Headline= Fighting+students+will+face+police+in+Venice+schools.

Alfonso, C. (2003, December 17). Guidelines issued for school use of video cameras. *Globe and Mail*. Available online: http://www.globeandmail.ca/servlet/ ArticleNews/ TPStory/LAC/ 20031217/VIDEO17/TPEducation/.

Alice Maxwell. Elementary School, Sparks, Nevada. (2005, March 24). *Violence in our schools.* Available online: http://www.columbine-angels.com/Shootings-2005-2009.htm.

Alito, S. A., Jr. (2001, February 14). *Saxe v. State College Area School District.* Available online: http://www.ca3.uscourts.gov/opinarch/994081.txt.

Amrhein, S. (2004, September 1). Ex-PTA head charged in $13,000 theft. *St. Petersburgh Times.* Available online: http://www.sptimes.com/2004/09/01/Hillsborough/Ex_PTA_head_charged_i.shtml.

Andersen, A. A. (2005, March 21). Benchmarking school security of the District of Columbia public schools. *DCWatch.* Available online: http://www.dcwatch.com/govern/ig050321.htm.

Anderson, C. A. (2003, October). Violent video games: Myths, facts, and unanswered questions. *Psychological Science Agenda*, 16(5). Available online: http://www.apa.org/science/psa/sb-anderson.html.

Ataiyero, K. T. (2005, January 5). Student faces threat charges. *Raleigh News-Observer.* Available online: http://www.newsobserver.com/news/story/1985285p-8367992c.html.

Atkins, K. (2005a, September 14). Parents claim teacher restrained kid. *Boston Herald.* Available online: http://news.bostonherald.com/localRegional/view.bg?articleid=102445.

Atkins, K. (2005b, October 16). Girl fights pack punch: Concern runs high among parents, teachers. *Boston Herald.* Available online: http://news.bostonherald.com/localRegional/view.bg?articleid=107265.

Ave, M. (2003, September 28). Bullied or not, Alexa's fear is all too familiar to many kids. *St. Petersburg Times.* Available online: http://www.sptimes.com/2003/09/28/Tampabay/Bullied_or_not_Alexa.shtml.

Baird, G. (2005, October 7). Parma firefighter accused of flashing schoolgirls. *The Plain Dealer.* Available online: http://www.cleveland.com/news/plaindealer/index.ssf?/base/cuyahoga/1128677950307921.xml&coll=2.

Baker, A. (1996, September 12). Instrument theft at school. *Point Reyes Light.* Available online: http://www.ptreyeslight.com/stories/sep12/dixie.html.

Banducci, E., Carreon, C., & Suryaraman, M. (2004, February 4). Student to face bomb plot charges. *San Jose Mercury News.* Available online: http://www.mercurynews.com/mld/mercurynews/news/local/7870862.htm/.

Banks, R. (1997). Bullying in schools. *ERIC Digest.* Available online: http://www.ericfacility.net/ericdigests/ed407154.html.

Banks, S., & Shields, N. (2005, July 6). Searching for lessons in Jefferson High melee. *Los Angeles Times.* Available online: http://www.latimes.com/news/local/la-me-jefferson6jul06,0,6512314.story?page=1&coll=la-home-headlines.

Barakat, M. (2004, March 18). Teenager battles his expulsion. *Richmond Times-Dispatch.* Available online:http://www.timesdispatch.com/servlet/Satellite?pagename=RTD%2FMGArticle%2FRTD_BasicArticle&c=MGArticle&cid=1031774363460&path=%21news&s=1045855934842.

Barayuga, D. (2003, May 28). Ex-bank exec gets probation in child sex assault. *Honolulu Star-Bulletin.* Available online: http://starbuletin.com/2003/05/28/news/story8.html.

Barnett, L. (2003, April 24). Student allegedly kills principal, self. *WGAL.* Available online: http://www.wgal.com/news/2155452/detail.html.

Barnhardt, L. (2003, June 6). Franklin Middle School teacher charged with having sex with pupil. *Baltimore Sun*. Available online: http://www.sunspot.net/news/education/bal-md.teacher06jun06,0,4809610.story?coll=bal-education-top.

Barry Goldwater High School. (2005). *Discipline and guideline procedures*. Available online: http://bghs.dvusd.org/rules_regulations/handbook_08.html.

Basehor-Linwood Public Schools. (2005). *Bus discipline regulations*. Available online: http://www.usd458.k12.ks.us/gres/handbook/busdiscipline.

Belcher, S. C. (2005). Tools for reducing school violence. *Teaching to change Los Angeles*. Available online: http://tcla.ucla.edu/reportcard/features/5-6/astor.html.

Biggs, P. (2003, December 9). Ex-teacher arrested in abuse of girl. *Arizona Republic*. Available online: http://www.azcentral.com/arizonarepublic/local/articles/1209tempearrest09.html.

Bir, P. (2004, February 19). Allegation against teacher continues to be investigated. *Indianapolis Star*. Available online: http://www.indystar.com/articles/9/121999–7049–009.html.

Blaha, K., & Adams, B. (2001, September 6). *Warning signs for school violence*. Available online: http://www.nwrel.org/comm/monthly/warning.html.

Boca Raton high school eases penalties for students' swearing. (2005, September 28). *Miami Herald*. Available online: http://www.miami.com/mld/miamiherald/news/state/12762036.htm.

Bomb survey. (2000). *Jefferson County Sheriff's Department*. Available online: http://www.cnn.com/SPECIALS/2000/Columbine.cd/Pages/BOMBS_TEXT.htm.

Bombs and school security. (2005). Available online: http://www.schoolsecurity.org/trends/school-bombs.html.

Bowie, L. (2005, November 30). A conflict over the pledge. *Baltimore Sun*. Available online: http://www.baltimoresun.com/news/education/bal-md.pledge30nov30,1,5857059.story?coll=bal-pe-maryland.

Boyd, C. (2003, December 10). Arden Hills: Bomb threat ends school early. *Pioneer Press*. Available online: http://www.twincities.com/mld/pioneerpress/7454308.htm.

Boys slapped with felonies in bus fight. (2005, May 23). *Washington Post*. Available online: http://www.washingtonpost.com/wpdyn/content/article/2005/05/23/AR2005052300488.html.

Brown, M. D. (2005, May 3). *National arson awareness week begins*. Available online: http://firechief.com/awareness/arson-aware ness-week 050205/.

Buchanan, W. (2004, December 17). Teacher is arrested in child porn probe. *San Francisco Chronicle*. Available online: http://www.sfgate.com/cgi-bin/article.cgi?f=/c/a/2004/12/17/BAGA6ACKUJ1.DTL&hw=Buchanan+child+porn&sn=002&sc=704.

Bullied Kansas teen wins $440K settlement. (2005, December 23). *Seattle Post-Intelligencer*. Available online: http://seattlepi.nwsource.com/national/1110AP_School_Bullying.html.

Bullying: What is bullying? (2005). *About*. Available online: http://homeworktips.about.com/library/weekly/aa011999.htm.

Bullying case costs Oregon school district $10,000. (2004, January 18). *Seattle Times*. Available online: http://seattletimes.nwsource.com/html/education/2001839182_bullying18.html.

Burnett, G., & Walz, G. (1994, July). Gangs in the schools. *ERIC Digest 99*. Available online: http://www.ericdigests.org/1995–1/gangs.htm.

Burwell High School. (2004). *Student handbook—2004–2005*. Available online: *Early warning, timely response: A guide to safe schools.*

Bustamante, M. (2005, January 26). Aftermath of school vandalism: Harmony restored. *Tucson Citizen*. Available online: http://www.tucsoncitizen.com/index.php?page=local&story_id=012604a5_rogers_update.

Cadiz, L. (2005, September 17). Ex-secretary in Howard charged in theft of $10,000 from school. *Baltimore Sun*. Available online: http://www.baltimoresun.com/news/education/balmd.ho.embezzle17sep17,1,5765197.story?coll=bal-education-k12.

Calgary boy fights to wear makeup to school. (2004, March 10). *The Cannon*. Available online: http://www.thecannon.ca/news_details.php?id=942.

Cardman, M. (2003, October 28). School violence rate leveled off since 2000. *Education Daily*, 36(201), 1.

Carr, C. (2004, June 23). Valley Center: A stunned community reacts to school vandalism. *North County Times*. Available online: http://www.nctimes.com/articles/2004/06/24/news/columnists/carr/22_14_306_23_04.txt.

Carreon, C. (2004, February 11). Arrest in threats at S.J. school. *San Jose Mercury News*. Available online: www.macon.com/mld/mercury news/news/local/7.

Carter, S. (2003, November 7). School officials use tools to halt violence, threats. *Oregonian*. Available online: http://www.oregonlive.com/news/oregonian/index.ssf?/base/news/106812414083310.xml.

Cauchon, D. (1999, April 13). Zero-tolerance policies lack flexibility. *USA Today*. Available online: http://www.usatoday.com/educate/ednews3.htm.

Cauvin, H. E., & Haynes, V. D. (2005, March 1). Second teen charged in spreading mercury. *Washington Post*. Available online: http://www.washingtonpost.com/wp-dyn/articles/A61802–2005Feb28.html.

Center for Effective Discipline. (2005). *Discipline at school*. Available online: http://www.stophitting.com/disatschool/100largest.php.

Center for Safe and Responsible Internet Use. (2005). *Mobilizing educators, parents, students, and others to combat online social cruelty*. Available online: http://www.cyberbully.org/.

Chang, A. L. (2005, June 9). Principal testifies against student in assault case. *Milwaukee Journal-Sentinel*. Available online: http://www.jsonline.com/news/racine/jun05/332635.asp.

Chellappa, V. (2004, February 19). Sherwood High School vandalized. *Silver Chips*. Available online: http://silverchips.mbhs.edu/inside. php?sid=2990.

Cheerleaders disciplined for putting feces on pizza. (2005, June 16). *Houston Chronicle*. http://www.chron.com/cs/CDA/ssistory.mpl/metropolitan/3227978.

Child abuse: Types, signs, symptoms, causes, and help. (2005). *Helpguide*. Available online: http://www.helpguide.org/mental/child_abuse_physical_emotional_sexual_neglect.htm.

Child abuse and neglect: Information for school employees. (2005). Denver: Colorado Department of Education.

Child maltreatment 2003—Summary of key findings. (2005). Washington, DC: National Clearinghouse on Child Abuse and Neglect Information. Available online: http://nccanch.acf.hhs.gov/pubs/factsheets/canstats.cfm.

Child pornography. (2005). *Wikipedia*. Available online: http://en.wikipedia.org/wiki/Child_pornography.

Child prostitution. (2004). *Children of the Night*. Available online: http://www.childrenofthenight.org/faq.html.

Child sexual abuse: What it is and how to prevent it. (1990). *Eric Digest*. Available online: http://www.ericdigests.org/pre-9217/sexual.htm.

Children and television violence. (2005). *Abelard*. Available online: http://www.abelard.org/tv/tv.htm.

Chu, D. (2005, September 15). School theft. *Youth Radio*. Available online: http://www.youthradio.org/education/kcbs2003_theft.Shtml.

Chute, E. (2005, May 17). Preschool expulsion rate triple K-12 rate, study says. *Pittsburgh Post-Gazette*. Available online: http://www.post-gazette.com/pg/05137/505593.stm.

Clarridge, C. (2005, October 3). New lawsuit alleges sex abuse at school. *Seattle Times*. Available online: http://seattletimes.nwsource.com/html/education/2002536131_briscoe03m.html.

Clemens, H. (2005). *School violence hotline—Missouri*. Available online: http://www.schoolviolencehotline.com/.

Code of conduct. (2005, December 2). *LaSalle Elementary School Website*. Available online: http://lasalle.lbpsb.qc.ca/conductsr.htm.

Cohen, J. (2000, January 30). Date-rape drug trial to start. *Detroit News*. Available online: http://www.detnews.com/2000/metro/0001/30/01300014.htm.

Colchester student shot by pellet gun, police say. (2005, March 17). *Burlington Free Press*. Available online: http://www.burlingtonfreepress.com/towns/colchester/12.htm.

Colias, M. (2005, April 27). Black student charged with racial threats. *Boston Globe*. Available online: http://www.boston.com/news/education/higher/articles/2005/04/27/black_student_charged_with_racial_threats/.

Collom, L. (2004, December 23). Two students are arrested in 9/11 hoax. *Arizona Republic*. Available online: http://www.azcentral.com/arizonarepublic/local/articles/1223EVhoax23.html.

Colorado Bureau of Investigation. (2005). *Things you should know about sexual offending*. Available online: http://sor.state.co.us/you.should.know.htm.

Colorado Department of Public Safety. (2003, December). *Reference guide for school personnel concerning juveniles who have committed sexually abusive and offensive behavior*. Denver, CO: Author.

Colorado Springs School District. (2003, August). *Student discipline regulations*. Available online: http://www.d11.org/boe/policies/jk-r.htm.

Columbine High School massacre. (2005). *Wikipedia*. Available online: http://en.wikipedia.org/wiki/Columbine_High_School_massacre.

Committee for Children. (2005). *Facts about bullying, school violence, and child abuse*. Available online: http://www.cfchildren.org/aboutf/mediaf/factsstats.

Constitutional Rights Foundation. (2005). *The challenge of school violence*. Available online: http://www.crf-usa.org/violence/school.html.

Cops say teen tried hacking into server. (2005, May 22). *Chicago Tribune*. Available online: http://www.chicagotribune.com/business/content/education/chi-0505220477may22,1,7488378.story?coll=chi-education-hed&ctrack=1&cset=trues.

Corcoran, K. (2005, September 22). Fired teacher gets 1 year in sex case. *Indianapolis Star*. Available online: http://www.indystar.com/apps/pbcs.dll/article?AID=/20050922/NEWS01/509220438.

Crane, J. P. (2005, June 30). Internet bullying hits home for teen. *Boston Globe*. Available online: http://www.boston.com/news/education/k_12/articles/2005/06/30/internet_bullying_hits_home_for_teen/?page=2.

Crary, D. (2005, January 24). Schools to take part in "No Name-Calling Week." *San Diego Union-Tribune*. Available online: http://www.signonsadiego.com/uniontrib/20050124/news_1n24names.html.

Crime of video voyerism. (2005). State of Idaho, House of Representatives. Available online: http://www3.state.id.us/oasis/H0047.html.

CSI: The classroom. (2004, January 30). *Weekly Reader*, 103(7), 4.

Currie, C. M. (1999, July 16). Unlocked doors lead to school vandalism. *Craig Daily Press*. Available online: http://www.craigdailypress.com/extra/archives/0712arc/n0716.html.

Daigle, J. (2005, May 2). Godchaux student fires handgun in class. *L'Observateur*. Available online: http://www.lobservateur.com/ar-ticles/2005/05/02/news/news04.txt.

Date rape drugs. (2005). *Women's Health*. Available online: http://www.4woman.gov/faq/rohypnol.htm.

Day, S. (2005, October 8). Mom, sons arrested in school theft case. *Statesman Journal*. Available online: http://www.statesmanjournal.com/apps/pbcs.dll/article?AID=/20051008/NEWS/510080333/1001.

Dean, M. M. (2004, February 13). School cops, teacher assaulted in separate incidents at Olney. *Philadelphia Inquirer*. Available online: http://www.philly.com/mld/daillynews/news/local/7943817.htm.

Dean, M. M. (2005a, March 1). Handcuffs here to stay in pupil arrests. *Philadelphia Daily News*. Available online: http://www.philly.com/mld/dailynews/news/local/11018890.htm.

Dean, M. M. (2005b, December 14). 4th-grader is arrested for trying to poison her teacher. *Philadelphia Daily News*. Available online: http://www.philly.com/mld/dailynews/13402699.htm.

Decker, J. (2005, June 8). Third-grader suspended for gun key chain. *Green Bay News-Chronicle*. Available online: http://www.greenbaynewschron.com/page.html?article=104279.

Defining sexual abuse. (2005a). Available online: http://www.uiowa.edu/~rvap/defining_sexual_abuse.html.

Defining sexual abuse. (2005b). Available online: http://www.geocities.com/CapitolHill/7836/defined.html.

Definitions of child abuse and neglect. (2005). Washington, DC: National Clearinghouse on Child Abuse and Neglect Information. Available online: http://nccanch.acf.hhs.gov/general/legal/statutes/define.cfm.

de Vise, D. (2005, July 27). "Expelled" no longer an empty punishment. *Washington Post*. Available online: http://www.washingtonpost.com/wpdyn/content/article/2005/07/27/AR2005072700768.html.

Discipline policy. (2005). Available online: http://jacobs.cps-k12.org/discipline.html.

Dissell, R. (2004, January 20). More teachers losing jobs over improper sex activity. *Plain Dealer*. Available online: http://www.cleveland.com/news/plaindealer/index.ssf?/base/news/1074605409156850.xml.

Dobbs, M. (2004, February 20). U.S. students still getting the paddle. *Washington Post.* Available online: http://www.washingtonpost.com/wp-dyn/articles/A59059–2004Feb20.htmls.

Dodd, D. A. (2003, October 18). Handgun found at school; girl arrested. *Atlanta Journal-Constitution.* Available online: http://www.ajc.com/saturday/content/epaper/editions/saturday/gwinnett_f309fabbe57990370072.html;COXnetJ SessionID=1UKhyrKiANfRoaavQxAe3ACDbHP8WFAJVHSPDCU3jvdN ktCu1aPp!.662747942?urac=n&urvf=10666829131540.4956217660791591.

Dodd, D. A. (2004, March 5.) Student suspended for hand gesture. *Atlanta Journal-Constitution.* Available online: http://www.ajc.com/friday/content/epaper/editions/friday/gwinnett_0484129bd0fff092 00ed.html.

Domestic sex trafficking of minors. (2003). U.S. Department of Justice. Available online: http://www.usdoj.gov/criminal/ceos/prstitu tion.html.

Donahue, M. C. (2004, April–May). Back off, bullies! *Current Health,* 2(8), 13.

Douglas, B. (2005, September 22). School theft. *KSN-TV.* Available online: http://www.ksntv.com/news/default.asp?mode=shownews&id=3552.

Douglas, J. (2005, February 14). Sword-wielding student cuts classmate. *WFAA-TV.* Available online: http://www.wfaa.com/sharedcontent/dws/wfaa/jdouglas/stories/wfaa050214_wz_lamarsword.a991d738.html.

Duncan, N. (2001, November). When should teachers report abuse? *Children's Voice.* Available online: http://www.cwla.org/articles/cv0111teachers.htm.

Durbin, D. A. (2005, June 11). School threat trial sails on unchartered waters. *Detroit News.* Available online: http://www.detnews.com/2005/metro/0506/11/metro-211993.htm.

Dwyer, T. (2004, February 11). A false accusation, and a fateful decision. *Washington Post.* Available online: http://www.washingtonpost.com/wp-dyn/articles/A34637–2004Feb11.html.

Eagan, M., & Gonzalez, R. (2005, Mary 19). Attack on coach resonates. *Hartford Courant.* Available online: http://www.courant.com/news/local/hc-coachattack 0519.artmay19,0,6741239.story?coll=hc-headlines-local.

Edo, T. (2004, January 13). Love letters land Holliston teacher in hot water. *Boston Herald.* Available online: http://news.bostonherald.com/localRegional/localRegional.bg?articleid=1184.

Eight Broad Ripple students arrested after 4 incidents. (2005, November 19). *Indianapolis Star.* Available online: http://www.indystar.com/apps/pbcs.dll/article?AID=/20051119/NEWS01/511190434/-1/ARCHIVE.

Eighth-grader accused of dealing OxyContin. (2005, December 2). *Chicago Sun-Times.* Available online: http://www.suntimes.com/output/news/cst-nws-contin02.html.

Epiphany, S. (2003, October 21). Mobile phones turn high school fights into near-riots. *Smart Mobs.* Available online: http://www.smatmobs.com/archive/2003/10/21/mobile_phones_t.html.

Epstein, R. J. (2003, November 7). School suspends teen for rap lyric. *Milwaukee Journal Sentinel.* Available online: http://www.jsonline.com/news/wauk/nov03/183108.asp.

Espanola incident. (2002, February 28). *The School Watch Network.* Available online: http://www.cybersnitch.net/schoolwatch/svstats.as;#2003.

Essoyan, S. (2004, March 3). Camera theft imperils school's newspaper. *Honolulu Star-Bulletin.* Available online: http://starbulletin.com/2004/03/03/news/story11.html.

Ex-schools chief denied bail in theft of $100,000. (2005, September 14). *Chicago Tribune*. Available online: http://www.chicagotribune.com/business/content/education/chi0509140235sep14,1,799104.story?coll=chi-education-hed.

Ex-student pleads guilty to hacking. (2005, June 17). *Chicago Tribune*. Available online: http://www.chicagotribune.com/business/content/education/chi-0506170169jun17,1,3879310.story?coll=chi-education-hed&ctrack=2&cset=true.

Ex-teacher pleads guilty to sex counts. (2005, September 29). *Los Angeles Times*. Available online: http://www.latimes.com/news/local/la-me-molest29sep29,1,3419409.story?coll=la-headlines-california.

Fahim, K. (2005, October 1). Teacher charged with rape killed himself, police say. *New York Times*. Available online: http://www.nytimes.com/2005/10/01/nyregion/01coach.html.

Fantz, A. (2005, December 7). Three knife-wielding girls arrested after school fight. *Miami Herald*. Available online: http://www.miami.com/mld/miamiherald/news/local/states/florida/counties/broward_county/13345357.htm.

Fargen, J. (2005, September 29). Sex, truth & videotape: Teen-tryst teacher admits to naked pix. *Boston Herald*. Available online: http://news.bostonherald.com/localRegional/view.bg?articleid=104726.

Fifth Judicial District of Pennsylvania. (2005). *School based probation*. Available online: http://www.alleghenycourts.us/family/juvenile/school_based_probation.asp.

Finn, K. V., & Frone, M. R. (2003). *Fights, vandalism related to drinking at school*. Available online: http://alcoholism.about.com/od/teens/a/blria040611.htm.

Finz, S. (2004, January 7). Settlement in gay suit. *San Francisco Chronicle*. Available online: http://www.sfgate.com/cgi-bin/article.cgi?f=/chronicle/archive/2004/01/07/BAGPD451UJ1.DTL.

Fla. student charged for biting off ear. (2005, April 14). *Raleigh News & Observer*. Available online: http://www.newsobserver.com/24hour/weird/story/2311926p-10520889c.html.

Flock, J. (2003, May 22). Two adults charged in violent hazing incident. *CNN.com*. Available online: http://www.cnn.com/2003/LAW/05/21/hazing.charges/.

Foderaro, L. W. (2005, November 19). In Mount Vernon, fights close a high school early. *New York Times*. Available online: http://www.nytimes.com/2005/11/19/nyregion/19fights.html.

Former coach sentenced in molesting case. (2005, October 7). *Boston Globe*. Available online: http://www.boston.com/news/local/connecticut/articles/2005/10/07/former_coach_sentenced_in_molestin g_case/.

Former Middleboro teacher charged with raping student. (2004, January 7). *Boston Globe*. Available online: http://www.boston.com/news/local/massachusetts/articles/2004/01/07/former_middleboro_teacher_charged_with_raping_student/.

Four juveniles accused of damaging school portable. *St. Petersburg Times*. Available online: http://www.sptimes.com/2004/07/25/Southpinellas/Four_juveniles_accuse.shtml.

Franklin, H. (2004, January 29). Assistant principal paddled 6-year-old. *Ledger-Enquirer*. Available online: http://www.corpun.com/uss00401.htm#12535.

Frantz, A. (2003, October 22). Son brings officer's gun, cuffs to school. *Miami Herald*. Available online: http://www.miami.com/mld/miamiheralnews/local/states/florida/counties/broward_county/7070964.htm.

Frantz, A., & Deutsch, K. (2004, February 6). Boys rape girl, 10, in school bathroom. *Miami Herald*. Available online: http://www.miami.com/mld/miamiherald/7887077.htm.

Freeh, L. J. (2005). *A parent's guide to internet safety*. Washington, DC: Federal Bureau of Investigation. Available online: http://www.fbi.gov/publications/pguide/pguidee.htm.

Fujimori, L. (2005, February 25). School fights in Kalihi allegedly tied to gangs. *Honolulu Star-Bulletin*. Available online: http://starbulletin.com/2005/02/19/news/story5.html.

Fulbright, L. (2004, January 9). Sledder hurt in accident may be arrested. *Seattle Times*. Available online: http://seattletimes.nwsource.com/html/localnews/2001833102_snowcrime09e.html.

Garner, J. (2003, December 13). Violent writings alarm school. *Rocky Mountain News*. Available online: http://www.rockymountainnews.com/drmn/state/article/0,1299,DRMN_21_2500512,00.html.

Garzia, V. (2000). Dennis Cotter receives summary disposition in school threat case in Oakland County Circuit Court. *Allmond v. Detroit Country Day School*, Oakland County Circuit Court Case Number 00–023605-NZ. Available online: http://www.vandeveergarzia.com/dbcsumdisp.htm.

Garza, C. L. (2004, January 12). Spare the rod? Not at many public schools. *Florida Times-Union*. Available online: http://www.corp un.com/uss00401.htm#12535.

Gates, N. (2003, December 2). Teacher is now held on counts of child sex. *Sacramento Bee*. Available online: http://www.sacbee.com/content/news/story/7887181p-8825894c.html.

Gaustad, J. (1992, December). School discipline. *ERIC Digest 78*. Available online: http://eric.uoregon.edu/publications/digests/digest078.html.

Gavin, T. A. (2000, March). Bringing SARA to school. *American School Board Journal*. Available online: http://.asbj.com/security/contents/0300gavin.html.

Gedan, B. (2003, October 23). Student admits to making hit list. *Boston Globe*. Available online: http://www.boston.com/news/local/articles/2003/10/23/student_admits_to_making_hit_list/.

Gilbert, H. (2005, October 14). Teacher takes plea in child abuse case. *Oregonian*. Available online: http://www.oregonlive.com/metronorth/oregnian/index.ssf?/base/metro_north_news/112928779131910.xml&coll=7.

Gillaspy, J. A. (2003, October 17). Boy suspended after list labeled "People to Kill" found. *Indianapolis Star*. Available online: http://www.indystar.com/print/articles/4/084015–1334–092.html.

Girls trash Kansas school art room. (2005, November 22). *Raleigh News & Observer*. Available online: http://dwb.newsobserver.com/24hour/weird/story/2924139p-11590587c.html.

Glod, M. (2005, April 27). Va. teacher accused of taking gun to school. *Washington Post*, B01. Available online: http://www.washingtonpost.com/wpdyn/content/article/2005/04/26/AR2005042601357.html.

Gormley, M. (2005, September 24). AP: Corporal punishment up in N.Y. schools. *Boston Globe*. Available online: http://www.boston.com/news/education/k_12/articles/2005/09/24/ap_corporal_punishment_up_in_ny_schools/.

Gottlieb, R. (2005a, November 30). Cracking down on cussing. *Hartford Courant*. Available online: http://www.courant.com/news/local/hc-cussfine1130.artnov30,0,1143016.story?page=2&coll=hc-headlines–home.

Gottlieb, R. (2005b, September 20). Fired teacher cleared in sexual assault case. *Hartford Courant*. Available online: http://www.courant.com/news/education/hc-hfdteacher0920.artsep20,0,74679 50.story? coll=hc-headlines-education.

Grant, D. G. (2004, August 4). Police arrest 4 in school vandalism. *Detroit News*. Available online: http://www.detnews.com/2004/schools/0408/06/b08d-231904.htm.

Green, M. W. (1999, September). *The appropriate and effective use of security technologies in schools*. Washington, DC: National Institute of Justice Research. Available online: http://www.ncjrs.org/school/home.html.

Guidance concerning state and local responsibilities under the gun-free schools act. (2004, January). *Gun-free schools act*. Available online: http://www.firn.edu/doe/besss/gunfree.htm.

Hanemann, M. (2004, February 8). Resource officer helps solve Mt. Hermon School theft. *The Daily News*. Available online: http://www.edailynews.info/articles/2004/02/08/news/news13.txt.

Hanna-Jones, N., & Biesecker, M. (2005, April 28). Mouth-taping alleged. *Raleigh News & Observer*. Available online: http://www.newsobserver.com/news/education/story/2353610p-8731294c.html.

Hanson, E. (2004, February 5). Sex offender's visits to schools prompt outrage. *Houston Chronicle*. Available online: http://www.raptorware.com/news/04%20news/news19.html.

Hendrie, C. (2003, April 30). States target sexual abuse by educators. *Education Week*. Available online: http://www.edweek.org/ew/ewstory.cfm?slug=33abuse.h22.

Herszenhorn, D. H. (2005, September 22). School janitor is arrested over $13,000 in phone calls. *New York Times*. Available online: http://www.nytimes.com/2005/09/22/nyregion/22school.html.

Hessler, C. (2004, March 29). Man blames mom for computer theft. *Pottstown Mercury*. Available online: http://www.pottstownmercury.com/site/news.cfm?newsid=11197751&BRD=1674&PAG=461&dept_id=18041&rfi=6.

High, B. (2005). Making the grade. *Bully Police USA*. Available online: http://www.bullypolice.org/grade.html.

High court rejects appeal in high school stalking murder. (2005, June 2). *CNN*. Available online: http://www.cnn.com/2005/LAW/06/02/stalking.murder.ap/.

High school student arrested after bomb threats (2003, November 6). *San Diego Union-Tribune*. Available online: http://www.signonsandiego.com/news/state/20031106-1420-ca-bombthreatarrest.html.

Highview Elementary School code of conduct. (2005). Available online: http://nanunet.lhric.org/highviewelem/MainOffice/HV%20Standards%20of%20Conduct.htm.

Hit list containing name of principal is turned in. (2004, April 24). *Indianapolis Star*. Available online: http://www.indystar.com/articles/6/140821-7536-009.html.

Hoover, N. C., & Pollard, N. J. (2000, August). *High school hazing*. Alfred, NY: Alfred University. Available online: http://www.alfred.edu/hs_hazing/executive_summary.html.

Howard, T., & Shinkle, P. (2005, May 24). Keeping suspended students in school. *St. Louis Post-Dispatch*. Available online: http://www.stltoday.com/stltoday/news/stories.nsf/stlouiscitycounty/story/33082E3424070A008625700B00209F23?OpenDocument.

Howell, J. C., & Lynch, J. P. (2000). *Youth gangs in schools*. Washington, DC: Office of Juvenile Justice and Delinquency Prevention. Available online: http://www.ncjrs.org/html/ojjdp/jjbul2000_8_2/con tents.html.

Howell students protest classmates' suspensions. (2005, May 11). *Detroit News*. Available online: http://hosted.ap.org/dynamic/stories/M/MI_PAINTED_ PHRASE_PROTEST_MIOL?SITE=MIDTN&SECTION=HOME& TEMPLATE=DEFAULT.

Hui, T. K. (2005, September 14). Five charged in Wake schools fraud case. *Raleigh News & Observer*. Available online: http://www.nsws observer.com/news/ crime_safety/wakefraud/story/2794916p-9235803c.html.

Hume, E. (2005, September 27). Racist graffiti found in Franklin High restroom. *Sacramento Bee*. Available online: http://www.sacbee.com.content/ news/story/13631858p-14474248c.html.

Ihejirika, M. (20005, June 16). Softball coach resigns after allegedly "mooning" girl. *Chicago Sun-Times*. Available online: http://www.suntimes.com/output/news/ cst-nws-mooned16.html.

Jacksonville police suspend Taser use. (2005, February 24). *St. Petersburg Times*. Available online: http://www.sptimes.com/2005/02/24/State/Jacksonville_police_s. shtml.

Jacobson, A. (2005, May 3). Marshall classroom dispute leads to girl's stabbing. *NBC-5*. Available online: http://www.nbc5.com/news/4446246/detail.html.

Jacques, S. (2005, June 9). Student must pay $5K for school vandalism. *Portsmouth Herald*. Available online: http://www.seacoastonline.com/news/ 06092005/news/46623.htm.

Johnson, T. W. (2004, March 10). A novel approach to end the taunting. *Baltimore Sun*. Available online: http://www.baltimoresun.com/news/education/bal-ho.noname10mar10,0,5095883.story?coll=baled ucation-k12.

Jones, S. (2003, November 7). Student caught with gun at Dunbar. *Lexington Herald Leader*. Available online: http://www.kentucky.com/mld/kentucky/ news/local/7203687.htm.

Judge rules in favor of Gwinnett County honor student. (2005, November 30). *San Jose Mercury News*. Available online: http://www.mercurynews.com/mld/ mercurynews/13291720.htm.

Juozapavicius, J. (2004, February 4). Schools must report suspected abuse. *Arizona Republic*. Available online: http://www.azcentral.com/families/education/ articles/0204mesaedabuseZ10-CP.html.

Karl & Associates. (2005). *Youth related computer crime*. Available online: http://www.karisable.com/crpcyouth.htm.

Keen, M. (2005, June 17). Sallisaw school hires five new teachers. *Sequoyah County Times*. Available online: http://www.corpun.com/uss00506.htm.

Kelley, M. (2005). Top 10 tips for classroom discipline and management. *About*. Available online: http://712educators.about.com/od/discipline/tp/ disciplinetips.htm.

Killackey, B. (2005, April 22). Boy, 8, arrested after attacking principal with wooden pole. *Journal Times*. Available online: http://www.journaltimes.com/ articles/2005/04/22/local/iq_3493863.txt.

Kim, C. W. (2005, September 24). Music teacher says he was told to resign or retire to avoid charges. *Register Citizen*. Available online: http://www.

registercitizen.com/site/news.cfm?newsid=15269871&BRD=1652&PAG=
461&dept_id=12530&rfi=6.

King, L. (2004, November 10). Students to testify against classmates. *Philadelphia Inquirer*. Available online: http://www.philly.com/mld/inquirer/10140605.htm.

Kirby, C. (2005a, November 18). Nicholas County student urinates in ice machine. *Lexington Herald-Leader*. Available online: http://www.kentucky.com/mld/kentucky/13198488.htm.

Kirby, C. (2005b, November 22). Student links urinating incident to bullying. *Lexington Herald-Leader*. Available online: http://www.kentucky.com/mld/kentucky/13230103.htm.

Klein, A. (2005, September 28). Two Md. teens accused of attempted rape. *Washington Post*. Available online: http://www.washingtonpost.com/wpdyn/content/article/2005/09/28/AR2005092802397.html.

Knich, D. (2005, October 15). County to hold parents responsible for school vandalism. *The Island Packet*. Available online: http://www.islandpacket.com/news/local/story/5256408p-4771601c.html.

Koch, W. (2005, November 30). More women charged in sex cases. *USA Today*. Available online: http://www.usatoday.com/printedition/news/20051130/a_femalesexcrimes30.art.htm.

Kostinsky, S., Bixler, E. O., & Kettl, P. A. (2001, September). Threats of school violence in Pennsylvania after media coverage of the Columbine High School massacre: Examining the role of imitation. *Archives of Pediatric & Adolescent Medicine*. Available online: http://www.ncbi.nlm.nih.gov/entrez/query.fcgi?cmd=Retrieve&db=PubMed&list_uids=11529800&dopt=Abstract.

Kovach, G. C. (2004, February 26). Officials: Students had gun, porn. *Dallas Morning News*. Available online: http://www.dallasnews.com/sharedcontent/dws/news/localnews/stories/022704dnmetnaughtytape.580d4.html.

Kutztown 13 plea bargain—High school drops felony charges. (2005, August 28). *Lockergnome*. Available online: http://channels. Locker gnome.com/net/archives/20050828_kutztown_13_plea_bargain_high_school_drops_felony_charges.phtml.

Lacour, G. (2005, February 9). Area schools rarely haul out the paddle. *Charlotte Observer*. Available online: http://www.corpun.com/uss00502.htm#15215.

Larsen, D. (2005). Schools can take action against date-rape. *About*. Available online: http://incestabuse.about.com/od/daterape/a/daterape.htm.

Lawrence, A. (2004, January 29). Ashland schools weighing cuts. *News Journal*. http://www.corpun.com/uss00401.htm#12535.

Leary, A., & Tobin, T. C. (2005, September 17). Child's afterschool tantrum thwarts officer. *St. Petersburg Times*. Available online: http://www.sptimes.com/2005/09/17/Southpinellas/Child_s_afterschool_t.shtml.

Leitch, S. (2004, September 22). Boy with disability banned from playground. *Boston Globe*. Available online: http://www.boston.com/news/education/k_12/articles/2004/09/22/boy_with_disability_banned_from_playground/.

Lerten, B. (2002, November 25). Students angry, staff frustrated by string of school vandalism. *Bend.com*. Available online: http://www.bend.com/news/ar_view.php?ar_id=7106.

Lewis, D. W. (2003, December 18). Class subdues teacher's attacker. *Atlanta Journal-Constitution*. Available online: http://www.ajc.com/thursday/content/epaper/editions/thursday/metro_f31eb522649d5 0a8000b.html.

Lindelof, B. (2004, March 6). Middle school student held after alleged death threat. *Sacramento Bee*. Available online: http://www.sacbee.com/content/news/education/story/8428622p-9357834c.html.

Literary luminaries write court on behalf of teen poet. (2003, November 9). *Sacramento Bee*. Available online: http://www.sacbee.com/state_wire/story/7755890p-8694994c.html.

Lombardi, F. (2004, November 9). A snapshot of cameras at schools. *New York Daily News*. Available online: http://www.nydailynews. com/11-09-2004/news/story/250961p-214899c.html.

Lopez, L. (2005, March 25). Shootings spur school building design changes. *The Oregonian*. Available online: http://www.oregonlive.com/news/oregonian/index.ssf?/base/front_page/1111748652291610.xml.

Lucas, B. (2003, May 13). Suspension raises questions about district policy. *East Valley Tribune*. Available online: http://www.eastvalleytribune.com/index.php?sty=4524.

Lyda, A. (2003, March 5). Ceremony marks two-year anniversary of school shooting. *San Diego Union-Tribune*. Available online: http://www.signonsandiego.com/news/metro/santana/200303059999_7m5sultans.html.

Lyda, A. (2004, March 9). Officials say student tip prevented shooting. *San Diego Union-Tribune*. Available online: http://www.signonsandiego.com/uniontrib/20040309/news_1m9lemon.html.

Madrid, O. (2005, September 23). District sends message on hazing issue. *ArizonaRepublic*. Available online: http://www.azcentral.com/arizonarepublic/local/articles/0923necoronado23.html.

Magee, M, & Hughes, J. (2005, April 27). Tip about gun at school leads to arrests. *San Diego Union-Tribune*. Available online: http://www.signonsandiego.com/uniontrib/20050427/news_7m27gun.html.

Mahoney, D., & Faulker, M. (1997, December 1). *A brief overview of pedophiles on the web*. Available online: http://www.prevent-abuse-now.com/pedoweb.htm.

Manual of rules. (2005). *Cather School/Grant School Website*. Available online: http://www.ncrel.org/sdrs/areas/issues/envrnmnt/drug free/sa2cathe.htm#One.

Marech, R. (2005, March 8). Reward offered for information on racist graffiti at middle school. *San Francisco Chronicle*. Available online: http://www.sfgate.com/cgibin/article.cgi?f=/c/a/2005/03/08/BAGBMBLTE81.DTL.

Martineau, P. (2002, December 19). Pushed around: Students lead the way in trying to prevent bullying at their schools. *Sacramento Bee*. Available online: http://www.gsanetwork.org/press/bullying. html.

Matzelle, C. (2005, September 21). Lorain ex-teacher faces new probe. *Plain Dealer*. http://www.cleveland.com/news/plaindealer/index.ssf?/base/lorain/1127295309122460.xml&coll=2.

McDonald, T. (2003, August 12). Teacher charged with sex abuse. *News and Observer*. Available online: http://www.newsobserver.com/front/story/2770532p-2567733c.html.

McElhatton, J. (2004, May 14). "Too much money" being spent on school security, Cafritz says. *Washington Times*. Available online: http://www.washtimes.com/metro/20040514-105900-5226r.htm.

Melendez, M. (2003, November 7). Boy with gun felt threat from gang. *Arizona Republic*. Available online: http://www.azcentral.com/arizonarepublic/local/articles/1107gun.html.

Menard, J., & Martindale, M. (2005, March 25). Bullying can push students over edge. *Detroit News*. Available online: http://www.detnews.com/2005/schools/0503/25/A01–128962.htm.

Meyer, K. (2003, June 14). Bill ensures vandals pay restitution. *Anchorage Daily News*. Available online: http://www.akrepublicans.org/meyer/23/info/meye2003061401i.php.

Middle school cook charged in threats. (2005, June 3). *Pioneer Press*. Available online: http://www.twincities.com/mld/twincities/news/local/11801040.htm.

Minnesota: Vandals strike educators, school in separate cases. (2003, November 11). *Pioneer Press*. Available online: http://www.twin cities.com/mld/pioneerpress/living/education/7232369.htm.

Missouri center for safe schools. (2001). *Intervening in student fights*. Available online: http://www.umkc.edu/safe-school/documents/monofght.pdf.

Molotov cocktail. (2005). *Wikipedia*. Available online: http://en.wikipedia.org/wiki/Molotov_cocktail.

Mongelli, L., & Martinez, E. (2005, March 11). Two teens stabbed in Bx. HS gang fight. *New York Post*. Available online: http://www.streetgangs.com/topics/2005/031105nybx.html.

Moran, K. (2003, December 10). Ex-teacher fined for belt around student's neck. *Houston Chronicle*. Available online: http://www.chron.com/cs/CDA/ssistory.mpl/metropolitan/2283504.

Morson, B., & Mitchell, N. (2005, December 7). Varying interpretations of what's required distort school-fights data. *Rocky Mountain News*. Available online: http://www.rockymountainnews.com/drmn/education/article/0,1299,DRMN_957_4295361,00.html.

Mueller, L. (2005, September 20). Teen's overdose leads to Pike principal's arrest. *Lexington Herald-Leader*. Available online: http://www.kentucky.com/mld/kentucky/12691468.htm.

Murray, J. (2005, February 8). Boy, 9, brings handgun to school. *Indianapolis Star*. Available online: http://www.indystar.com/articles/3/220674-3853- 102.html.

Music instructor facing abuse claims gets another teaching job. (October 2, 2005). *Kansas City Star*. Available online: http://www.kansascity.com/mld/kansascity/12801326.htm.

Nadeau, T. (2003, October 23). School threat causes a drop in attendance. *Sacramento Bee*. Available online: http://www.sacbee.com/content/news/education/story/7651049p-8591332c.html.

Napolitano, J. (2005, November 10). Oak Lawn High suspends hackers. *Chicago Tribune*. Available online: http://www.chicagotribune. com/technology/chi-051110computerhacking,1,1706537.story?coll= chi-news-hed.

National Clearinghouse on Child Abuse and Neglect Information. (2003). *Foster care national statistics*. Available online: http://nccanch.acf.hhs.gov/pubs/factsheets/foster.cfm.

National Clearinghouse on Child Abuse and Neglect Information. (2004). *What is child abuse and neglect?* Available online: http://nccanch.acf.hhs.gov/pubs/factsheets/whatiscan.cfm.

National Education Association. (2005). *National bullying awareness campaign*. Available online: http://www.nea.org/schoolsafety/bullying.html.

National School Safety and Security Services. (2002). *School-related deaths, school shootings, & school violence incidents, 2001–2002.* Available online: http://www. schoolsecurity.org/trends/school_violence 01–02.html.

National School Safety and Security Services. (2005a). *School safety implications of No Child Left Behind Law's "persistently dangerous school" definitions.* Available online: http://www.schoolsecurity.org/trends persistently_dangerous.html.

National School Safety and Security Services. (2005b). *Zero tolerance.* Available online: http://www.schoolsecurity.org/trends/zero_tol erance.html.

Nealis, L. (2003, November). "Persistently dangerous schools" and other problematic NCLB provisions. *NASP Communiqué*, 32 (3). Available online: http://www. nasponline.org/publications/cq323 nclbnealis.html.

Nebraska teen's bomb plot foiled. (2004, March 18). *USA Today.* Available online. http://www.usatoday.com/news/nation/2004–03–18-school-nebraska_x.htm.

Nelson, R. (2005, March 27). Character-focused program is planned. *Times-Picayune.* Available   online: http://www.nola.com/search/index.ssf?/base/library-73/ 111190661796260.xml?nola.

Newbury, U. (2004, February 27). Student is charged in high school gun incident. *Kansas City Star.* Available online: http://www.kansascity.com/mld/kansascity/ news/local/8052183.htm.

New York State Government. (1999, July 9). *Governor: Legislation cracks down on false threats at schools.* Available online: http://www.state.ny.us/governor/press/ year99/july9_1_99.htm.

Nguyen, H. D., & Portner, J. (2003, December 5). Teens arrested in school blaze. *San Jose Mercury News.* Available online: http://www.bayarea.com/mld/ mercurynews/news/local/states/california/the_valley/7420156.htm.

No kirpans in school, Quebec court rules. (2004, March 5). *CBC News.* Available online: http://www.cbc.ca/story/canada/national/2004/03/05/kirpan040305. html?print.

Nuwer, H. (2000). *Excerpt from high school hazing.* Available online: http://www. stophazing.org/nuwer/hshexcerpt.htm.

O'Donnell, P. (2005, June 11). Strongsville ex-student accused of school threat pleads no contest. *Plain Dealer.* Available online: http://www.cleveland.com/ news/plaindealer/index.ssf?/base/cuyahoga/111848256218491.xml&coll=2,

Office of Juvenile Justice and Delinquency Prevention. (2004). *Model programs guide.* Available online: http://www.dsgonline.com/mpg_non_flash/intermediate_ sanctions.htm.

O'Hare, P. (2004, February 3). Fifth-grader shoots self in class. *Houston Chronicle.* Available online: http://www.chron.com/cs/CDA/ssistory.mpl/ metropolitan/2386327.

Okoben, J. (2005, April 12). Administrator, student hurt in brawls at South High. *The Plain Dealer.* Available online: http://www.cleveland.com/education/ plaindealer/index.ssf?/base/isedu/1113305452146660.xml.

Olberliesen, E. (2005, April 12). Schools help kids stand up to bullies. *Detroit News.* Available online: http://www.detnews.com/2005/lifestyle/0504/12/E06– 147379.htm.

Olweus, D. (2001, December). *General information about the Olweus bully/victim questionnaire, PC program, and teacher handbook.* Bergen, Norway: Dan Olweus. Available online: www.colorado.edu/cspv/blueprints/model/BPP_OrderForm.pdf.

Olweus bullying prevention program. (2005). Washington, DC: Substance Abuse and Mental Health Services Administration, U.S. Department of Health and Human Services. Available online: modelprograms. samhsa.gov/pdfs/FactSheets/Olweus%20Bully.pdf.

O'Malley, M. (2004, January 7). Vandals slash tires on 25 buses; classes go on in North Royalton. *Cleveland Plain Dealer*. Available online: http://www.cleveland.com/education/index.ssf?/base/isedu/1073480105167150.xml.

O'Neal, K. (2003, November 11). Two boys charged with shouting bomb alert. *Indianapolis Star*. Available online: http://www.indy star.com/articles/0/091706–3970–103.html.

Ore. girls charged with attempted murder. (2005, September 20). *Atlanta Journal-Constitution*. Available online: http://www.ajc.com/news/content/sTharedgen/ap/National/Rat_Poison_Milk.htm.

OSERS. (2005). *Early warning, timely response: A guide to safe schools*. Available online: http://www.ed.gov/about/offices/list/osers/osep/gtss.html.

Osinski, B. (2004, January 9). Threats tricky area for psychologists. *Atlanta Journal Constitution*. Available online: http://www.ajc.com/friday/content/epaper/editions/friday/gwinnett_f3ef0668c1bc701f 00e2.html.

Padilla, H., & Shah, A. (2003, May 2). Minneapolis teacher charged with sex abuse practiced black magic, complaint says. *Minneapolis Star Tribune*. Available online: http://www.startribune.com/stories/462/3859805.html.

Patchin, J. W., & Hinduja, S. (2005, October 11). *Cyberbullying study*. Available online: http://www.cyberbullying.us/.

Pathway Courses. (2005). *Bullying case studies*. Available online: http://pathwayscourses.samhsa.gov/bully/pdfs_bully/case-study-2.pdf.

Patterson, S. (2005, October 14). Conviction of student who imitated Nazi upheld. *Chicago Sun-Time*. Available online: http://www.suntimes.com/output/news/cst-nws-nazi14.html.

Paul, K. (2002, April 30). Bus hijacker's plan "rudimental." *Las Vegas Sun*. Available online: http://www.lasvegassun.com/sunbin/stories/sun/2002/apr/30/513381592.html.

Paulson, A. (2003, December 30). Internet bullying. *Christian Science Monitor*. Available online: http://www.csmonitor.com/2003/1230/p11s01-legn.html.

Peeping incident. (1999, October 28). *UCLA Daily Bruin*. Available online: http://www.dailybruin.ucla.edu/db/issues/99/10.28/news.1930s.html.

Pelley, S. (2000, March 7). Murder in the first grade. *CBS News*. Available online: http://www.cbsnews.com/stories/2000/03/07/60II/main168970.shtml.

Perry, J. L. (2001, August 8). School vandalism beyond belief. *NewsMax*. Available online: http://www.newsmax.com/archives/articles/2001/8/7/190918.shtml.

Pilcher, J. (1999, May 21). Teen wounds six fellow students. *Boulder Daily Camera*. Available online: http://www.boulderdailycamera. com/shooting/21ashoo.html.

Pinzur, M. I., Santana, S., & Rabin. C. (2004, February 4). Boy killed at school; classmate charged. *Miami Herald*. Available online: http://www.miami.com/mld/miamiherald/7868956.htm.

Pittsburgh schools suspend 2nd-grade girl for saying "hell." (2004, February 5). *Plain Dealer*. Available online: http://www.cleveland.com/news/plaindealer/index.ssf?/base/news/1075982128305080.xml.

Police warning cancels school's blues festival. (2005, June 6). *Buffalo News*. Available online: http://www.buffalonews.com/editorial/20050606/5060694.asp.

Post, T. (2004, September 24). Rocori High School marks shooting anniversary. *Minnesota Public Radio*. Available online: http://news.minnesota.publicradio. org/features/2004/09/24_postt_rocori a year later/.

Principal resigns, counselor suspended in high school cheating. (2003, November 4). *Chicago Flame*. Available online: http://www.chicagoflame.com/media/ paper519/news/2003/11/04/NewBriefs/Principal.Resigns.Counselor. Suspended.In.High.School.Cheating-546438.shtml.

Pritchard, O. (2004, February 5). Judge won't watch videotape in spanking case. *Philadelphia Inquirer*. Available online: http://www.philly.com/mld/inquirer/ news/local/7877279.htm.

Pupil suspended for swinging skunk at schoolmates. (2005, October 1). *Boston Globe*. Available online: http://www.boston.com/news/education/k_12/articles/ 2005/10/01/pupil_suspended_for_swinging_skunk_at_schoolmates/.

Randall, K. (2001, August 3). Another Florida teenager receives harsh adult prison sentence. *World Socialist Website*. Available online: http://www.wsws.org/ articles/2001/aug2001/flor-a03.shtml.

Real life cases of bullying. (2005). *Teacher Net*. Available online: http://www.teachernet. gov.uk/wholeschool/behaviour/tacklingbullying/examplesofbullying/.

Recognizing child abuse and neglect: Signs and symptoms. (2003). Washington, DC: National Clearinghouse on Child Abuse and Neglect Information. Available online: http://nccanch.acf.hhs.gov/pubs/fact sheets/signs.cfm.

Reed, E., & Okoben, J. (2003, November 9). Numbers may not tell whole story of assaults against teachers, staff. *Cleveland Plain-Dealer*. Available online: http:// www.cleveland.com/education/index.ssf ?/base/isedu/1068377581229620.xml.

Reese, P. (2005, February 11). Corporal punishment in state schools declines. *Arkansas Democrat-Gazette*. Available online: http://www.corpun.com/ uss00502.htm#15215.

Reid, S. A. (2003, December 10). School probed in fatal abuse case. *Atlanta Journal-Constitution*. Available online: http://www.ajc.com/wednesday/content/ epaper/editions/wednesday/metro_f36dacd0329aa07a0073.html.

Renze-Rhodes, L. (2004, March 24). Student arrested after taking BB gun and hit list to school. *Indianapolis Star*. Available online: http://www.indystar. com/articles/4/132027–8024–009.html.

Richie, K. (2005, June 14). Board approves specifications for spanking. *Press-Herald*. Available online: http://www.corpun.com/uss00506.Htm.

Rockdale school vandal leaves prison after 4 years. (2005, June 16). *Atlanta Journal-Constitution*. Available online: http://www.ajc.com/metro/content/metro/ dekalb/0605/16vandals.html.

Rollins, J. (2005, May). Before and after. *Counseling Today*. Available online: http://www.counseling.org/Content/NavigationMenu/PUBLICATIONS/ COUNSELINGTODAYONLINE/MAY2005/May_2005_Counseling.htm.

Rolly, P., & Jacobson-Wells, J. (2004, December 17). Rolly & Wells: Horseplay lands kids in court *Salt Lake Tribune*. Available online: http://www.sltrib.com/ utah/ci_2490327.

Rosario, R. (2005, October 3). Unproven accusations devastate a teacher. *Pioneer Press*. Available online: http://www.twincities.com/mld/twincities/news/local/ 12802891.htm.

Rothstein, K. (2004, January 13). Teens accused of gang rape: Prosecutor: Trio plied classmate with booze. *Boston Herald.* Available online: http://news.bostonherald.com/localRegional/localRegional.bg?articleid=1191.

Rozek, D. (2004, March 4). Girls stay home from school after complaints of groping. *Chicago Sun-Times.* Available online: http://www.sun times.com/output/news/cst-nws-grope05.html.

Rubenstein, S. (2001, May 18). 2 teens suspended in school vandalism. *San Francisco Chronicle.* Available online: http://www.sfgate.com/cgi-bin/article.cgi?f=/c/a/2001/05/18/MNL227495.DTL.

Rutledge, M. (1997). Fireworks give fun a tragic spin. *Cincinnati Post.* Available online: http://www.cincypost.com/news/1997/firewk062687.html.

Ryckaert, V. (2005, April 8). History teacher charged with intimidating student. *Indianapolis Star.* Available online: http://www.indystar.com/articles/8/235289-9898-103.html.

Sanchez, L., & Arner, M. (2005, October 21). Schools trying to head off violence. *San Diego Union-Tribune.* Available online: http://www.signonsandiego.com/news/education/20051021–9999–7m21grosviol.html.

Santos, F. (2005, September 21). Protest over metal detectors gains legs as students walk out. *New York Times.* Available online: http://wwwnytimes.com/2005/09/21/nyregion/21walkout.html?oref=login.

Schneider, T. (2001, February). Newer technologies for school security. *ERIC Digest 145.* Available online: http://cepm.uoregon.edu/publications/digests/digest145.html.

Schoepf, M. (2004, November 9). Fake pistol causes two suspensions. *Pioneer Press.* Available online: http://www.twincities.com/mld/twincities/news/local/10131967.htm.

School anti-vandalism task force. (2005). *School District 42.* Available online: http://www.sd42.ca/community-antivandal.html.

School bus driver shot to death; teen charged. (2005, March 3). *Arizona Republic.* Available online: http://www.azcentral.com/arizonare public/news/articles/0303schoolbus03.html.

School fights. (2005). *Responding to violence in schools.* Available online: http://www.colorado.edu/cspv/publications/factsheets/safeschools/FS-SC14.html.

School suspends most 6th-graders for mass rowdiness. (2004, March 26). *Arizona Republic.* Available online: http://www.azcentral.com/families/education/articles/0326StudentsSuspended26-ON.html.

School violence prevention. (2002, October). U.S. Department of Health & Human Services. Available online: http://www.mentalhealth.samhsa.gov/schoolviolence/.

School violence statistics. (2000). *Security World.* Available online: http://www.securityworld.com/community/statistics/schoolviolence.html.

School won't erase "beautiful" vandalism. (2005, June 2). *Houston Chronicle.* Available online: http://www.chron.com/cs/CDA/ssistory.mpl/nation/3208158.

Schools may move Friday night games to avoid violence. (2005, October 21). *Houston Chronicle.* Available online: http://www.chron.com/cs/CDA/ssistory.mpl/metropolitan/3406998.

Schwisow, A. (2005, July 21). Mich. teen gets prison time for threats. *eWoss News.* Available online: http://news.ewoss.com/articles/D8BG5BSG0.aspx.

Schworm, P. (2004, February 12). Teen charged under antiterror law after school threat. *Boston Globe.* Available online: http://www.boston.com/news/

education/k_12/articles/2004/02/12/teen_charged_under_antiterror_law_after_school_threat/.

Scott, M. (2004, March 12). Rap CD puts school on edge. *Cleveland Plain Dealer*. Available online: http://www.cleveland.com/news/plaindealer/index.ssf?/base/news/1079087976253912.xml.

Secure Computing Corporation. (2005, September 7). *Nearly 800 plagiarism web sites make school cheating easier than ever*. Available online: http://biz.yahoo.com/bw/050907/75311.html?.v=1.

Sedlak, A. J., & Broadhurst, D. D. (1996). *Executive summary of the third national incidence study of child abuse and neglect*. Washington, DC: U.S. Department of Health and Human Services. Available online: http://nccanch.acf.hhs.gov/pubs/statsinfo/nis3.cfm.

Selekman, J., & Vessey, J. A. (2004, May–June). Bullying: It isn't what it used to be. *Pediatric Nursing*, 30 (3), 246.

Seven suspended in taped school bus beating. (2004, February 13). *Boston Globe*. Available online: http://www.boston.com/news/education/k_12/articles/2004/02/13/7_suspended_in_taped_school_bus_beating/.

Sexual abuse. (2005). *California adoptions*. Available online: http://glossary.adoption.com/sexual-abuse.html.

Sexual Assault Crises Center. (2005). *Child sexual abuse*. Author. Available online: http://www.thesacc.org/pdfs/Child_Sex_Abuse.pdf.

Sexual victimization. (2005). University of Florida Counseling Center for Human Development. Available online: http://usfweb2.usf.edu/counsel/self-hlp/daterape.htm.

Shea, K. B. (2003, May 30). Former teacher waives hearing on sex charges. *Philadelphia Inquirer*. Available online: http://www.philly.com/mld/inquirer/news/local/5972635.htm.

Sheehan, C. (2005, October 21). Chicago hearing debates rise in attacks by girls. *Chicago Tribune*. Available online: http://www.chicagotribune.com/news/local/chi0510210148oct21,1,1986495.story?coll=chi-news-hed.

Sherman, M. (2005, November 21). School crimes decline, US report says. *Boston Globe*. Available online: http://www.boston.com/news/nation/washington/articles/2005/11/21/school_crimes_decline_us_report_says/.

Sierra, T. (2005, October 13). Ex-principal rejects district allegations. *San Diego Union-Tribune*. Available online: http://www.signonsandiego.com/news/education/20051013–9999–6m13ncmiddle.html.

Smulevitz, H. (2005, June 14). Kids get alternative to suspension. *Indianapolis Star*. Available online: http://www.indystar.com/apps/pbcs.dll/article?AID=/20050614/ZONES04/506140337/1026/ZONES04.

Snyder, D. (2005, April 21). Girl accused of writing threats at Md. School. *Washington Post*, p. B03. Available online: http://www.washingtonpost.com/wp-dyn/articles/A6228-2005Apr20.html.

Soto, O. R. (2004, March 30). Hearings for boys in school-plot case to be public. *San Diego Union-Tribune*. Available online: http://www.signonsandiego.com/news/education/20040330–9999news_1m30pa lm.html.

St. Gerard, V. (2003, December). *Corrections Compendium*, 28(12), 23.

Stacom, D. (2005, September 1). Schools closed after bus vandalism. *Hartford Courant*. Available online: http://www.courant.com/news/local/hc-thombus0901.artsep01,0,320909.story?coll=hc-headlines-local.

Staten, C. (1996, January 6). "Roofies," the new "date rape" drug of choice. *Emergency Net News.* Available online: http://www.emergency.com/roofies.htm.

Stearns, J. (2003, December 12). Threat puts Vineyard high school on alert. *Boston Globe.* Available online: http://www.boston.com/news/education/k_12/articles/2003/12/12/threat_puts_vineyard_high_school_on_alert/.

Stelzer, A. (2005, February 17). Taser concerns grow as death, injuries mount. *The New Standard.* Available online: http://newstandard news.net/content/?action=show_item&itemid=1486.

Student accused of sending note. (2005, May 19). *Richmond Times Dispatch.* Available online: http://www.timesdispatch.com/servlet/Satellite?pagename=RTD%2FMGArticle%2FRTD_BasicArticle&c=MGArticle&cid=1031782802346&path=%21news&s=1045855934842.

Student accused of taking gun to school. (2003, October 22). *Lexington Herald-Leader.* Available online: http://www.kentucky.com/mld/kentucky/news/local/7072187.htm.

Student expelled for gun can return. (2004, January 22). *Indianapolis Star.* Available online: http://www.indystar.com/articles/2/113773–6322-093.html.

Student stabbed, school guard hurt. (2005, September 22). *Chicago Sun.* Available online: http://www.suntimes.com/output/news/cst-nw s-farragut22.html.

Study finds zero tolerance policies put thousands of children on school-house to jailhouse track. (2003, May 14). *Find Law.* Available online: http://news.findlaw.com/prnewswire/20030513/14mqy2003164331.html.

Substitute teacher fired for taping mouths. (2005, May 26). *Boston Globe.* Available online: http://www.freerepublic.com/focus/f-news/1411385/posts.

Sullivan, J. (2004, December 17). Slain teen's mom settles suit; schools to alter threat policy. *Seattle Times.* Available online: http://seattle times.nwsource.com/html/snohomishcountynews/2002220555_jasmer26m.html.

Sung, E. (2004, December 17). Melee erupts at school. *Raleigh News-Observer.* Available online: http://www.newsobserver.com/news/story/1938072p-8294638c.html.

Swahn, M. H., Lubell, K. M., & Simon, T. R. (2004, June 11). *Suicide attempts and physical fighting among high school students—United States, 2001.* Available online: http://www.cdc.gov/mmwr/preview/mm wrhtml/mm5322a3.htm.

Taylor, M. (2003, October 24). Student expelled over diary. *Atlanta Journal Constitution.* Available online: http://www.ajc.com/friday/content/epaper/editions/friday/news_f3894cef913af08000a5.html.

Teacher aide accused of abusing student. (2005, May 22). *St. Petersburg Times.* Available online: http://pqasb.pqarchiver.com/sptimes/access/843158571.html?dids=843158571:843158571&FMT=FT&FMTS=ABS:FT&date=May+22%2C+2005&author=&pub=St.+Petersburg+Times&edition=&startpage=3.B&desc=Teacher+aide+accused+of+abusing+student.

Teacher charged in molestation of 6 pupils. (2005, June 16). *Los Angeles Times.* Available online: http://www.latimes.com/news/local/la-me-rbriefs.1jun16,1,786488.story?coll=la-headlinescalifornia&ctrack= 1&cset=true.

Teacher charged with sexual relationship with 11-year-old. (2004, January 8). *CNN.* Available online: http://www.con.com/2004/LAW/01/08/teacher.charged.ap/index.html.

Teacher pleads guilty in sex case. (2003, August 11). *San Diego Union-Tribune*. Available online: http://www.signonsandiego.com/news//metro/20030811–1221-teacher.html.

Teacher rebuked for showing film about teen lesbian couple. (1994, May 13). *Richmond Times-Dispatch*, B-4.

Teacher suspended during pornography investigation. (2005, June 2). *Boston Globe*. Available online: http://www.boston.com/news/education/k_12/articles/2005/06/02/teacher_suspended_during_pornography_investigation/.

Teen said to threaten to shoot 5 classmates. (2003, December 7). *Boston Globe*. Available online: http://www.boston.com/news/education/k_12/articles/2003/12/07/teen_said_to_threaten_to_shoot_5_classmates/.

Teen sentenced for intentionally vomiting on teacher. (2005, August 2). *Chicago Sun-Times*. Available online: http://www.suntimes.com/output/news/cst-nws-vomit02.html.

Teens get jail for fireworks prank gone too far. (2005, October 26). *Chicago Sun-Times*. Available online: http://www.suntimes.com/output/news/cst-nws-jail26.html#.

Thermos, W. (2005, December 9). Boy, 17, admits he booby-trapped pens. *Los Angeles Times*. Available online: http://www.latimes. com/news/local/la-me-pens9dec09,1,3510118.story?coll=laheadline s-california.

Thomas, R. M. (1995). *Classifying reactions to wrongdoing*. Westport, CT: Greenwood.

Thomas, R. M. (2003). New frontiers in cheating. In *Encyclopaedia Britannica book of the year*, pp. 206–207. Chicago: Encyclopaedia Britannica.

Thompson, C. (2005, April 1). Student jailed in bomb plot. *Arizona Republic*. Available online: http://www.azcentral.com/arizonarepublic/news/articles/0401schoolplot01.html.

Three grade-schoolers held in plot on classmate. (2004, March 9). *Arizona Republic*. Available online: http://www.azcentral.com/arizonarepublic/news/articles/0319schoolplot19.html.

Three students convicted in school fights. (2002, November 20). *Associated Press*. Available online: http://linuslibrary.appstate.edu/lumbee/4/TH43001.htm.

Three threats of school violence within weeks. (2005, May 3). *WKYC-Channel 3*. Available online: http://www.wkyc.com/news/news/-fullsory.asp?id=34282.

Tobin, T. C. (2005, April 23). Textbook case of discipline viewed with praise, criticism. *St. Petersburg Times*. Available online: http://www.sptimes.com/2005/04/23/Southpinelas/Textbook_case_of_disc.shtml.

Torres, K. (2003, December 10). Hacking gets teen 10-day school time-out. *Atlanta Journal-Constitution*. Available online: http://www.ajc.com/wednesday/content/epaper/editions/wednesday/metro_f36dac50329af0bf0003. Html.

Trela, N. (2004, June 4). Contractor admits guilt in school theft scandal. *Detroit Free Press*. Available online: http://www.freep.com/news/locway/stone4_20040604.htm.

Tripp loses appeal of sentence in classmate's murder. (2005, June 8). *Kansas City Star*. Available online: http://www.kansascity.com/mld/kansascity/news/local/11845520.htm.

Tucker, D. Q. (2005, May 26). Mother, daughter face trials in school fight. *Saginaw News*. Available online: http://www.mlive.com/news/sanews/index.ssf?/base/news-2/1117117247228370.xml.

Two juveniles arrested for JLS Middle School vandalism and hamster killing. (2004, March 1). *City of Palo Alto.* Available online: http://www.cityofpaloalto.org/press/New%20Releases/20040301.htm.

Two students arrested in Columbine-style plot. (2004, January 13). *CNN.* Available online: http://www.cnn.com/2004/US/South/01/13/creating.columbine.ap/index.html.

USA school violence statistics. (2005). *School Violence Watch Network.* Available online: http://www.cybersnitch.net/schoowatch/svstats.asp#2003.

Vaishnav, A. (2003, November 6). School threats seen straining town budgets and patience. *Boston Globe.* Available online: http://www.boston.com/news/education/k_12/articles/2003/11/06/school_threats_seen_straining_town_budgets_and_patience/.

Vandalism. (2005). Available online: http://www.btpolice.com/vandal ism.htm.

Vandals at Conant High do $100,000 in damage. (2005, June 2). *Chicago Tribune.* Available online: http://www.chicagotribune.com/busibess/content/education/chi-0506020297jun02,1,536964.story?coll=chi-educationhed&ctrack=2&cset=true.

Vanderford, J. (2005, September 3). School vandalism investigated. *KOLN/KGIN.* Available online: http://www.kolnkgin.com/news/features/1/1830967.html.

Vendel, C. (2005, September 21). Fight at charter school spurs arrests of teens. *Kansas City Star.* Available online: http://www.kansascity.com/mld/kansascity/news/local/12698637.htm.

Violence in our schools. (2005, March 21). Available online: www.col-umbine-angels.com/Shootings-2005-2009.htm.

Vitello, P. (2005a, September 27). Ex-schools chief pleads guilty to huge theft. *New York Times.* Available online: http://www.nytimes.com/2005/09/27/nyregion/27roslyn.html.

Vitello, P. (2005b, October 6). A suspicious clerk and a school scandal. *New York Times.* http://www.nytimes.com/2005/10/06/nyregion/06roslyn.html?ex=1129435200&en=56194a255a977839&ei=5070.

Wagner, A. (2005, November 15). School evacuated after boy, 10, sets fire in bathroom. *Washington Times.* Available online: http://www.washtimes.com/metro/20051114-112156-8258r.htm.

Waite, M. (2003, August 23). Suspect in bus hijacking to be tried as an adult. *View.* Available online: http://www.viewnews.com/2002/VIEW-Aug-23-2002/pahrump/19449435.html.

Walsh, D. (2001). *Video game violence and public policy.* Available online: http://culturalpolicy.uchicago.edu/conf2001/papers/walsh.html.

Walsh, J. (2004, January 8). Ex-teacher pleads guilty in sex case. *Arizona Republic.* Available online: http://www.azcentral.com/arizonarepublic/local/articles/0108sexteach08.html.

Walton, E. R. (2003, September 9). Judge says school system erred in expulsion. *Greenville News.*http://greenvilleonline.com/news/2003/09/09/x2003090913949.htm.

Weiss, E. M. (2003, November 5). Va. teacher charged after bomb threat prank. *Washington Post*, B03. Available online: http://www.washingtonpost.com/wp-dyn/articles/A1140-2003Nov4.html.

Welles, K. (2005, April 28). Beating, kicking, bullying ongoing at local schools. *WPIX-TV*. Available online: http://www.wpxi.com/targe t11/4426745/detail. html.

Westley, M. N. (2005, April 28). Assault allegation probed at school. *Salt Lake Tribune*. Available online: http://www.sltrib.com/utah/ci_2692538.

What is child abuse and neglect? (2004). Washington, DC: National Clearinghouse on Child Abuse and Neglect Information. Available online: http:// nccanch.acf.hhs.gov/pubs/factsheets/whatiscan.cfm.

Whiting, B. (2003, October 23). Boy is held in Arizona massacre plot. *Arizona Republic*. Available online: http://www.azcentral.com/arizonarepublic/ local/articles/1023wvthreats23.html.

Wichita Public Schools. (2005). *Emergency preparedness and homeland security*. Available online: http://www.usd259.com/safeschools/homeland-security.

Wilbur, D. Q. (2005, April 22). 15-year-old charged in charter school arson. *Washington Post*. Available online: http://www.washington post.com/wp-dyn/ articles/A7958–2005Apr21.html.

William B. Travis Academy/Vanguard for the Academically Talented and Gifted (Middle School), Dallas, Texas. (2005, April 1). *Violence in our schools*. Available online: http://www.columbine-angels.com/shootings-2005-2009.htm.

William Gladden Foundation. (1992). *Juvenile gangs*. York, PA: Author.

Williamson, E., & Aratani, L. (2005, June 14). As school bus sexual assaults rise, danger often overlooked. *Washington Post*. Available online: http://www. washingtonpost.com/wpdyn/content/article/2005/06/13/AR2005061301642. html.

Willmsen, C. (2005, October 4). Court backs identifying teachers accused of sexual misconduct. *Seattle Times*. Available online: http://seattletimes.nwsource. com/html/education/2002538092_records04 m.html.

Wilstein, S. (2003, December 18). Wilstein: Coaches sexually abusing girls. *Boston Globe*. http://www.boston.com/news/education/k_12/articles/2003/12/ 18/wilstein_coaches_sexually_abusing_girls/.

Woodall, M. (2005, April 19). Student stabbed at high school. *Philadelphia Inquirer*, B-08.

Woolf, M. (2004, August 4). No-blame approach to bullies comes under attack. *Independent*. Available online: http://news.independent.co.uk/uk/politics/ story.jsp?story=547700.

Yettick, H. (2005, May 19). Teacher charged in taping incident. *Rocky Mountain News*. Available online: http://www.rockymountainnews.com/drmn/ education/article/0,1299,DRMN_957_3789844,00.html.

Youth gets life in school murder. (1997, June 11). *St. Louis Post-Dispatch*. Available online: http://www.rickross.com/reference/mountain_park/mountain_ park27.html.

Yuen, L. (2004, May 26). Three charged with felonies in school bomb threats. *Pioneer Press*. Available online: http://www.twincities.com/mld/pioneerpress/ news/local/8760006.htm.

Zuiga, J. A. (2003, October 23). Blind eye of zero tolerance fuels criticism. *Houston Chronicle*. Available online: http://www.chron.com/cs/CDA/ssistory. mpl/metropolitan/2176204.

Index

About the Author

R. MURRAY THOMAS is Emeritus Professor at the University of California, Santa Barbara, where he taught educational psychology and headed the program in international education for three decades. His professional publications over a 56-year period exceed 370, including such books as *Moral Development Theories: Secular and Religious*, *What Wrongdoers Deserve*, *Classifying Reactions to Wrongdoing*, and *Religion in Schools: Controversies Around the World*.